Digital Revolution Tamed

Hyojung Sun

Digital Revolution Tamed

The Case of the Recording Industry

palgrave
macmillan

Hyojung Sun
Creative Industries Institute
Ulster University
Belfast, UK

ISBN 978-3-030-06571-3 ISBN 978-3-319-93022-0 (eBook)
https://doi.org/10.1007/978-3-319-93022-0

Softcover re-print of the Hardcover 1st edition 2019

Cover credit: David Kozlowski

Printed on acid-free paper

This Palgrave Macmillan imprint is published by the registered company Springer International Publishing AG part of Springer Nature
The registered company address is: Gewerbestrasse 11, 6330 Cham, Switzerland

For Jeong-In

Acknowledgements

This book is an updated version of my Ph.D. thesis from Science, Technology and Innovation Studies at the University of Edinburgh. Huge gratitude goes to my supervisors, Prof. Robin Williams and Dr. James Stewart, who guided me with insightful comments, constructive criticism and great patience. Great appreciation also goes to the interviewees who have taken time out of their busy schedules to share insights with me. Their input has played a vital role in bringing this book together, and this would not have been possible without their generosity. I am also grateful for Music 2025 team, particularly Peter Jenner and Paul O'Hagan who gave life to this research and rekindled my academic interest in the digital music industry. Special thanks go to David Humphries for his emotional and practical support.

Contents

Abbreviations

A&R	Artist and Repertoire
ADA	Alternative Distribution Association
AHRA	Audio Home Recording Act
AIM	Association of Independent Music
ASCAP	American Society of Composers, Authors and Publishers
A2IM	American Association of Independent Music
CI	Consolidated Independent
DIY	Do-It-Yourself
DMCA	Digital Millennium Copyright Act
DRM	Digital Rights Management
DSP	Digital (Music) Service Provider
D2F	Direct-To-Fan
HADOPI	Haute Autorité pour la Diffusion des œuvres et la Protection des droits d'auteur sur Internet
IFPI	International Federation of the Phonographic Industry
IM	Instant Messaging
IMPALA	Independent Music Companies Association
IODA	Independent Online Distribution Association
ISP	Internet Service Provider
MCPS	Mechanical Copyright Protection Society
MLP	Multi-Level Perspective

MPAA	Motion Picture Association of America
P2P	Peer-To-Peer
PPL	Phonographic Performance Limited
PPV	Pay-Per-View
PRS	Performing Rights Society
RIAA	Recording Industry Association of America
RPM	Rotations Per Minute
SACEM	Societé des Auteurs, Compositeurs et Editeurs de Musique
SCMS	Serial Copy Management System
SDMI	Secure Digital Music Initiative
SNS	Social Network Sites
SPP	Swedish Pirate Party
SST	Social Shaping of Technology
STS	Science and Technology Studies
TPM	Technical Protection Measures
TRIPS	Trade Related Aspects of Intellectual Property Rights
VOD	Video-On-Demand
WCT	WIPO Copyright Treaty
WIN	Worldwide Independent Network
WIPO	World Intellectual Property Organisation
WPPT	WIPO Performances and Phonograms Treaty
XML	Extensible Markup Language

List of Figures

1

Introduction

1.1 Digital Disruption in the Recording Industry: The Quest for a New Perspective

By enabling the duplication and sharing of cultural products at no cost with no degradation of quality, digitalisation suggested there would be a major shift in the way cultural contents are produced, distributed and consumed. The recording industry has been the first of the cultural industries to confront the changes posed by digital technology. The debut of Napster, the pioneering digital music service based on Peer-To-Peer ("P2P") technology, promoted widespread predictions of an imminent and radical transformation within the music industry. The concept of radical innovation brings to mind Schumpeter's concept of innovation as involving "gales of creative destruction," a process of far-reaching changes to existing frameworks, technologies and institutions "that incessantly revolutionizes the economic structure by incessantly destroying the old one, incessantly creating a new one" (Schumpeter 1950, p. 83).

This radical change was claimed to bring about the "networked information economy" that could offer individuals "greater autonomy,

H. Sun, *Digital Revolution Tamed*, https://doi.org/10.1007/978-3-319-93022-0_1

political communities greater democracy, and societies greater opportunities for cultural self-reflection and human connection" (Benkler 2006, p. 473). P2P technology had the potential for decentralising the commodification and commercial control of capital-intensive intellectual property, and was celebrated as a way to build a "communal innovation," in which individual information sharing and filtering mechanism would diversify user tastes through exposure to lesser-known artists (Pasquale et al. 2002).

However, the path of technological innovation is by no means straightforward. The unauthorised use of copyrighted material has undermined the recording industry's business structure, which was based upon distributing and selling cultural content embedded in physical artefacts, through which an artificial scarcity created as a rival good was used to control distribution and consumer price. The possibility of infinite reproduction and distribution of free music, in conjunction with the ease of music recording, presented a great challenge to the recording industry, potentially displacing the conventional gatekeepers or rendering them redundant. The immediate consequence was manifested in the decreasing revenue from record sales. The recording industry cultivated the so-called digital crisis rhetoric to lobby for longer and stronger copyright protection. The "war" on piracy was launched to stamp out P2P file-sharing, criminalising all forms of file-sharing activities. Napster was shut down, and a plethora of subsequent P2P services remained on the outskirts of the marketplace as "darknet" (Biddle et al. 2002). While iTunes and a myriad of other digital music services arose to valorise music on the digital music networks, a large proportion of digital music users remained unwilling to pay for digital content.

Since Napster was closed down, a series of digital initiatives were launched, and through trial and error, the recording industry entered a new phase in which consumers were attracted to legitimate digital music services, and not the free, often illegal, options. Central to this change is the growth of the freemium-based streaming music business service initiated by Spotify. Spotify's proclaimed legal and superior quality to P2P file-sharing, as well as access to a large number of legal catalogues, have proved enticing enough to engage almost 100 million paid users (IFPI 2017). The recent changes in the recording industry, such as newly adjusted rights and services suitable for digital formats and the diversification of revenue streams, have prompted some commentators to proclaim that a successful new technological model has been established in the music industry (Roberts 2011). Indeed, streaming services are increasingly perceived to be an answer to the industry's battle to eliminate piracy (Page 2013; Aguiar and Waldfogel 2015; Wlömert and Papies 2016), signalling the economic recovery of the recording industry as a whole (IFPI 2017).

However, this pattern of development deviates from the initial predictions of digital disruption in the recording industry. Why did this mismatch between predictions and what actually happened arise? What factors shaped this development? Is the growth of the digital music business a response to digital innovation or an outcome of a restrictive copyright regime? There are sharp dichotomies in assessments of the recent changes emerging in the digital recording industry. Studies focusing on the legal impacts tend to emphasise the constrained aspect of the innovation. Drawing upon the continuity of the conventionally run technological, legal and societal structure, these studies argue that as long as the major labels retain control over the market built around copyright, innovation is difficult to attain. On the contrary, many media accounts have placed a greater emphasis on the discontinuity which have enabled new forms of production, distribution and consumption outside the well-established industry structure. Focusing on a few notable changes or cases, these accounts portray a utopian picture of the contemporary digital recording industry.

However, both views offer a techno-centric vision, which places P2P distribution as the central focal point of analysis. In contrast, this book argues that technological innovation in the recording industry entails a complex interplay amongst a diverse array of factors such as digital technology, copyright regulation and the more or less conflicting interests between heterogeneous players such as major labels, intermediaries, music consumers and artists. Despite the overall popularity of the subject, there has been a dearth of enquiry into these complex interactions between law, society and technology in the digital recording industry. This book attempts to fill that gap by mapping out the interplay amongst a diverse array of actors and factors involved in the actual innovation process. To do so, the book explores the early history and addresses contemporary developments from a number of viewpoints in the sector.

The study has adopted a qualitative data analysis of 55 interviews with a wide range of entrepreneurs and innovators, focusing upon two successful innovation cases within different locales within the digital recording industry: (1) Spotify: a digital music service and (2) INgrooves: an independent digital music distribution service provider whose system is also used by Universal Music Group. This book is largely inspired by the Social Shaping of Technology (SST) (MacKenzie and Wajcman 1985; Williams and Edge 1996) and its extension into the Social Learning in Technological Innovation (SLTI) perspective ("SLTI") (Sørensen 1996; Williams et al. 2005). SST guides this study in investigating the heterogeneous and dispersed process of innovation through which the negotiations amongst the diverse actors and factors drive choices in the direction of technological development. SLTI as an extension to SST provides an insightful conceptual tool to explore the gradual process of technological change arising over a period of time and the reflexive efforts to ensure technologies are implemented, appropriated and domesticated in the market. The insights from SST to SLTI as well as an in-depth analysis of two layers within the industry—digital music service and distribution—allow this study to investigate a broader range of settings for innovation and a wider array of players involved in the innovation of the recording industry.

1.2 What I Mean by the "Recording Industry"

Before advancing the discussion, I will clarify the scope of the research this book covers by giving a definition of what I mean by the recording industry. Amongst academia, the term "music industry" has been defined in a number of ways. The music industry has therefore been covered by many different terms including forming part of the creative industries, the cultural industries and the copyright industry.[1] Williamson and Cloonan (2007) particularly raised the discussion on defining the music industry. Questioning the simplicity compressed in the term, they suggest "music industries" (as a plural) as a more practical term to convey the complexity and plurality of the tenets in the music business sparked by digitisation. While there is an increasing adoption of this concept (Marshall et al. 2013), and acknowledging the disputes around the term, in referring to recording industry, for this book I define the recording industry as that which does not include the business unit of music publishing. The recording and publishing businesses often share many canons of music business practices. However, publishing has its own characteristics that this book did not cover. The music industry is used when it is considered appropriate to describe the overall state of the industry in general. The music business on the other hand refers to the specifics of the business side of the music industry.

1.3 Major Predictions of the Digital Recording Industry

The process of technological innovation is imbued with uncertainty, contingency and complexity. Understanding digital technology requires a sophisticated and intricate understanding of the relationship between technology and society; analysis must attend to the interplay between heterogeneous players who have differing power and interests (Williams et al. 2005). So far, however, two very distinct discourses have dominated the discussion of understanding technological innovation in the recording industry: Is it a creative destruction or a destructive creation? Prevalent linear understandings of technological change focusing on the impact of technology on society produced a dichotomy between utopian and dystopian views of the way the industry would develop. This book seeks to overcome the shortcomings of these partial accounts by providing a detailed examination of the innovation process in which

[1]Wikström (2013) gives a more detailed discussion on each term from pp. 12–18.

the complex set of interactions amongst heterogeneous players with conflicting interests and differing commitments involved in the digital music networks guides diverging choices in relation to particular market conditions and user requirements.

To this end, I critically examine the prevalent accounts that technology would induce disintermediation. These accounts advance three broad predictions about the digital revolution in the recording industry. First, digital technology will shorten the value chain in the music industry by diminishing the roles of intermediaries or rendering them redundant. Secondly, disintermediation will enable artists to connect with their fans directly through digital distribution networks and retain the legal rights for their own sound recordings. This will lead to the overturn of the major labels' control built through access to Intellectual Property Law. Thirdly, music fans can enjoy ubiquitous access to an unlimited music supply known as the "Celestial Jukebox," combined with peer review and viral impact on the Internet, which would in turn help music fans discover lesser-known or unknown music. This will contribute to achieving the beloved cultural attribute where diversity of music choices will flourish. Informed by a concern about assessing these three major predictions, this book investigates what has actually happened in the market.

1.4 Outline of the Book

This book is structured as follows. Chapter 2 provides an overview of the approach this book employed to develop a more sophisticated account of the story than the prevailing view. It reviews the relevant literature that has been used to discuss disruptive technology and illustrates the limitations. The section moves on to a discussion of the way this book sought to move beyond the simplistic view of the industry and explains how SST and its extension SLTI can provide a useful insight to understand digital disruption in the recording industry as a main theoretical framework. I then present "Socio-technical constellation of the digital recording industry" as a new way of conceptualising the digital recording industry. This chapter finishes with a brief discussion on the key methodologies. In Chapter 3, I trace the history of the recording industry that has evolved in the context of economic, cultural, legal and institutional changes and show how the dominant discourse surrounding the digital recording industry has developed. It first summarises the way the recording industry has changed in the context of technological advances, Intellectual Property (IP) Law and organisational practices. In the following section, the view is extended to discuss the conventional value networks in the recording industry in a wide range of settings for innovation. The chapter ends with existing views on the digitalisation of music and their limitations. It presents the dichotomy of understanding the digital recording industry induced by techno-centric views, the widely discussed views focused on P2P technology's impact on the market and the technological trajectory of P2P technology that has deviated from the prediction.

The empirical findings are presented from Chapters 4 to 7. Chapter 4 looks at the detailed process of innovation involved in the evolution of digital music services. The chapter sketches the early history of the digital music services developed since Napster up to current digital music services and demonstrates the uneven trajectory of business model developments in the digital recording industry. The early history is characterised as major labels' contradictory response to digital novelty. On the one hand, they resisted the change, but at the same time, they also sought to ensure that they were not displaced by new forms of digital distribution. Their survival strategies are discussed in two measures: the Secure Digital Music Initiative ("SDMI") project, forged to secure technological control of burgeoning digital recording devices, and early digital music services such as PressPlay, MusicNet, Rhapsody and EMusic and their limitations. It then discusses how iTunes arose as an alternative business model to valorise digital music. Although iTunes' download model of a lowered price for legal catalogues was successful to a certain degree, it also left a space for a new generation of experimentation with new business models. This new type of digital music service model, including Last.fm and YouTube, is covered in order to demonstrate how firms with similar advertising-based free music offerings had different fates depending on their strategies for coping with challenges, such as licensing deals with major labels. The chapter finishes with a brief overview of the recent changes prompted by streaming service business models.

Following on the discussion on the evolution of digital music services, in Chapter 5, I provide an in-depth view of the recent changes with a focus on the case of Spotify. Spotify's case illustrates how the company built a commercially viable digital music service in the midst of piracy's golden era. The story begins with Daniel Ek's vision to develop a digital music service better than piracy and the way this innovation became possible in Sweden, the stronghold of piracy. The section continues with the specific solutions Spotify developed to compete against piracy, as well as its strategies to overcome challenges in making the technology work in the market. This is followed by the changes Spotify has made in the digital recording industry, such as reduced piracy, increased paying subscribers and subsequent changes. The section goes on to examine the changing strategies in relation to music discovery and its implications. The final part of the section discusses the problems Spotify has yet to solve.

Chapter 6 focuses on the changes in digital music distribution networks since Napster. The chapter begins with a brief overview of the lack of matching innovations left by Napster's technological leap. The arrival of iTunes quickly changed the situation by laying out the foundation of the legitimate digital music distribution infrastructure. The development of this system was made possible by allowing major labels to maintain their control over the distribution. In the independent sector, considerable changes took place, notably with the emergence of a new breed of intermediaries, digital music aggregators. The chapter then explores the changes to digital music networks brought about by the digital affordances known as Direct-To-Fan (D2F), as well as the challenges prompted by an abundance of choice, leading both discontinuity and continuity to converge in digital music distribution networks. I then broaden the perspective to examine how the digital music convergence is bringing about changing dynamics in the recording industry. The complex interplay amongst the diverse arrays of actors and factors in the digital recording industry is discussed in terms of four major networks—creativity, reproduction, distribution/promotion and consumption.

In Chapter 7, I delve into the detailed process of the reintermediation that took place in digital music distribution networks. The first part looks at the way a large-scale digital music distribution, sparked by iTunes' growth, allowed digital music aggregators to emerge and serve as a new middleman between digital music services and independent labels. The second part discusses the partnership between INgrooves and Universal Music Group, which reveals the unexpected problems arising in the digital era, followed by INgrooves' evolving roles as a distributor and a promoter. By detailing INgrooves' innovation process that parallels the process digital music distribution networks have become reintermediated, this chapter highlights the uneven and constantly changing business environment that is far removed from the linear view.

Chapter 8 recapitulates the main theme and argument of this book. It reviews the approach this book drew upon so as to move beyond the linear understanding of digital disruption in the recording industry. It moves on to the discussion that underscoring the mismatch between the prediction and the tamed digital revolution was the complexity of valorisation processes involved in the development of digital music distribution and services. I then recount how the "Socio-technical constellation of the digital recording industry" framework served to provide a more sophisticated understanding of the subject and finish the book with a few forward-thinking remarks.

References

Aguiar, L., and J. Waldfogel. 2015. Streaming Reaches Flood Stage: Does Spotify Stimulate or Depress Music Sales? Working Paper No. 21653, National Bureau of Economic Research.

Benkler, Y. 2006. *The Wealth of Networks: How Social Production Transforms Markets and Freedom*. New Haven, CT: Yale University Press.

Biddle, P., P. England, M. Peinado, and B. Willman. 2002. The Darknet and the Future of Content Distribution. *ACM Workshop on Digital Rights Management*.

IFPI. 2017. IFPI Global Music Report 2017: Annual State of the Industry. Available from http://www.ifpi.org/news/IFPI-GLOBAL-MUSIC-REPORT-2017.
MacKenzie, D.A., and J. Wajcman. 1985. *The Social Shaping of Technology: How the Refrigerator Got Its Hum*. Milton Keynes: Open University Press.
Marshall, L., J. Williamson, and M. Cloonan (eds.). 2013. Contextualising the Contemporary Recording Industry. In *The International Recording Industries*. Milton Park: Routledge.
Page, W. 2013. Adventures in the Netherlands: New Spotify Study Sees Encouraging Downwards Trend in Music Piracy in the Netherlands. *Spotify Press*.
Pasquale III, F.A., K.G. Weatherall, and M.B. Fagin. 2002. Beyond Napster: Using Antitrust Law to Advance and Enhance Online Music Distribution. *Boston University Journal of Science & Technology Law* 8 (2): 451–573.
Roberts, R. 2011. Critic's Notebook: With Spotify, the Future of Music Is Here. *LA Times Blogs—Pop & Hiss*.
Schumpeter, J.A. 1950. *Capitalism, Socialism and Democracy*. London: G. Allen & Unwin.
Sørensen, K.H. 1996. *Learning Technology, Constructing Culture: Socio-Technical Change as Social Learning*. Trondheim: University of Trondheim, Centre for Technology and Society, No. 18/96.
Wikström, P. 2013. *The Music Industry: Music in the Cloud*, 2nd ed. Cambridge, England: Polity.
Williams, R., and D. Edge. 1996. The Social Shaping of Technology. *Research Policy* 25 (6): 865.
Williams, R., J. Stewart, and R. Slack. 2005. *Social Learning in Technological Innovation: Experimenting with Information and Communication Technologies*. Cheltenham: Edward Elgar.
Williamson, J., and M. Cloonan. 2007. Rethinking the Music Industry. *Popular Music* 26 (2): 305–322.
Wlömert, N., and D. Papies. 2016. On-Demand Streaming Services and Music Industry Revenues—Insights from Spotify's Market Entry. *International Journal of Research in Marketing* 33 (2): 314–327.

2

Towards a More Sophisticated Account

This chapter focuses on theoretical backgrounds that guided this research to achieve a more sophisticated account than prevailing studies. It begins by critically examining the earlier and existing approaches in understanding disruptive technology and addressing the limitations of these approaches. In the following section, I discuss more specifically the theoretical frameworks that have guided the research. By elaborating on the general concepts and some accompanying key concepts, the section reviews how Social Shaping of Technology ("SST") (MacKenzie and Wajcman 1985; Williams and Edge 1996) and its extension into Social Learning in Technological Innovation ("SLTI") (Sørensen 1996; Williams et al. 2005) serve as valuable frameworks to understand digital disruption in the recording industry. Drawing upon these theoretical approaches, I present "Socio-technical Constellations of the Digital Recording Industry" as a framework of demonstrating a more complete and sophisticated account of the digital recording industry.

H. Sun, *Digital Revolution Tamed*, https://doi.org/10.1007/978-3-319-93022-0_2

2.1 Understanding Disruptive Technology

2.1.1 Technological Paradigms and Revolutions

In understanding disruptive technology, a wide range of analysts of innovation and technological change have drawn attention to discontinuities whereby extended periods of stability are interspersed by periods of revolutionary change.

The concept of "creative destruction" has been widely used to describe the process of radical transformation that has been presumed to characterise the change in the music industry in the digital era. Advanced by Schumpeter (1950), the term "creative destruction" refers to the revolution of an economic structure achieved by the turn of the innovation cycle. After periods of economic stability, as possibilities for innovation within an industry become depleted, a cluster of developments over a certain period of time, involving an interaction between technological and institutional change, tends to lead to a discontinuous pattern of growth through a process "that incessantly revolutionizes the economic structure by incessantly destroying the old one, incessantly creating a new one" (Schumpeter 1950, p. 83). The new combinations of change required across all sectors of the economy have the disruptive effects of sweeping away old structures and bringing about creative motion of change.

Concepts such as technological paradigm or techno-economic regimes/technological revolution are understood in this vein. Developed from Kuhn's (1970) scientific paradigm, Dosi (1982) introduced a concept of technological paradigm that refers to a pattern that firms follow in finding solutions to techno-economic problems in selective principles. Technological paradigms "define the technological opportunities for further innovations and some basic procedures on how to exploit them" (Dosi 1988, p. 226). The development of particular technologies is patterned by the technological paradigm giving rise to a distinctive technological trajectory, shaped by various factors such as economic and technical conditions conditioned by the paradigm (Dosi and Orsenigo 1988). A similar notion of "techno-economic paradigm" is presented by Freeman (Freeman and Perez 1988; Freeman 1992). It describes the pervasive effect of a technology, which could bring about a major change not just in sectors but in the whole economy, opening up an exceptionally wide range of opportunities for economic growth. Techno-economic paradigm, also called technological revolution, parallels Schumpeter's idea of creative destruction, which stresses the long wave, with more emphasis on "a painful process of structural change" (Freeman and Perez 1988, p. 47).

Other writers in technology studies have also sought to explain periods of continuity in the development of technology as well as periods of discontinuity. The concept of "technology regimes" advanced by Rip and Kemp (1998) seeks to explain how regimes become entrenched by capturing expectations, motivations and regulations contributing to the shaping of technological development. They place a focus on the emergence of sociotechnical systems and stress the dynamics of sociotechnical change. To this end, they use the concept of "technological regime," "the rule-set or grammar embedded in a complex of engineering practices, production process technologies, product characteristics, skills and procedures, ways of handing relevant artefacts and persons, ways of defining problems" (Rip and Kemp 1998, p. 338). Nelson and Winter (1977) place more importance on the gradual evolution in innovation. They reject neoclassical economists' view, which regards firms as making rational decisions, and adopt ideas such as "procedural" and "bounded rationality" to describe firms' anomalous behaviour as arising from the complicated nature of innovation. From their view, technological development unfolds following its own logic of "natural trajectories," and technology progresses according to the pattern of companies' problem-solving activity, depending on the selection environment. They define this as "technological regime," which explains why different industrial sectors have different patterns of technological development (Nelson and Winter 1982).

Understanding technological change within a framework of a paradigm, however, tends to presume that technologies develop according to the technological "trajectory" of finite techno-economic logic and therefore ignores the social circumstances influencing the technological development, failing to explain why technologies develop differently in different circumstances (MacKenzie and Wajcman 1985). What appears to be a new technology is in fact an outcome of a gradual change and new combinations of existing technology (MacKenzie and Wajcman 1985). Gilfillan's (1970) study of the gradual evolution of the ship from a floating log to the modern motor ship demonstrates that technological change is an accretion of small incremental details. Rosenberg (1982) also underscores a weakness of the view, which characterises technological change as developing within paradigms, interrupted by radical discontinuities. His rich account of the complex process involved in the process of technological change, in which both radical and incremental innovations cross over each other, highlights that technological changes arise as an accumulation of many interrelated innovations rather than as a shift detached from existing technologies. All this points to the fact that existing technologies serve as an important foreground to be modified, improved and turned into new technologies (Edge 1974).

The contingency, complexity and diversity involved in the innovation process often make the process of technological development uneven. The multiple interests and power involved in the innovation process often cause the process of alignment and stabilisation of technology to be prolonged and produce unexpected outcomes. While these approaches can be useful in capturing certain patterns and regularities of technological change, we need to investigate the more detailed dynamics that occur in particular settings. Here, I turn to SST, which seeks to address a more comprehensive understanding of innovation and the complexity of interactions amongst the wide range of players and different phases of innovation.

2.1.2 Social Shaping of Technology ("SST")

Early studies of understanding technology were based upon markedly simplistic models of the relationship between technology and society, conceiving technological progress analogous to social progress. One strand regards technology as an autonomous force developing according to its own inner logic. Implicit in this notion is that technology is the most important force of social changes. These approaches were criticised by SST as "technological determinist." An equally deterministic view was advanced by neoclassical economics. Based on the belief that firms will choose the technology that will bring about maximum profits, they presume that technical capacities are readily available to all firms and that the most efficient technologies will thus diffuse across markets. Neoclassical economists treat technology as an exogenous variable and offer little insight into our concerns.

SST emerged to provide frameworks for analysing the relations between technology and society. In order to transcend the limitations of these earlier attempts, SST provides a broader perspective in understanding the complexity involved in technological innovation. SST rejects the simplistic models of innovation whose focus was on the "impacts" of technology on society, and stresses the coupling of society and technology. In this period, various major frameworks arose to analyse the relations of technology and society.

MacKenzie and Wajcman's (1985) book, *The Social Shaping of Technology*, ignited the discussion of SST. They emphasise the diverse choices available throughout innovation processes from the development to the implementation of technologies. Moving beyond the technology's "impact" on society, they stressed the need to take into account a wide range of factors such as economic, political, social, cultural and organisational settings influencing choices and the subsequent social implications. More recent SST has widened the perspectives integrating diverse research areas under the rubric of "a broad church," including evolutionary economics, politics, history and cultural studies, and seeks to provide a more sophisticated approach to demonstrating the diversity and complexities in sociotechnical factors influencing technological innovation (Williams and Edge 1996). Law (1987) describes the multifaceted aspect of interactivity between social and technical factors as "heterogeneous network." In Hughes' (1986) terms, it is "social-technical systems" or a "seamless web," which refers to all elements enabling technology to be intertwined within the structures of social, economic, political and technical spheres.

SST understands the development of technology as a heterogeneous and dispersed process in which technologies rarely diffuse straightforwardly as conceived from the outset at the design stage. Instead, technologies are subject to complex influences, unpredictable circumstances and a wide range of actors and activities. The contingency, complexity and diversity of technological innovation underpinned by SST imply the difficulty of achieving technological changes. In other words, the heterogeneous players and different power and interests involved in the technological development make the alignment and stabilisation of technology inevitably contentious and prolonged. SST stresses that the trajectory of innovation is composed of "choices" that unfold in different routes and produce different outcomes through a "garden of forking paths" (Williams and Edge 1996). In order to demonstrate how innovation proceeds in the course of complex selection processes, SST attends to the detailed processes involved in technological innovation. The detailed case studies, in conjunction with SST's broad scope, offer a useful analytical framework for observing how alignments of diverse interests lead to technological change and the negotiation process through which innovators change their strategies and modify selections in response to the particular environment (Russell and Willams 2002).

The uncertainty, contingency and complexity involved in the process of technological innovation for digital media require a sophisticated and intricate understanding of the relationship between technology and society and the interplay amongst the heterogeneous factors and players involved in it (Williams et al. 2005). The music industry was the first of the cultural industries to confront the challenges of digital technology. The trajectory of technological innovation in the music industry has been a contested process of learning in which heterogeneous factors are influencing the (re)shaping of business settings. The possibility of digital revolution has been compounded by the major players' propensity to extend the existing framework. The SST perspective is therefore deemed appropriate to explore the dispersed and heterogeneous process of technological innovation arising from the diverse array of actors and factors in the digital recording industry.

Building upon the core concepts of SST, the SLTI framework (Sørensen 1996; Williams et al. 2005) examines gradual improvements in technological changes and focuses upon reflexive practices involved in technological development. The SLTI perspective is particularly useful for understanding why the promises of revolutionary change have not materialised. The traditional technology-driven view presumes that finished solutions will somehow match user requirements and thus can be readily applied in the market. The hype surrounding digital revolution in the recording industry can be understood in this vein. The predictions of revolutionary change in the recording industry presupposed that the possibilities enabled by the decreased costs of music recording and distribution would materialise in the market without much difficulty. However, the societal uptake and use of digital technologies turned out to be much more complex than widely assumed because the social adoption of new technologies inevitably involves decision-making processes characterised by ambiguity and uncertainty and thus inherently difficult to predict from the outset (Williams 1997).

The transformation of society is not achieved solely by technology. What it hints at is the discrepancy between the supply and the adoption arising from the learning process in which technologies are actually adopted, employed and embedded in the society. Characterised as "the serendipity of innovation," technologies are rarely diffused as conceived at the outset in the design stage, and radical innovations carry particular challenges to predict the direction of technological development because they have no existing ground—customers, previous products or markets—upon which to rely (Williams et al. 2005, p. 13). A suggested solution is to move beyond traditional studies' focus on design and deployment, and instead to attend to the actual "learning" process of technological innovation composed of experimentation, discovery and struggles taking place at the micro-level of technological innovation. This can be an effective tool to address the complexity of choices inherent in the cycle of technological design, development and adoption. As a result, we can discover the multiple interests and visions involved in the innovation process that is often complicated and contested, unfolding through negotiation amongst diverse players who have different power and interests (Williams et al. 2005).

2.2 Sociotechnical Constellation of the Digital Recording Industry

The innovation of the digital recording industry is highly complex, arising from the interplay of a wide-ranging collection of actors and factors. The complexity, contingency and uncertainty involved in the process of innovation in the recording industry typically make the process of technological development unpredictable and protracted. To move beyond the prevailing linear account of understanding, this book examines the detailed process of innovation and the uptake of a particular digital technology in the recording industry. A particular focus of the study is a multifaceted intertwining of choices involved in designing and developing technologies in heterogeneous networks, as well as the gradual process of technological change and the reflexive efforts made by actors responding to changing circumstances.

To that end, a conceptual framework of "socio-technical constellation of digital recording industry" was drawn up. It is built upon the concept "socio-technical constellation" (Williams et al. 2005), which emphasises the heterogeneity and loose coupling of players involved in the development of technologies. This metaphor describes not only the closely organised arrays of players but also the loosely connected linkages amongst players, especially with some groups who remain on the fringe. With divergent motivations and interests, these players strive to achieve their goals.

In understanding complex technologies such as digital media, it is important to understand that as a whole, these networks, linking heterogeneous and loose connections, contribute to the complete dynamics of technological innovation. Drawing upon this framework, this investigation is centred on the entire circuit of the innovation process in which heterogeneous players struggled to stabilise their location in relation to a changing environment. From this, we will examine the complexity of interactions that is subject to negotiation amongst players with divergent motivations, interests and power. In understanding the constellation of the digital recording industry, this study identified four major factors: digital technology, copyright law, users and business models.

In this way, we will capture the interrelations and the interdependencies of a wide range of actors involved in the innovation, as well as providing a detailed understanding of the way diverging expectations, visions, sets of rules and interests are aligned in the process of innovation.

In the following section, I will introduce some of the concepts drawn from the SLTI approach, which are particularly useful in exploring the intricate dynamics of the digital recording industry.

The common problems in developing digital media systems are related to the dominant "technocratic" design, which is driven by engineers with little understanding of user requirements (Williams et al. 2005). In understanding how digital technology has been reconfigured in digital music services, attention has been mostly drawn to the roles of legal regulations or the major labels, and therefore, the contribution of music consumers has not been adequately recognised. In the digital music business, the gulf between the supply and the users' demand has protracted the process of building a commercially successful digital music business. In assessing how digital recording industry arrived at finding a solution, this book rejects the widely believed presumption that users are sufficiently understood in technological design from the outset, and seeks to understand that consumption is an active and creative process through which products are appropriated and integrated into societal settings (Sørensen 1994). In this regard, users are not passive and adaptive receivers of technical supply, but play a crucial role in shaping and redirecting innovation.

2.2.1 Innofusion and Domestication

To understand users' vital role in the evolution of digital music services, this study draws insights from concepts such as "innofusion" and "domestication." The concept "innofusion" refers to "the processes of technological design, trial and exploration, in which users' needs and requirements are discovered and incorporated in the course of the struggle to get the technology to work in useful ways, at the point of application" (Fleck 1988, p. 4). This concept refutes the widely accepted notion of diffusion of innovation as a passive process of adoption and stresses that the implementation of technology takes place during the course of making it work. At the centre of this process lie users' struggles to come to terms with new technologies, finding meanings or values and integrating them into their everyday life. This is called "domestication," which refers to "the way in which technical capabilities are explored, meanings attributed and practices developed as artefacts are integrated within local social settings" (Williams et al. 2005, p. 57). Domestication, therefore, highlights the active roles users play as "attributed agency," constructing and reconstructing technology in the context of their own culture and social relations (Lie and Sørensen 1996).

2.2.2 Learning by Doing, Learning by Using and Learning by Interacting

Additional concepts important to understand users' contribution to innovation are "learning by doing" (Arrow 1962) and "learning by using" (Rosenberg 1982). Both concepts stress that productivity growth is achieved through incremental innovation over a long period through a "learning curve," with "learning by doing" referring to the productivity gain arising from the producer's past production experience and "learning by using" emphasising the stochastic process through which technology improves through producers' knowledge of users' experience. The concept of "learning by interacting" emphasises the reciprocity of the innovation process through which technologies develop, informed by feedback from users and vice versa (Sørensen 1996). These notions imply that linkages between users and producers can contribute to successful innovation. The concept of "configurations" (Fleck 1988) helps us understand the interplay between the supply of digital technology and the specific social settings in which technology is appropriated. The rapidly changing nature of digital technology is highly heterogeneous and therefore carries the tension between the promises and what actually happens in the market. By perceiving technologies as a range of components that are assembled to configure particular purposes, the concept of configurational technology helps us understand how contradictory visions and interests are negotiated in its appropriation.

2.2.3 Learning by Regulating

While assessing the role of copyright is essential to understand the digital recording industry, current scholarship has so far paid a great deal of attention to the law's impact on the market. Developed from the notion of technology regime advanced by Rip et al. (1995), Sørensen's (1996) concept of "learning by regulating" seeks to explicate how expectations, visions, rules and regulations contribute to the development of new technologies (Williams et al. 2005). Drawing upon this concept, this study explores the process of innovation in relation to copyright regulations, expectations and visions amongst various players.

2.2.4 Intermediaries

In understanding sociotechnical constellations, concepts of "intermediaries" help us map out the complex interactions of relations involved in the innovation process. The concept of "intermediaries" seeks to explain the crucial role certain players have in bridging the "generic" technological offerings and consumers' appropriation by configuring technologies to make them relevant to consumers. The significance of intermediaries is their ability to make the constellations happen. Their roles are twofold: first, they play an enabling role for the service by, for example, lowering barriers to access and reducing costs, which is crucial to including non-specialist users. Secondly, they play a crucial role in the services' inclusion by refining and developing new productions. The crucial traits that intermediaries require in order to make intermediation successful range from the ability to mobilise knowledge and resources to the capacity to cross different spaces and different knowledge communities. By positioning themselves to acquire "know-who" (knowing the right people), they can exert an influence on future markets and reputation building.

2.2.5 Meso-level Interactions

Networked multimedia applications typically require a diverse range of resources and knowledge from infrastructure for content distribution to information about the user context (Williams 2000). Multimedia developments therefore often require mediation amongst a range of actors. The SLTI approach therefore seeks to address the complexity of interactions amongst a wide range of players and between different phases and the broader institutional settings through the multi-layered model (Sørensen and Levold 1992). In a large-scale technological system, institutional arrangements involved in technological innovation require intermediaries who can build inter-organisational systems. SLTI's particular emphasis on the "meso-level" of interactions between organisations helps this study to look at the process of intermediation through which varying kinds of supply are distributed, used and appropriated.

Technological innovation in the recording industry entails the complex interplay of a diverse array of factors such as digital technology, copyright regulation and conflicting interests between heterogeneous players such as labels, other intermediaries, music consumers and artists. Following insights from the above-mentioned concepts drawn from SLTI's extended focus of enquiry, this book will observe the multiplicity of locales of innovation and the entire circle of the innovation process, through which diverging interests, motivations and power are negotiated (Fig. 2.1).

2.2.6 Networks of Music Economy

SST and the Social Learning approach provide a generic account of the processes by which technologies are shaped in particular historically structured contexts and configurations of actors. However, it does not provide specific accounts of the changing landscape of the digital music economy. Here, I turn to the substantive literature in this domain and in particular Leyshon's (2001) networks of music economy. Developed upon Attali's (1985) political and economic music value framework, Leyshon's (2001) value networks explore the allocation of the different

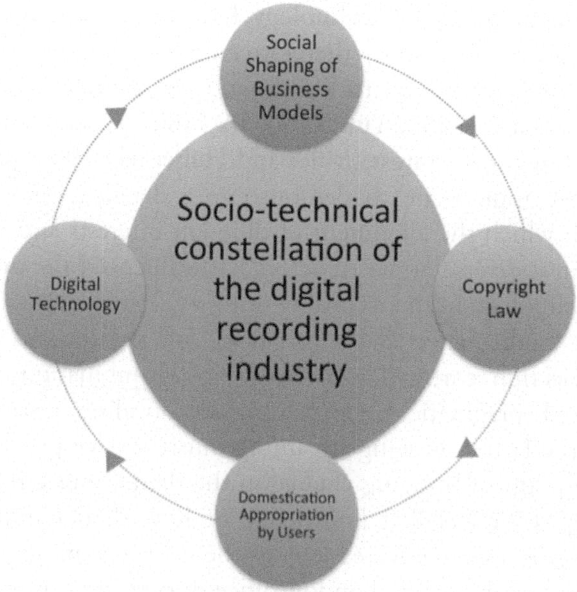

Fig. 2.1 Sociotechnical constellation of the digital recording industry

functions of the industry in four musical networks. His networks of musical economy depict the constellations of four major networks in the music industry. This framework is useful for depicting the complex relationship amongst heterogeneous forces and the blurred interaction amongst the four major networks in the music industry. Drawing upon this framework, this book demonstrates how these networks are undergoing changes in the digital era.

2.3 Case Study

The digital recording industry has predominantly been studied by legal scholars whose main concern is focused on law's impact on the industry. The primary purpose of this study is to move beyond this prevailing account and provide a rich account of the innovation process through which a diverse array of interests, motivations and visions involved in the development of digital technology have been reconfigured in the recording industry. This study therefore employed the case study methods, which are widely used to understand the complexity of the case in question (Blaikie 2009; Yin 2009). Its "'thick descriptions' that are vivid, nested in a real context (Miles and Huberman 1984, p. 19)" were deemed most appropriate to demonstrate a detailed innovation process through which the alignment of different interests and negotiation power amongst diverse arrays of actors has influenced the development of digital technology in the recording industry.

Two case studies selected for this book are Spotify and INgrooves. The case selection emerged as a result of a combination of strategic planning and pragmatic opportunism surrounding research access. Spotify, as the fastest growing streaming music service provider, as well as the focal point of bringing change in the digital music industry, was chosen to provide detailed knowledge of how digital music services evolved. INgrooves was selected later as the fieldwork progressed when I secured an internship at its London office during the summer of 2013. Napster's largest impact was on the distribution networks, and the control of distribution was essential in overcoming the uncertainty and risk involved in the production of music in the conventional recording business. INgrooves, a fast-growing independent digital music distributor whose distribution platform was also used by Universal Music Group, was chosen as a window into a detailed account of changes on the digital distribution networks. Through multiple case studies of Spotify and INgrooves—two leading players, with different locations in the newly emerging digital recording industry—this book delivers different "viewpoints" in a sector that can be a set of heuristics to explore important sites of technological development arising over time, and over multiple locations in a broader context (Pollock 2009; Hyysalo 2010; Williams and Pollock 2012). Triangulating between these provides the basis for a richer and more robust understanding of developments and the way these were negotiated amongst an array of players in diverse and changing locations across the sector.

2.4 Data Collection

The book draws upon qualitative data analysis of 55 interviews with a wide range of music entrepreneurs and innovators.[1] The data collection was conducted over an extended period from January 2013 to May 2014 by attending major music festivals, industry workshops and a work placement. They include Midem, the largest European annual music industry conference held in Cannes (26–29 January 2013), France, field trip to New York (March 2013), the Great Escape, one of the major British music in Brighton, UK festival (16–18 May 2013), Internship at INgrooves (July–August 2013), Wide Days, Scotland's music convention held in Edinburgh from (9–10 April 2014), and a field trip to Stockholm (May 2014).

References

Arrow, K.J. 1962. The Economic Implications of Learning by Doing. *The Review of Economic Studies* 29 (3): 155–173.

Attali, J. 1985. *Noise: The Political Economy of Music*. Manchester: Manchester University Press.

Blaikie, N.W.H. 2009. *Designing Social Research: The Logic of Anticipation*, 2nd ed. Cambridge, UK and Malden, MA: Polity.

Dosi, G. 1982. Technological Paradigms and Technological Trajectories: A Suggested Interpretation of the Determinants and Directions of Technical Change. *Research Policy* 11 (3): 147–162.

Dosi, G. 1988. The Nature of the Innovative Process. In *Technical Change and Economic Theory*, ed. G. Dosi, C. Freeman, N. Richard, S. Gerald, and S. Luc. London: Pinter Publishers.

Dosi, G., and L. Orsenigo. 1988. Coordination and Transformation: An Overview of Structures, Behaviours and Change in Evolutionary

[1]Reflecting the fast-changing business environment, there have been many changes in the interviewees' role since the time the interviews took place. Since the interviewees spoke on behalf of the companies they worked for, this book noted the interviewees' career positions at the time of the interviews.

Environments. In *Technical Change and Economic Theory*, ed. G. Dosi, C. Freeman, N. Richard, S. Gerald, and S. Luc. London: Pinter Publishers.
Edge, D. 1974. Technological Metaphor and Social Control. *New Literary History* 6 (1): 135–147.
Fleck, J. 1988. *Innofusion or Diffusation? The Nature of Technological Development in Robotics*. Edinburgh: Research Centre for Social Sciences, University of Edinburgh.
Freeman, C. 1992. *The Economics of Hope : Essays on Technical Change, Economic Growth and the Environment*. London: Pinter.
Freeman, C., and C. Perez. 1988. Structural Crises of Adjustment: Busines Cycles and Investment Behaviour. In *Technical Change and Economic Theory*, ed. G. Dosi, C. Freeman, R. Nelson, G. Silverberg, and L. Soete. London: Pinter Publishers.
Gilfillan, S.C. 1970. *The Sociology of Invention: An Essay in the Social Causes, Ways and Effects of Technic Invention, Especially as Demonstrated Historicly in the Author's 'Inventing the Ship'*. Cambridge, MA: MIT Press.
Hughes, T.P. 1986. The Seamless Web: Technology, Science, Etcetera, Etcetera. *Social Studies of Science* 16 (2): 281–292.
Hyysalo, S. 2010. *Health Technology Development and Use from Practice-Bound Imagination to Evolving Impacts*. New York, NY: Routledge.
Kuhn, T.S. 1970. *The Structure of Scientific Revolutions*, 2nd ed. Chicago: University of Chicago Press.
Leyshon, A. 2001. Time-Space (and Digital) Compression: Software Formats, Musical Networks, and the Reorganisation of the Music Industry. *Environment & Planning A* 33 (1): 49.
Lie, M., and K.H. Sørensen. 1996. *Making Technology Our Own?: Domesticating Technology into Everyday Life*. Oslo: Scandinavian University Press.
MacKenzie, D.A., and J. Wajcman. 1985. *The Social Shaping of Technology: How the Refrigerator Got Its Hum*. Milton Keynes: Open University Press.
Miles, M.B., and A.M. Huberman. 1984. *Qualitative Data Analysis: A Sourcebook of New Methods*. Beverly Hills: Sage.
Nelson, R.R., and S.G. Winter. 1977. In Search of Useful Theory of Innovation. *Research Policy* 6 (1): 36–76.
Nelson, R.R., and S.G. Winter. 1982. *An Evolutionary Theory of Economic Change*. Cambridge, MA: Belknap Press.
Pollock, N. 2009. *Software and Organisations: The Biography of the Enterprise-Wide System or How SAP Conquered the World*. London: Routledge.
Rip, A., and R. Kemp. 1998. Technological Change. In *Human Choice and Climate Change*, ed. S. Rayner and E.L. Malone. Columbus, OH: Battelle Press.

Rip, A., T.J. Misa, and J. Schot. 1995. *Managing Technology in Society: The Approach of Constructive Technology Assessment*. London: Pinter.
Rosenberg, N. 1982. *Inside the Black Box: Technology and Economics*. Cambridge: Cambridge University Press.
Russell, S., and R. Willams. 2002. Social Shaping of Technology: Frameworks, Findings and Implications for Policy with Glossary of Social Shaping Concepts. In *Shaping Technology, Guiding Policy: Concepts, Spaces, and Tools*, ed. K.H. Sørensen and R. Williams. Cheltenham: Edward Elgar.
Schumpeter, J.A. 1950. *Capitalism, Socialism and Democracy*. London: G. Allen & Unwin.
Sørensen, K.H. 1994. Adieu Adorno: The Moral Emancipation of Consumers. In *Domestic Technology and Everyday Life—Mutual Shaping Processes: Proceedings from COST A4 Workshop in Trondheim, Norway, October 28–30, 1993*, ed. A.-J. Berg and M. Aune. Brussels: Europese Commissie, Directorate General Science, Research and Development.
Sørensen, K.H. 1996. *Learning Technology, Constructing Culture: Socio-Technical Change as Social Learning*. Trondheim: University of Trondheim, Centre for Technology and Society, No. 18/96.
Sørensen, K.H., and N. Levold. 1992. Tacit Networks, Heterogeneous Engineers, and Embodied Technology. *Science, Technology and Human Values* 17 (1): 13–35.
Williams, R. 1997. The Social Shaping of Information and Communications Technologies. In *The social shaping of information superhighways: European and American roads to the information society*, ed. H. Kubicek, W.H. Dutton, and R. Williams. Frankfurt and New York: Campus Verlag St. Martin's Press.
Williams, R. 2000. Public Choices and Social Learning: The New Multimedia Technologies in Europe. *The Information Society* 16 (4): 251–262.
Williams, R., and D. Edge. 1996. The Social Shaping of Technology. *Research Policy* 25 (6): 865.
Williams, R., and N. Pollock. 2012. Research Commentary—Moving Beyond the Single Site Implementation Study: How (and Why) We Should Study the Biography of Packaged Enterprise Solutions. *Information Systems Research* 23 (1): 1–22.
Williams, R., J. Stewart, and R. Slack. 2005. *Social Learning in Technological Innovation: Experimenting with Information and Communication Technologies*. Cheltenham: Edward Elgar.
Yin, R.K. 2009. *Case Study Research: Design and Methods*, 4th ed. Thousand Oaks, CA: Sage.

3

The History of Technological Developments in the Recording Industry

This chapter explores how the dominant discourse surrounding the digital recording industry has developed. It begins by demonstrating how the recording industry has evolved in the framework of technological advances, intellectual property (IP) and organisational practices. In the following section, I extend the view to the perspective of the entire network of the recording industry and discuss a broader range of settings for innovation and a wider array of players involved in the innovation of the recording industry. Close attention in this section is paid to illustrating how diverse, often conflicting, interests are negotiated. To juxtapose the changes that have emerged in the digital era (which are discussed in Chapter 6, Sect. 6.3), this section focuses on the dynamics in pre-digital settings. This chapter finishes with existing views on the digitalisation of music in three dimensions: the techno-centric dichotomy in understanding the digital recording industry, the discourse of Peer-To-Peer (P2P) technology's impact on the market and the technological trajectory of P2P technology that has deviated from the prediction.

H. Sun, *Digital Revolution Tamed*, https://doi.org/10.1007/978-3-319-93022-0_3

3.1 Evolution of Music Technologies

3.1.1 Fifteenth Century–Eighteenth Century

3.1.1.1 The Invention of the Printing Press

In the mid-fifteenth century, Johannes Gutenberg, a German goldsmith, invented a movable metal type of printing press. William Caxton, a British merchant and diplomat, introduced the machine to England in 1476, and with it brought a dramatic shift in the intellectual, political and religious landscape of the West (Feather 2006). The improved literacy made possible by the proliferation of books, pamphlets and other printed materials sparked an increased demand for new printed products, and thus, the number of printers and booksellers expanded. The wide dissemination of printed material combined with a diversification of content, including heretical and blasphemous content, reached a broad audience. Controlling the printing industry became increasingly difficult. The British government decided to bestow privilege upon the Stationers' Company, a guild of stationers, to regulate the printing of books. The first of its kind was the Royal Charter granted by Philip and Mary in 1557. The protection of the business was given only to the stationers, who, in turn, were required to check every book before printing. Publishers, whose business accompanied substantial risk, welcomed this legal decision, which could guarantee the prevention of competition. They, therefore, "were to become ardent lobbyists for decrees of censorship as a means to sustain their control of the book trade" (Patterson 1968, p. 39).

3.1.1.2 The Statute of Anne, the First Modern Copyright Law

The monopoly enabled by the aforementioned royal privilege later caused problems such as price gouging and an enormous barrier to entry into the market. The controversy surrounding the book trade culminated in the grant of the Licensing Act of 1662, which made it illegal to publish anything without first securing a licence from the appropriate authority. The act is considered to be the linear descendant of the various printing ordinances and decrees dating back to press regulation (Rose 1993). As problems with the monopoly intensified, the British government decided not to renew the act, and the perpetual right granted to the publishers ended in 1695. In order to tackle these problems, the Statute of Anne, the first modern copyright law, was created in 1709. Under this act, exclusive publication was granted for 21 years on books already published, and 14 years on books yet to be published, with a one-time renewal of 14 years. When the protection duration expired, all works were to enter the public domain.

The interpretation of the original intention of this act is still subject to debate. Scholars such as Deazley (2004) and Kaplan (1966) emphasise that the primary purpose of the act was the promotion of public interest. They believe this idea is elucidated well in the preamble of the Statute of Anne, which stated its intention as "an act for preventing the frequent abuses in printing seditious treasonable and unlicensed books and pamphlets and for regulating of printing and printing presses." As an act regulating printers in order to prevent the printing and sales of "heretical schismatical blasphemous seditious and treasonable Books Pamphlets and Papers," they argue, its concern was "the encouragement of learning" through "continued production of socially useful books" (Deazley 2003, p. 128). Other copyright historians, however, try not to over-emphasise its significance. Patterson (1968) states that the Statute of Anne, modelled after prior acts of censorship such as the Licensing Act of 1662 and the Star Chamber Decree of 1637, was nothing more than a trade regulation designed to restore order in the book trade and to prevent monopoly. Kaplan (1966) agrees that it was designed to regulate printers in order to prevent the printing and sale of heretical publications. Bently (1994) goes even further and stresses that the main purpose of the Act of Anne was to allow publishers to "print and reprint" books; therefore, it would be misleading to conceive the Act of Anne as a "copyright."

3.1.1.3 Copyright and Authors

It is now widely believed that copyright should protect authors and artists, in order for them to be remunerated and thus stimulate creativity. Claims about artists' earnings in the music business are often rooted in this belief. However, copyright being an author's right is a notion that was formulated over time. Behind the history of how copyright began as a royal privilege bestowed upon publishers but became defined as an author's right lies in the so-called battles of booksellers (Deazley 2004; Rose 1993). From 1706 onwards, booksellers, who were seeking to restore the government's perpetual protection through the revival of the 1662 Act, decided to shift their major rhetorical theme. Instead of appealing for regulation by underscoring the financial risks they faced, the publishers placed authors (whose plight as artists looked more noble and sympathetic by comparison) at the centre of the debate in the petitions and pamphlets that they sent to the government (Deazley 2004; Rose 1993). Deazley (2010)'s remark explains the background of this shift in rhetoric. He says "[N]ot only was it reasonable that an author should have all the advantage that may possibly [be] allowed him for his writings, but, without a secure property in books, no bookseller would be able to give a consideration even for the most valuable copies of books: by which means, learned men will be wholly discouraged from propagating the most useful parts of knowledge and literature. In addition, there was also an author's family and dependents to consider" (Deazley 2010, p. 47).

In regard to the matter of this change, two landmark cases are worth mentioning. The first is the case of Millar v. Taylor in 1769. Andrew Millar, a bookseller, filed a suit against Robert Taylor for printing James Thompson's poem "The Seasons." Andrew Millar purchased the publishing rights for "The Seasons" in 1729, and its term for protection granted by the Statute of Anne had already expired when Robert Taylor began publishing it. By the decision of the Court of the King's Bench led by Lord Mansfield, an author's copyright in common law was approved. Copyright lasted in perpetuity. Patterson (1968) notes that the Millar case decision was a watershed moment in the evolution of copyright as both a philosophy and a legal practice, as "it is the first case in which the problem of the meaning of copyright was judicially delineated. Because the court was concerned with the copyright of authors, it was almost inevitable that thereafter copyright should be treated as an author's right" (Patterson 1968, p. 169).

Five years later, this decision was overturned. In Donaldson v. Beckett, a legal action was brought to the King's Bench for the same work, "The Seasons," which was, it can be inferred, a cash cow for the myriad of players across the spectrum of publishing. Through this legal suit, Alexander Donaldson, a publisher in Edinburgh, attempted to acquire the right to publish the work whose perpetual right for publishing was granted to Beckett and his partners. This decision confirmed that the duration of copyright existed for twenty-eight years and the copies were in public domain thereafter. This long legal development left two important legacies: authors' rights and public domain (Feather 2007).

Opinions remain divided on this decision. Clair (2004) claims the Donaldson case as "the most decisive event in the history of reading in England since the arrival of printing 300 years before" (Clair 2004, p. 109) for this decision transformed what was once a highly monopolistic industry into a much more competitive and prosperous one. As a result, he argues, the price of books decreased, the industry enjoyed a fourfold growth in production from the increased book consumption and reading. Raven (2007), however, counters this claim and states that "the 1774 Lords' ruling has gained an importance in histories of the trade quite in excess of its true worth." For him, this ruling should be interpreted as a continuation of the earlier business output, and that it is "less a 'watershed' than a point in a much longer and more complex course of development" (Raven 2007, p. 232).

Despite the dispute, copyright has firmly become an author's right. Many scholars remain concerned about this change. Many argue that copyright as an author's right is a misconstrued conception advanced by the publisher for their benefit and deprives us of the "basis for distinguishing between the interest of the author and that of the publisher" (Feather 2006, p. 226). Patterson (1968) agrees that the concept of copyright as an author's right is an outcome propagated by publishers, not authors, who "in their quest for perpetual copyright, promoted the idea that the author had a common-law copyright based upon his natural rights as author" (Patterson 1968, p. 151). He states that since the copyright stemmed from the right to copy—which meant to publish—copyright is "a right of the publisher only," and "not until after the Statute of Anne did the modern idea of copyright as a right of the author develop" (Patterson 1968, p. 5). From his perspective, authors were not members of the Stationers' Company, and they had no role in developing and shaping the stationer's copyright. Other scholars argue that there is a belief that this change of copyright as an author's right is the consequence of the romanticised concept of authors. For example, Rose (1993) argues that copyright, far from being a moral issue, is the product of modern printing technology and the economic interests surrounding it. Through the Donaldson decision, he continues, "the representation of the author as a creator who is entitled to profit from his intellectual labor came into being through a blending of the literary and legal discourses in the context of the contest over perpetual copyright" (Rose 1993, p. 6). Marshall (2005) shares this idea and states that the concept of romantic authorship can be attributed to the historical and societal changes that flowered during the Romantic period. During this period, an author was elevated to a profession, and the increased signficance conceived as masters of one's domain subjected authors to a copyright debate. He argues that this romanticism situates the commodification of art at the centre of the copyright discussion and became subsumed in the rhetoric for both condemning copyright infringement and demanding stronger copyright protection.

3.1.1.4 Copyright for Music

Legal protection for music, like that of publishing, took shape over a long period of time as a result of the interplay between technological advances, power struggles and social needs. Even after the enactment of the first modern copyright law, the Statute of Anne, music was not subject to copyright protection because music did not belong to any of the three subject matters it covered: books, plays and maps (Rosen 2008).

The first attempt to achieve copyright protection for music was made in England in 1777 by Johann Christian Bach (Johann Sebastian Bach's younger son), and, as a result, copyright protection was conferred upon music under the category of books and other writings (Kretschmer et al. 1999). However, this decision did not lead to a common practice of legal protection for music. Music publishers by and large did not lobby for statutory protection during this period; instead, they endeavoured to strike market deals that, through strategies such as limit pricing (setting prices below the threshold of profit maximisation), prevented new entrants from establishing themselves. According to Hunter, this was because "for music publishers, the maintenance of copyright protection over 14 or 28 years was unnecessary, as most musical works would not remain in fashion that long" (Hunter 1986, p. 276).

The means of making a living for composers included working for churches, conducting, teaching and even "marrying a rich widow, as in the case of Debussy" (Peacock and Weir 1975, p. 21). Patronage from rich noblemen, rather than royalties from copyright, had long been the honourable and (once acquired) most important source of income for composers. Some composers relied on institutional mechanisms, but most musicians, even distinguished ones such as Joseph Haydn, worked for either noblemen or churches. During this period of time, copyright was remotely related either to artists' earnings or stimulation of creative works. In fact, substantial volumes of classical music, including some of the greatest masterpieces, were produced when no copyright protection existed (Boldrin and Levine 2002).

3.1.1.5 The Emergence of Publishers

The mechanisation of printing introduced an era of mass communication that led to a fundamental change in society, including the music industry. The invention of sheet music printing in 1501 allowed music admirers to enjoy music by playing what they heard at concerts or operas. The publishing business, however, required an extensive degree of expertise and upfront capital, which made an investment in it risky. Moreover, its potential customers were confined only to an elite of aristocrats, and thus, it was, at best, a side business for those pursuing other enterprises (Scherer 2004). The eighteenth century witnessed the emergence of the middle class, whose purchasing power transformed a nation of cultural deprivation into a culture-craving society (Plumb 1973). Pianos increasingly became essential status symbol of honourable home (Ehrlich 1985). As concerts and theatre life began to grow, distribution of sheet music for public performances in concerts or operas became an important business for music publishers. As a consequence, concert promoters and publishers began to exert strong influence over the music that could reach the public, commercial success of songs and therefore financial gains for artists (Napier-Bell 2014). This interplay between the burgeoning music publishing business and the growth of concert culture established the industrial basis for the music industry (Tschmuck 2012a).

3.1.2 Nineteenth Century—1910

The market structure built around music publishers lasted until the end of the nineteenth century, and sheet music was the driving force for the mass production of music as a commercial form (Garofalo 1999). At the heart of the music industry during the last third of the nineteenth century were music publishers and promoters, whose market power depended on the technological base of music concerts and the subsequent distribution of music through mass-produced sheet music (Tschmuck 2012a, p. 10). In the case of USA, this market power was well manifested in the Tin Pan Alley, a collection of music publishers and songwriters who exerted great power over the fortunes of artists.[1] With their close proximity to the vaudeville theatres, they dominated the mainstream through a near perfect distribution system in which they controlled contracts with composers, distribution and the plugging of diverse avenues for sheet music (Kernfeld 2011, p. 18).

[1]Napier-Bell (2014) argues that music halls in the UK played an equivalent role to Tin Pan Alley.

Listening to music had long been "a temporal, fleeting experience – and a rare treat…most often heard in church and perhaps at home, if someone had talent, not to mention a piano" (Coleman 2004, p. 1). Edison brought music to the home by inventing the phonograph in 1877. It became possible to record sounds, which had theretofore been limited to a single performance and thus always ephemeral. The sounds, fixed in place, became multiplied and distributed to the public. Like many other technologies, however, the phonograph was not conceived in order to perform the primary utility for which it is now most popularly known. In an 1878 publication of the North American Review, Edison published an article on the 10 intended uses of his invention, and music—either the playing or recording of—did not even make the top three. Stenography was the phonograph's first and primary function; sound recording came a distant fourth (Garofalo 1999; Tschmuck 2012b, p. 11). This initial vision is well reflected in the name of the company Edison founded in 1878: the Edison Speaking Phonograph Company. He regarded the phonograph as "a mere toy with no commercial value," and shifted his attention to developing electric light (Negus 1992, p. 21).

3.1.2.1 Phonographic Industry

The first commercial value of this technology was recognised when the Columbia Phonograph Corporation licensed and developed it as a "nickel-in-the-slot" machine. This first pay-per-play machine was introduced in 1899 by Louis Glass and allowed people to listen to a recording for a nickel. It proved to be very popular. Prompted by its unexpected commercial success, other distribution companies joined the business and spread the machine to other public places such as saloons, amusement parks, retail shops and train stations. Tschmuck (2012b) suggests that this accidental innovation is owed to the relative infancy of the industry, in which diverse experimentation was allowed. With the commercial success of the nickel-in-the-slot and jukebox, it became evident that the future of the phonographic industry did not lie with dictation technology but instead with the development of sound recordings.

A series of developments for the phonograph ensued, and sound recordings officially became its main function. Edison's phonography was developed from wax cylinders, which were not ideal for mass production. To produce a thousand albums, performers had to sing the same song 100 times with 10 phonography machines. Mass production of cylinders was not yet viable, and there were more demands for sheet music than for cylinders. Royalties from the sales of recorded music were not considered significant to writers or publishers (Kretschmer 2000). This changed with Emile Berliner who envisaged that artists could earn revenues from phonograph as "a machine for home entertainment and mass production of music discs" (Frith 1987, p. 96). He replaced the cylinder with a flat disc and named it the gramophone. A fierce rivalry between the cylinder and flat disc brought a stream of technical improvements. Edison eventually gave up the cylinder and introduced a diamond disc, but the gramophone won the competition. The creation of a master recording opened up an easy and less expensive way of duplicating and distributing sound recordings. Negus (1992) suggests that Berliner's prophecy of the technology meshed better with the industrialisation of music because "[the gramophone] was better suited to the capitalist system of production and distribution because it was harder to make pirate copies and, hence, the companies were able to control its manufacture more easily" (p. 22).

During this period, technological advances drove recording companies forward. This is a recurring theme in the history of the recording industry. It was particularly so in the early phase of the development of the recording industry: the recording companies were managed and owned by engineers and were remotely related to the previously predominant music entities such as publishing houses, theatres, artists and artist management companies (Frith 1987). The music that was released was chosen by technicians (Huygens et al. 2001), and Berliner was one of the few entrepreneurs with an interest in music (Frith 1987). As part of the "electrical goods industry," the recording companies also had to provide a wide range of technologies from recording to consumption (Gronow 1983).

3.1.3 1910–1930

3.1.3.1 Radio

Two further technological developments, radio and sound in cinema, pushed the recording industry to become its own entertainment industry (Negus 1992). Radio eventually became an important destination for recording promotions. The cinema was an important link between songs and entertainment media (Negus 1992). The way radio became a popular medium for music listening, however, is imbued with struggles and power negotiations. Many artists and producers resisted having their music played on this new medium, assuming that free play of their music would displace the need to purchase their albums. For example, Bing Crosby, the most popular crooner in early Radio era stamped "Not licensed for radio airplay" on his records (Peterson 1990, p. 105). Likewise, radio stations had a great disdain for playing "canned music" (Peterson 1990, p. 105). However, the advent of television in the 1940s took advertising income away from radio, and radio could therefore no longer afford expensive forms of programming. Radio stations decided to rely on records as a low-cost yet appealing form of programme. The record companies soon realised that radio airplay directly correlated with an increase in the sales of a record. As radio became an increasingly important gatekeeper that dictated which songs would grab consumers' attention, record companies were naturally keen to get their artists on the airwaves in order to move more units (Burnett 1996). This led to the practice of "payola," in which record companies sent out free copies of new albums or even bribed radio DJs for airplay on the radio. Top 40 playlists were developed to make sure that listeners would stay tuned. These efforts to keep listeners loyal to stations produced an "ever-narrowing chart-based play-list" (Frith 1987, p. 131). The two forged a symbiotic relationship that would persist for decades. It was not long before radio became the dominant music consumption medium, and the royalties resulting from this phenomenon became a significant source of profit for the industry (Frith 1987). By the end of the nineteenth century, royalties from sound recordings well superseded revenue from sheet music sales (Kretschmer 2000).

3.1.3.2 Collecting Societies

Prior to the invention of phonography, the only avenues by which musical performances could be monetised were theatres and concert halls: avenues that, by their very nature, were highly visible, heavily promoted and therefore easily monitored by publishers, artists and other rights holders. Performance royalty systems were common practice in Paris throughout the era predating phonograph and gramophone technology (Kretschmer 2000). In the years following the invention and proliferation of new technologies, especially radio, it became clear that although recorded sound was potentially lucrative, it was also, unlike live performance, exceedingly difficult to monitor. There was no way that individual composers could monitor each and every use of their music. Therefore, publishers, composers and songwriters attempted to form an organisation to secure an effective performance royalty system. It was kindled by an incident in Paris in 1847, when composers Ernest Bourget and Victor Parizot visited the Paris concert café Ambassadeur. Surprised at Bourget's own piece being played by an orchestra who never attempted to obtain performance permissions, they refused to pay the bill for their drinks, arguing, "You consume my music, I consume your beverages, property against property" (Kretschmer 2000, p. 211). In the following legal suit, the Tribunal de Commerce de la Seine prevented the café owner from playing the works of the composer without consent and upheld the performing rights. In the same year, the first collecting society for music, Societé des Auteurs, Compositeurs et Editeurs de Musique (SACEM), was established in Paris. This society laid the foundation for utilising performing rights for works played on sound recordings; furthermore, the society and its legislative achievements, albeit in embryonic fashion, provided a practical way to monitor sound usage and distribute royalties accordingly (Kretschmer 2000). Later, in 1914, the Performing Rights Society (PRS) was founded in the

UK to work on behalf of copyright holders in the music field. In the same year, the American Society of Composers, Authors and Publishers (ASCAP) was established in the USA.

By the 1910s, it was clear that records would become a powerful cultural force (Garofalo 1999). The record sales of classical music in both the local and international market enabled the recording industry to blossom on a global scale (Laing 2013). The 1911 Copyright Act was enacted in the UK to grant composers and publishers control over public performance of their works. In order to collect payments for the use of sound recordings, which became possible with the introduction of the 1911 Copyright Act, music publishers established the Mechanical Copyright Protection Society (MCPS) in 1924. In the lawsuit of Cawardine v. the Gramophone Company, the court ruled in favour of the Gramophone Company (which later became EMI) and ordered Stephen Cawardine & Co., a café in Bristol, to pay royalties for the playing of the Gramophone Company's sound recordings. The Gramophone Company's victory laid the groundwork for subsequent changes that guaranteed royalties for rights holders deriving from the broadcasting and public performance of sound recordings. As a result, Phonographic Performance Limited (PPL) was established to administer collective management of performance rights, through which recording companies could charge a royalty when their record was used for a public performance. As the use of radio became widespread in the 1920s, revenue generated from the licensing of the rights of record recordings increased. Collecting societies were conceived as a convenient and efficient mechanism for collecting and distributing revenue to rights holders. However, it was not without its problems or critics. Kretschmer (2000) emphasises that the establishment of collecting societies resounds with the development of copyright—which was driven by publishers, not authors or artists—in that they, in an effort to boost their own bottom lines, "used the now familiar rhetoric of authors' rights to foster their own ends" (Kretschmer 2000, p. 212). It is also argued that it ultimately led to a record-dependent music industry and the pay-per-use-driven business model which was hit hard in the digital era (Burkart and McCourt 2006).

3.1.4 1940–1950

3.1.4.1 Magnetic Tape and Multi-track

With the 1940s advent of magnetic tape, transistor and long play technology, recording structures were forced to recalibrate and reorganise. Magnetic tape was conceived to improve sound reproduction. Not only could tape be reused and edited with ease, but also it allowed for a greater length of recording compared to previous mediums. It was more portable and durable, not to mention less expensive. Multi-track recording, which soon followed magnetic tape's implementation, entirely changed the technical process of recording music and, inasmuch as it freed songs from the shackles of single-take recording, allowed artists to explore new frontiers of music production. Prior to multi-track recording, music production relied heavily, if not entirely, on the musician or musicians delivering a perfect performance for the microphone in one take. Even a single mistake meant scrapping the take and starting from scratch, which made the production time-consuming, frustrating and costly. Multi-track technology enabled artists to record sections or layers of a song, piece by piece, and combine parts to create the whole: a process known as "overdubbing." These new splicing, mixing and editing techniques enabled musicians to overcome the previous limitations and even to create wholly unique, organically impossible sounds. The Beatles' "Sergeant Pepper" LP set the standard for the complexity of eight-track recording technology (Frith 1986). Ironically, this increased reliance on technological advances moved control of the creative part from the artists to studio engineers and music producers (Toynbee 2004).

In 1947, the transistor was developed by Bell Telephone as a replacement for fragile vacuum tubes. Though initially for military uses, e.g. radar, it was less expensive, lighter and better for mass production and hence rapidly became adopted in commercial electronic products. It gave portability to the phonograph and mobility to radios. It brought high fidelity into the homes and sparked the Top 40 revolution (Coleman 2004).

Another important audio technology introduced around this time was long play. Shellac, the main ingredient in gramophone records, experienced a wartime shortage and was replaced by vinyl, which was less costly but more durable (Coleman 2004). Using vinyl as their base, CBS invented high fidelity 33-RPM (rotations per minute, pertaining to the speed at which the disc revolved on the player) records that increased the duration of audio that could fit on a record. RCA created 45-RPM in response, thus creating a marketplace competition. Following the "battle of the speeds," 45-RPM discs became the standard for the industry; they proved to be more durable yet lighter and therefore could be shipped easily at lower cost. Following the development of a two-track system, the high fidelity stereo was brought to the home. The confluence of these technological advances coincided with the emergence of rock and roll, independent labels and celebrity culture in the music industry. The low cost and ease of use enabled by tape recording lowered the entry barrier for smaller recording companies, and thus, new players entered the scene with fresh ideas, un-beholden to corporate interests (Jones 1992). The new possibilities in editing tape recordings and the emergence of home stereo systems both facilitated new, experimental music styles and allowed these styles to be enjoyed in privacy, on demand and in direct reflection of the consumer's specific taste. Niche music and niche demography were born. The reduced cost of shipping enabled by the microgroove record bred a host of distribution companies that helped small record companies distribute their albums to retail stores around the world (Peterson 1990).

3.1.4.2 Emergence of Piracy and International Conventions

The combination of technological developments and cultural influences, in the next decades, such as the increased popularity of magnetic tape and television in the 1940s, the growth of American rock and roll in the 1950s and the "British Invasion" from the Beatles to Stones in the 1960s, brought Western music sweeping across the globe. The unexpected consequence was the rampant bootlegging and home-taping which the music industry claimed to cause a decline in sales. The technological advances that ensued continued to refine bootlegging and home-taping even further, rendering it difficult to distinguish unauthorised copying and private sharing, both of which were condemned as "piracy" by the industry, nonetheless (Marshall 2004).

Music, by nature, easily crossed linguistic and cultural barriers; therefore, music publishers tried to seek international legal protection in order to ensure they could generate income from abroad and prevent pirated editions (Laing 2004). Even though reproduction technologies were still in their infancy, a few countries already had laws in place to deal with the reproduction of musical works by mechanical means (Laing 2004). While bilateral agreements were drawn up between neighbouring countries in Europe, they were not a well-organised way of securing international copyright protection (Ricketson 2006). Claims were made that mechanical recordings had cut employment opportunities for performers and that this could bring about the eradication of the profession. Existing laws were considered insufficient to cover the newly emerging practice of unauthorised use of sound recordings (World Intellectual Property Organization 1981). This developed into a major issue, feared by the recording industry, who lobbied hard to protect performers against unauthorised use of their performances (Davies 1979). The remedy proposed was to establish international legal protection to monitor the use of recorded or broadcast performers (Thompson 1986).

Copyright protection for literary and artistic works was first recognised across national boundaries through the Berne Convention, established in 1886. However, the derivative nature of performances or musical arrangements whose works are derived from an original musical composition could not satisfy the requirements for protection under the Berne Convention (Boytha 1993; Bently 2008). After a 50-year-long gestation, the Rome Convention was signed in 1961 and came into force in 1964, with about twenty contracting states. It provided protection, for the first time at an international level, of the three principal categories of neighbouring rights: performers, producers of phonograms and broadcasting organisations.

The intrinsic nature of neighbouring rights—rights neighbouring on copyright—required the collection of royalties to be exploited by way of licensing the public performance of records to the users. Collecting societies, which worked on behalf of copyright holders, enabled users to access the societies' collection of sound recordings through blanket licences. These licences, as opposed to single-use licences, saved time and therefore improved income for rights holders, who no longer had to examine each individual use on a case-by-case, micro level. The Rome Convention laid the foundation for granting the right of exploitation of sound recordings to relevant parties under the norms of copyright, and thus, the economic incentive for copyright owners to control their works was born (Teller 1990). From the Rome Convention onwards, the expansion of protection for music continued. In 1992, the EC Rental Directive was legislated and enforced in European countries by the Rome Convention.

3.1.5 1960–1980

3.1.5.1 Cassette Tape and CD

The magnetic tape improved the process of recording and editing of sounds, but its reel-to-reel format was not ideal for playback (Laing 2013). Philips, a Dutch electronic firm, improved the format to a self-contained cassette to which a tape is inserted, enabling playback. With the arrival of cassettes, the landscape of popular music changed entirely (Frith 1986). It made music portable and recordable. The lowered cost and less complex method of production, duplication and dissemination of music bred new and small labels in the market. More significantly, this technology facilitated changes in the relationship between the creator and the public by blurring the line between the creators and the users. It allowed users to copy music from radio and an ability to record their own music. An associated product, Sony's Walkman, a portable cassette player launched in 1979, heralded the age of nomadic and private music listening and played a crucial role in cassettes becoming a sustainable music listening format (Nathan 1999). Although it enabled the recording industry to reach every corner of the world and become a transnational industry, the cassette tape was a double-edged sword. The decentralised control over the production and consumption of music enabled by this technology made the issue of home-taping and bootlegging even more acute. The industry realised the significance of this change only later, which is claimed to be "another example of the multinationals' ignorance of the implications of their own inventions" (Frith 1986, p. 87).

The introduction of the music video in the late 1970s enhanced the importance of television and, in tandem, the imagery associated with popular music (Negus 1992). Images of artists portrayed in visual media such as film and television became an integral part of a song's popularity. The significance of visual media reached its peak in 1983 when Michael Jackson's music video for "Thriller" was released. As one of the most expensive, as well as influential, music videos, "Thriller" helped the same-titled album achieve sales surpass 40 million copies, an unprecedented record. In the face of the financial constraints generated by the recession of this era, major labels were in need of cost-cutting measures. "Thriller" suggested that superstar economy could be an answer to this concern by generating enormous amount of income from a small number of artists (Garofalo 1999). It also signalled a shift in the focus of recording companies' business from production to copyright exploitation (Garofalo 1999).

In 1982, the CD was introduced. It was far superior to the LP in many ways: crisper sound quality, greater durability and simpler usage. The barrier of buying new CD hardware delayed its market penetration, but soon it successfully replaced the vinyl LP. In fact, not only did the CD replace vinyl for new albums, but also the sales of back catalogues became a lucrative revenue stream for recording companies. Consumers purchased records they already owned on LP in the CD format. The major labels promoted this new format vigorously (McLeod 2005), only to realise later that it allowed users to "retrieve digital music information for new uses" and "undermine[d] the material distinction between production and reproduction on which copyright law rests" (Toynbee 2004, p. 3).

3.1.5.2 Mergers and Acquisitions

Over the past few decades, a series of mergers and acquisitions has characterised the recording business structure. A major "merger mania" began in the 1960s, with rock and roll swaying the market and independent record companies achieving unprecedented growth (Garofalo 1999). In the 1980s and 1990s, the recording industry market underwent a series of consolidations in which smaller labels were purchased by or merged with larger firms. The commercial success of American music and the rise of the superstar system bred a multinational recording business driven by US recording companies (Laing 2004). By 1999, "the Big Five"—Warner, EMI, Sony, BMG and Universal—dominated and became the basis for the multinational recording industry (Garofalo 1999). The music industry was firmly controlled by this oligopoly of five major international record companies, which dominated 70–80% of global sales (Burnett 1996). Through this process of market consolidation, copyright became an integral part of the global music business (Frith 1978; Negus 1992; Bettig 1996). Multinational music companies adopted rights-based business structure where economies of scale built through vertical integration could bring enough profits to overcome the endogenous sunk costs (Bakker 2012).

3.1.5.3 Copyright as an Economic Incentive

In the 1980s, the recording industry shifted its attention from international conventions to lobbying trade regulations (Laing 2004). Through subsequent international conventions, protection for neighbouring rights became consolidated. World Copyright Treaty (WCT) and WIPO Performances and Phonograms Treaty (WPPT) granted phonogram producers the right to equitable remuneration for broadcast or communication to the public and the exclusive right to make their recordings available. Copyright exploitation has become vitally important for the global recording business (Frith 1988).

What followed is a well-established notion of copyright as an economic incentive (Towse 2001). The economic justification of copyright is to provide an incentive to artists to continue to create artistic works by guaranteeing commercial exploitation and, as a result, financial compensation. The substantial financial investment required to produce music, compounded by consumers' fickle and unpredictable musical tastes, makes the music business particularly high risk, with a high ratio of failures. This market condition is associated with the market failure that creative works carry as public goods. That is, as a public good, music is non-excludable and non-rival. Listening to music does not diminish its value or exclude its usage. By being packaged in physical formats, music is turned into a rival good. This leads to the argument that the absence of protection could result in a "tragedy of the commons"—where no exclusive right to common goods would eventually lead to the destruction of the common resource (Hardin 1968). To counteract these problems, the government can intervene and grant exclusive rights to the owner of the property as a remedy to the threat of over-consumption. Posner (1998) argues that the absence of legal protection for property rights would result in less or no incentive for investment. An efficient use of resources and continuous production is emphasised in order to ensure the recovery of the cost of development through exclusive rights. Another important economic aspect of copyright is that it is a trade of interests between costs and benefits (Towse 2004). No benefit of copyright, in other words, will reduce the incentive to produce works, because the benefit will increase the price. Therefore, in determining copyright policy, it is of the utmost importance to strike a balance between the protection of artists and the costs of copyright in order to maximise creative output (Landes and Posner 1989). However, the way to overcome the dilemma of copyright as a mechanism for incentive to create access to users while avoiding concentration of copyright ownership in enterprises with excessive market power is still a matter of dispute (Towse 2004).

From the artist's perspective, royalties generated from copyright are increasingly conceived as an important source of revenue. Under the terms of a standard contract, artists receive an agreed percentage of profit derived from record sales only after all upfront expenses—recording, marketing, manufacturing, advance, etc.—have been recouped (Caves 2002). A few scholars have raised questions relating to copyright as a reward for creators. Towse and Kretschmer provided empirical research on copyright and artists' earnings to determine whether or not copyright is economically beneficial for artists. Towse (1999) demonstrated that the different interests of authors and publishers as well as the asymmetries in power, including risk-bearing ability and information, lead to an imbalance in power amongst the parties involved in music. She observed a skewed distribution of royalties amongst individual musicians across the fame spectrum; the majority of royalties collected by PPL are distributed to top-tier musicians. Kretschmer et al. (1999) identified that the bargaining power between the parties surrounding the rights granted by copyright is the determinant factor of the location of intellectual property rights (IPR). The digital technology that is posing challenges to the existing structure of the industry, they argued, threw up questions about the need to sustain the traditional flow of the rights. In an article, "Intellectual Property in music," Kretschmer (2000) illustrated that publishers and a few established authors were the driving force behind the evolution of copyright and observed that the major portion of the earnings of the artists distributed by PRS are paid to a few top artists. This favourability to the few and the skewed bargaining power of the parties involved brings into question whether copyright operates under the widespread notion that it serves to help artists gain financial returns. It also highlights the fact that a more sophisticated examination is essential to understand the spectrum of artists that are benefiting from the copyright system and to gain a more balanced view of copyright's role in artists' earnings.

3.2 The Conventional Music Value Networks

Technological innovation in the recording industry entails a complex interplay of a diverse array of factors including digital technology, copyright regulation and conflicting interests between heterogeneous players such as major labels, other intermediaries, music consumers and artists. This section demonstrates the organisational structure and features of the recorded music industry, paying special attention to the intricate relationship amongst its diverse actors. This section focuses on the

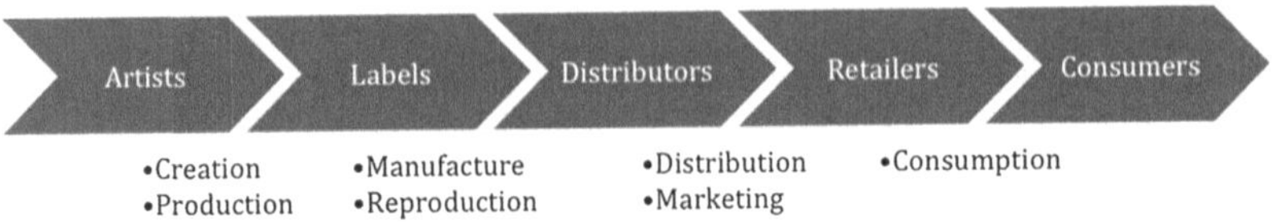

Fig. 3.1 Conventional music business value chain

dynamics in pre-digital settings in order to juxtapose the changes that emerged during the digital era (discussed in Chapter 6, Sect. 6.3).

Value chain analysis determines the value-creating logic in an industry. The publication of Porter's (1980) value chain framework signalled a new understanding of the way firms achieve a competitive advantage by differentiating their product or service in value-adding processes. The value chain framework has thus been widely used to study the music industry. Kretschmer et al. (1999, 2001) probed the role of IPR in music value creation. Combining this with many other business perspective works (Rapaport 2003; Hull 2004; Parker 2004; Weissman 2010), the conventional value chain in the music industry can be shown in Fig. 3.1. This value chain was established around the 1930s, when publishers emerged at the heart of the music business as intermediaries between composers, performers and recording companies. Concomitant with the development of new technologies, new intermediaries have been added to the chain. The basic structure of the chain, however, has changed little since the first model (Wallis 2006).

This value chain provides a useful framework to understand the process by which music is created and delivered to consumers in the market; in each of the stages, value is added. The chain begins with the creation of musical works, the right of which to exploit in most cases is assigned to intermediaries such as labels or publishing companies. When the music is recorded and manufactured, it is distributed, marketed and promoted to the final users, who purchase the products at retail outlets. In the music industry, IPRs play a crucial role in adding value to the chain by enabling the right of use of the contents to be transferred to the next process (Kretschmer et al. 1999; Towse 2014).

Although the value chain is useful for understanding value creation logic, it is not sufficient for comprehending the interplay between innovation actors and their interaction in the economic, cultural, legal and institutional context. In mapping out these complicated dynamics, this book draws upon Leyshon's (2001) network of musical economy. Developed upon Attali's (1985) political and economic music value framework, Leyshon's (2001) value networks explore the allocation of the different functions of the industry in four musical networks. The constellations of four major networks in the music industry depicted in this framework are particularly valuable for capturing the complex relationship amongst heterogeneous forces and the blurred interaction amongst the four networks. As a geographer, Leyshon places the location at the centre of the analysis of musical value networks. In this book, I place more focus on the sociotechnical aspects in the recording industry and provide complex and intricate dynamics of the recording industry in the context of the whole network.

3.2.1 Networks of Creativity

Leyshon (2001) defines networks of musical creativity as "centres of musical knowledge, both in the sense of being a repository of the requisite technical competencies to be able to compose, perform, and record music, but also of knowledge of what different compositional, performative, and recording styles signify within a wider cultural and subculture context. They are, as such, not only centres of production, but also of interpretation. As such, networks of musical creativity influence the ways in which musical forms circulate and are recombined through acts of creativity" (p. 62). Drawing upon this concept, this subsection discusses two features within the networks of creativity that have close relevance to this research: production and the relationship between record labels and artists.

3.2.1.1 Music Production

Up until the 1960s, music production was a well-structured process in which A&R agents discovered talent, developed and trained them and signed them by contract to labels. Artists' aptitude for live performance had to be strong enough to be pressed on a disc. Therefore, the artists' performance was of prime importance in the quality of sound recordings. A dramatic change in recording came with the development of multi-track recording in the 1960s (Cunningham 1998). The introduction of new mixing and editing techniques enabled the creation of otherwise "impossible music" and also brought about a drastic reorganisation of production. The studio's significance increased, as a space to separate and control both artists and sound; sound engineers became an essential part of the recording process for sound layering (Théberge 1997). From Hennion's (1989) perspective, studios became the axis to which music's collective apparatus was anchored: the networks of creativity, therefore, became intermediated by music producers, whose role as negotiators between artists, engineers, facilities and consumers gave them enormous power. The intrinsic value of producers, he argues, is embodied in their ability to associate with the public and thereby to produce hits. In this setting, "pop musicians have increasingly taken on the more detached, evaluative role of the producer in assessing the commercial potential of their material" (Théberge 1997, p. 221).

3.2.1.2 Relationship Between Artists and Record Companies

Record companies play an essential role in the networks of creativity by providing the resources necessary for artists to focus on their artwork instead of finances or logistics. These resources include a specialised workforce including sound engineers, producers and high-quality recording facilities. Normally, a record company signs a contract with an artist and provides them with an advance, so they can concentrate on their career without needing to engage in part-time jobs or other means of ancillary income. All this takes a substantial amount of financial investment, which an average artist cannot afford. Just as record companies are crucial in providing the wherewithal for artists' creative activity, artists are also instrumental in record companies' survival. Releasing projects by established artists is often preferable because it is a safe bet that record labels will accrue money from them without much risk. These projects often generate the capital necessary to discover, nurture and launch new talent, who are, although riskier from an investment standpoint, crucial to the future of any recording company (Hull 2004). Since the music business relies heavily on the fickle nature of popular taste, it is continually essential to seek the "next big sound" (Hull 2004). If a new artist becomes successful, the label not only earns a considerable return on their investment, but also improves their own leveraging power for future projects. Since new artists do not have a proven record of success, the royalty rates and advances paid out to them are normally lower than those offered to established artists. The label, moreover, can also bind the artist to the contract during the most lucrative period of her career. Contractual agreements are common forms of sharing risk, distributing incentives and rewards between artists and labels (Caves 2002). In theory, royalties are paid to artists when the advance is recouped through the sales of albums. However, in reality, very few releases sell enough copies to recoup the initial investment made in production, marketing and so forth. It is argued that less than 10% of releases sell enough copies to cover the loss made by the other 90% (Cummings 2010).

Historically, the relationship between artists and gatekeepers has often been subject to conflict of interests over the ways in which musical products are exploited (Peacock and Weir 1975). This owes to the power imbalance tilted towards labels, with the exception of a few established top-echelon stars that command considerable leverage when negotiating deal points. These stars are the exception, however, and the vast majority of artists—especially those of the fledgling variety—have little to no say in the content of their contracts. "Take it or leave it" is the operating principle in most cases. In all contractual negotiations within the music industry, regardless of either party's stature at the table, the bargaining power of the artist is determined by the extent to which the interested label must hedge their bets at each stage of value creation. When new music is created and produced, artists and labels negotiate their power. Artists trade their artistic talents for labels' financial capacity and knowledge. Artists' recorded output then becomes labels' asset in further negotiations with other parties such as publishers, synchronisation licensing firms and advertising agencies. Once music is ready to be marketed, the key to the negotiation is reaching the widest possible leverage of intended audiences (Burnett 1996). This power imbalance, as well as the often insurmountable technical and logistical hurdles faced by new artists, meant that the majority of artists have traditionally been obligated to sign contracts with labels in order to elevate themselves from amateur to professional status.

3.2.2 Networks of Reproduction

In networks of reproduction, economies of scale become a crucial element of the music business. Due to the initial sunk cost of building the manufacturing infrastructure, it is imperative to ensure mass production. This mass production can be beneficial not only to reducing the overhead cost, but also to overcoming the fickle demands of consumers (Leyshon 2001). The record labels undertake the responsibilities of providing the means of resolving the financial burdens involved in the production, manufacturing, reproduction and distribution of a record. Economies of scale, which require an enormous capital resource, put the major labels in a more advantageous position than independent labels in controlling the market. The substantial cost involved in reproduction has contributed to the rise of the star system suited to multinational firms.

One consequence of brick-and-mortar reproduction features is the impact on innovation and the diversity of cultural products. Some research shows that there is an inverse correlation between market concentration and diversity of popular music production (Peterson and Berger 1975). Burnett (1993) contends that market control in the hands of a few large corporations is closely related to the extent to which major labels control innovation and cultural diversity.

The internationalisation and concentration of the entertainment conglomerates have made this issue particularly contentious. For example, Burnett (1996) examines the internationalisation of the media conglomerates and their control of global distribution and demonstrated that large recording organisations are better positioned to effectively utilise and capitalise on the newly emerging open modes of music production, which he defined as a "global jukebox." On the other hand,

Frith (1986) argues that the conditions of manufacturing infrastructure contributed to the control of the major companies, but stresses the need for the divergent effects of technology. He argues:

> Technology, the shifting possibility of mechanical reproduction, has certainly been the necessary condition for the rise of the multinational entertainment business, for ever more sophisticated techniques of ideological manipulation, but technology has also made possible new forms of cultural democracy and new opportunities of individual and collective expression. (Frith 1986, p. 91)

3.2.3 Networks of Distribution/Promotion

The music business could be characterised as a combination of two strands—uncertainty and contingency. The uncertainty of the business stems from the features carried by all brick-and-mortar business. To overcome the uncertainty, the processes of music distribution have become more streamlined by adding more windows as illustrated in Fig. 3.2. In the process of music distribution—manufacturing, mass production of physical products, storing products at a warehouse and finally delivering products to retailers—"each of these technologies was initially expensive, specialized, and not accessible to individuals" (Kernfeld 2011, p. 14).

The distribution system, built around physical copies of sound recordings, creates high barriers to entry. It entails a distribution system with wide coverage, warehouses and storage space and thus requires a substantial amount of finance (Hull 2004). For recording companies who invest a significant amount of money, maximising the exposure of their products is essential to recouping their investment. The control of distribution, therefore, becomes essential to eliminating—or at least reducing—the uncertainty entailed in the investment (Hirsch 2000). This control has long been in the hands of the major labels in the form of oligopoly (Negus 1992). This subsection describes the different approaches employed by major labels and independent labels in distributing their works.

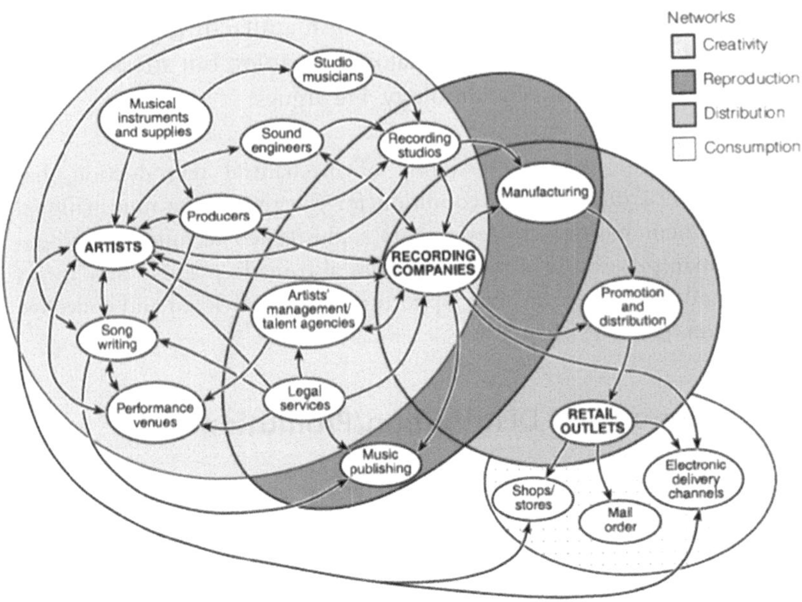

Fig. 3.2 Value networks in the conventional music industry (Leyshon 2001)

3.2.3.1 Distribution Networks for Major Labels

Major labels distribute large quantities of records. In order to justify the large overhead of their operations, they own their own distribution networks. Their distribution operations are geared towards selling large quantities of hit albums by established artists. The major labels distribute not only their own product but also recordings owned by some independent labels. The major label in-house distribution systems, in pursuit of the maximum number of units, are also beholden to the largest retailers, who are in the position to order the most product (Weissman 2010, p. 15).

The major labels have built their own distribution systems, in which publishing, record label, manufacture and distribution units are integrated into their own business structure. Known as vertical integration, this system is defined as "the combination of technologically distinct production, distribution, selling, and/or economic processes within

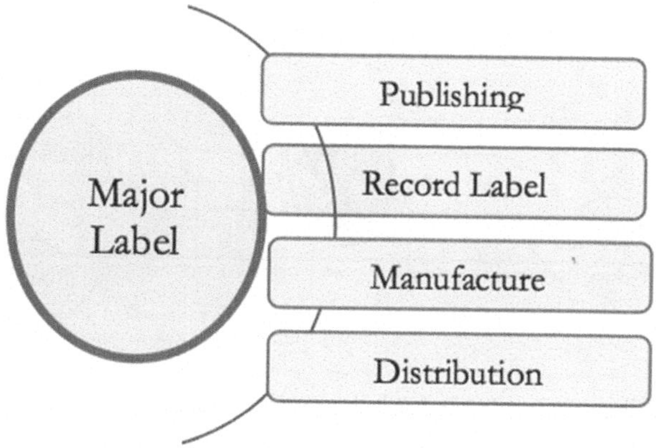

Fig. 3.3 Distribution networks for major labels

the confines of a single firm" (Porter 1980, p. 300). Companies build vertical integration "in circumstances where small-numbers bargaining would otherwise obtain and where, in sequential decision-process has optimal properties" (Williamson 1975, p. 104). The first and most important reason for vertical integration is for economic benefit, which is achieved "by harmonizing interests and permitting a wider variety of sensitive incentive and control processes to be activated" (Williamson 1975, p. 104). However, other strategic issues, which are not often easily calculated in numbers, also come into play (Porter 1980, p. 301). The control stems from "the distribution of marginally differentiated products" and enables them to "link available input to reliable and established distribution channels" (Hirsch 1972, p. 646) (Fig. 3.3).

3.2.3.2 Distribution Networks for Independent Labels

On the other hand, independent labels focus on nurturing fewer releases, to be distributed in smaller quantities to niche retailers via independent distributors. No individual label sells enough product or has a large enough catalogue to justify the costs of self-distribution, but when combined with other labels under one umbrella, enough product can be pooled to keep an independent distributor in business

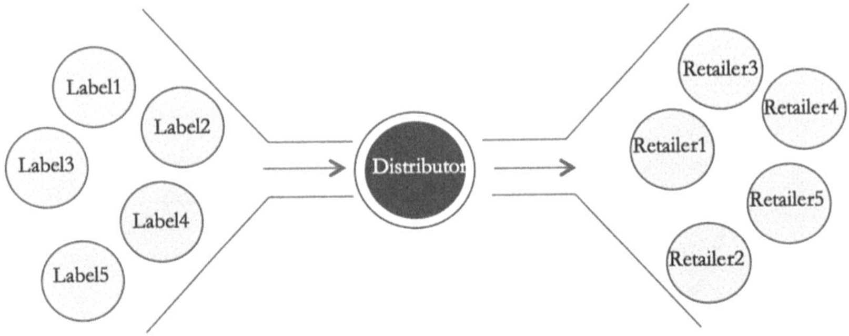

Fig. 3.4 Distribution networks for independent labels

(Weissman 2010, p. 15). Independent labels vary in size, but as a rule, they manage smaller quantities of records than major labels and are not controlled by corporate shareholders. Independent distributors help independent labels achieve retail coverage for their music in markets that, unassisted, would be impossible to reach. In the conventional system, numerous and diverse distributors and retailers exist in order to cover as many regions as possible. Since the majority of independent labels do not have album-manufacturing equipment, often the role of distributors begins with the manufacturing of albums. The crucial factors influencing the relationship between labels and distributors are specialities, coverage and advances. The competitive advantages of independent labels lie in expertise in niche genres; distribution of indie albums, therefore, requires a special network and knowledge in that particular niche market. Small-scale distributors in particular, known as "boutique" distributors, provide much more bespoke services for labels than comparatively larger distributors (Fig. 3.4).

In general, labels are defined as independent when they are not owned by a major label, and when their albums are sold through independent distributors (Passman 2011). In the mid-1980s, the term "independent" increasingly acquired subjective connotations of genre and style in addition to its objective characteristics (Hesmondhalgh 1997). Although "independent" music, in both scope and definition, has evolved alongside the development of rock and roll, it has always carried the connotations of "authentic," "different" and "alternative" compared to the output of major labels (Frith 1981). The need for a more nuanced approach to this concept has thus been suggested (Frith 1990). A similar view was expressed by Lee (1995) who observed that the ideology and distribution network that distinguished independents from majors has dissolved, and moreover, major labels have appropriated the style and aesthetic of independents in their eternal quest for cool. In his view, the current distinction between "indie" and "major" is arbitrary and nostalgic at best: a "sign post to a different era that treated the concepts of artistry, independence and audience as somehow shared" (Lee 1995, p. 15).

The exploitation of copyright has proven to be crucial to the success of music companies (Frith 1987; Negus 1992; Bettig 1996; Litman 2001; Towse 2004). This means that the size and range of any label's repertoire, whether major or independent, has a direct correlation to the label's profits. This motivated many independent labels to build links with major labels (Negus 1992), and as a result, the structure of the music industry has experienced a high degree of consolidation and concentration in the past decade. During the half century following the invention of phonograph, a scant few companies—companies that held patents for technologies, such as Edison, Columbia and Victor—dominated the music business (Laing 2013). Smaller recording companies that catered to niche markets arose in the mid-1920s, but they were eventually bought by major companies like Victor, Decca and Columbia in the 1930s (Weissman 2010). From that point until the early 1950s, American popular music dominated the world's music marketplace. The sudden surge of rock and roll in the mid-1950s, combined with major labels' lack of enthusiasm, led to the emergence of independent record labels and loosened the early music business' oligopoly (Weissman 2010). However, the next 20 years saw extensive acquisitions and mergers which were built to assert control over distribution (Hull 2004, p. 123). After a series of acquisitions and mergers in which smaller labels were absorbed by powerful entertainment conglomerates, a tight oligopoly was firmly established by 2000 (Hull 2004, p. 124).

3.2.3.3 Marketing and Promotion

Once music is recorded, the important next step is to have it heard, known and sold. Despite the commonly held idea that the cream always rises to the top, without effective promotion it, in many cases, remains at the bottom and dissolves. Three methods of music marketing and promotion played a crucial role in the conventional system: pre-filtering, publicity and radio.

The substantial costs and the added windows of distribution led the record business to be perceived as risky. To overcome this risk, the recording industry hedged their bets on a few big hits by overproducing diverse musical products. Subsequently, the music industry became structured as a network of complex organisations in which discovery and filtering was processed at each level of the network (Hirsch 1972). Consumers' access to music therefore was considerably restricted by the filtering process that was subject to negotiations of conflicting interests and power relations. Underpinning this pre-selection was the emphasis on the control of distribution channels, through which recording companies could ensure sufficient exposure for their products and in turn maximise revenue. As Turow (1997) write:

> [They] could be sure that the material their firm produced would have at least the opportunity to make its costs back in places they considered appropriate…[and] accumulate a great deal of power within the mass media system and still not be subject to restrictions on monopolies that authorities might enforce if they tried to control individual mass media industries. (p. 687)

DiMaggio (1977) was particularly concerned with the way the uncertainty involved in the music business influences the creative process. Since this uncertainty arises from external conditions, he suggested, the supply of cultural goods came as a consequence of the constant negotiations of the social, cultural and regulatory embodied in the creative process and personnel. He states:

> The market structure of an industry, in particular the degree of what economists call 'seller concentration' determines the degree of control

> over the market that firms hold and the certainty of corporate managers that their products will be sold. This, in turn, strongly influences the independence granted popular-culture creators which, in turn, affects the degree of innovation and diversity in the products that the industry manufactures. (p. 438)

3.2.3.4 Pre-Selection

In his book *The Structure of the Popular Music Industry*, Hirsch (1969) investigated the industrial mechanism behind the way that certain songs become popular. By demonstrating the interdependent relationship between record companies and commercial radio stations, he defined the recording industry as "The Top 40 Music Industry." His pre-selection framework, shown in Fig. 3.5, encapsulates the features of the popular music industry he conceives. He identified four important agents that play a crucial role in this process of filtering: the A&R agent, the record company, the promoter/distributor and the radio station/media outlet. In this model, each stage of the pre-selection system entails a large amount of filtering. Wikström (2013) well recapitulated it:

> Only a small fraction of all artists are ever able even to meet an A&R agent, and only very few out of all the acts that an A&R agent ever listens to attract the attention of the record executive. Eventually, only one artist 'in a million' will be heard by the mainstream audience on commercial radio stations. (Wikström 2013, p. 53)

3.2.3.5 Publicity

The purpose of publicity is to increase the exposure of the product to the widest possible audience, normally through media coverage. The history of music promotion began with sales of sheet music for songs heard through recordings or public performances. The basic principle is to increase the odds of commercial success by providing positive impressions of albums to consumers. This means the campaign "can 'reach' sufficient numbers of their target market with the 'frequency' necessary

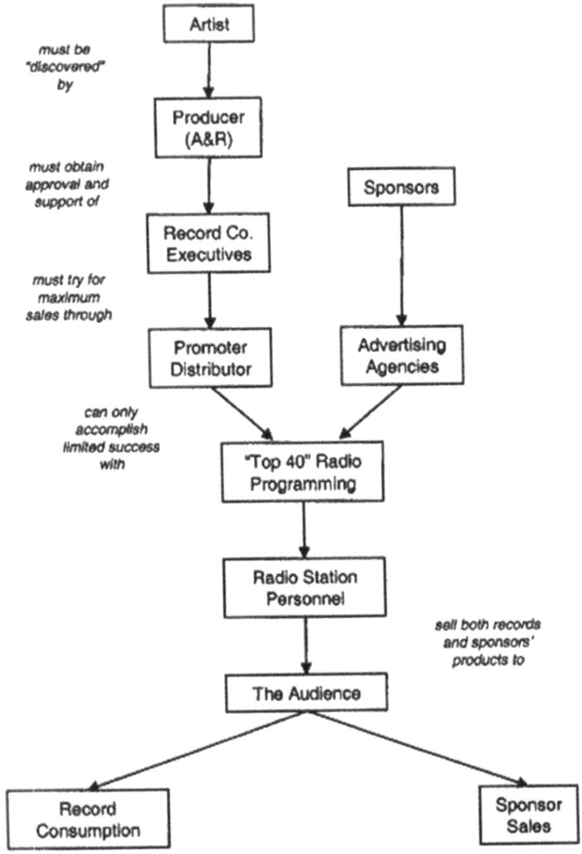

Fig. 3.5 The organization of the pop music industry (Hirsch 1969)

for them to remember the message and act by purchasing" (Katz and Hepworth-Sawyer 2009, p. 213). The significance of publicity comes from its credibility as information rather than as a commercial product for which an advertisement is designed. Even though publicity is not influenced by market spending as much as advertising is, it would be naïve to believe that it is not somewhat affected by the power of marketing. Major labels have departments for this specific job, or sometimes hire independent publicists who have the capacity to promote their music to other promotion outlets. The extent of their capacity as publicists is directly correlated with the pedigree of their contacts within major media. Large independent labels also have their own publicity departments, but often publicity firms are outsourced for specific projects. The objectives of publicity can be successfully achieved through the ripple effects of media exposure. In order to make maximum impact in the market, record companies usually undertake record promotion in tandem with publicity (Spellman 1996).

3.2.3.6 Radio

Since becoming popular in the 1950s, radio has been the most influential outlet for our engagement with music. Frith (2002) calls it "the most significant twentieth-century mass medium" and emphasises that "radio is still the most important source of popular musical discourse, defining genres and genre communities, shaping music history and nostalgia, determining what we mean by 'popular' music in the first place" (p. 201). Ever since radio emerged as a music discovery channel in the 1950s, radio airplay has been a crucial part of music promotion. The significance of the radio's role in record sales was so great that record companies bribed disk jockeys to play their recordings. Known as "payola," this practice was exposed and has been forbidden. The significance of the radio, however, has not withered, because of its essential ripple effect throughout media, which can ultimately lead to the success of record sales.

The importance of airplay begs the question of the way radio stations choose playlist. The task of getting a track on the radio in the first place is exclusive to market specialists called independent promoters, also known as pluggers. Lathrop (2007) gives a clear explanation for the way this process works:

> The placement of songs on commercial Top-40 and rock radio is handled virtually exclusively through the independent promotion system. Independent promoters establish close relationships with stations and networks that may involve making promotional payments for adding

> songs to playlists. And independent promoters may gain a 'lock' on a station or cluster of stations and become a kind of exclusive gateway between the stations and the record labels who want their songs played on those stations. With fewer 'clusters' around, the indie promoter with a lock on one wields a huge amount of clout and can command huge payments from record companies. (p. 176)

Different radio stations have different priorities and characteristics and hence have different measures to consider what songs to play. Commercial radio stations, however, are primarily concerned with the commercial interest, specifically the revenue from advertisement. As a general rule, that means radio stations tend to play music that can gratify the widest possible audiences. In addition, people's penchant for familiar tunes rather than new ones makes it difficult for radio stations to play experimental music (Frith 2002). What came as a consequence is the practice of "settl[ing] for what is easy and familiar" (Crisell 2002, p. 132), also known as the lowest common denominator (Burnett 1993).

3.2.4 Networks of Consumption

By enabling the recording of the ephemeral experience of performance, the phonograph signalled a shift in music consumption. Music listening and consumption were initially a public activity and a signal of status. Technological developments, in conjunction with societal change, have brought about significant changes in music consumption. The phonograph signalled the emergence of music listeners who enjoyed music on their own terms in time and space. The subsequent technologies of mass production and distribution enabled the industry to make music more affordable. This led to an increase in the number and strata of listeners with access to music. As a result, the demarcation between serious and non-serious music listeners became blurred. Adorno (1976) believed that the musical experience, which requires a deep emotional commitment, is demeaned by the accessibility and affordability of music: music has become an easy pleasure, enjoyed by passive listeners whose consumption behaviour is concealed by the manipulation of taste by capitalist production. Critics of this approach place importance on the diverse social conditions affecting the music listening experience. For example, Hennion (2001) argued that taste in music is not entirely determined by external elements, but is conditioned by factors that inherently exist as a social being. Although music is a very personal experience that functions as emotional agency, Frith (2002) stressed, musical activities are in essence a vehicle for communication and social activity, orchestrating the way we experience the world and therefore helping us understand who we are. From this perspective, the reasons why we like certain music or why certain music is popular are not an objective means of determining objective aesthetics of music, but a socially determined preference. The "popularity" of a song, therefore, is less an outcome of an absolute aesthetic definition than a socially determined collective consumption.

Since musical experience is such a collective and social activity, music is also deeply intertwined with the way we relate to society, other listeners and our identity. In other words, music listening is often a reflexive social practice in which tastes develop in the context of social relations (Hennion 2001). However, this does not mean that musical activity is confined to separate special occasions such as concert halls or theatres. Rather, music listening is a practice that anchors music in our common mundane everyday experience (DeNora 2000). In this context, music listening is not exclusively either active or passive, but both for the majority of listeners. Bergh and DeNora (2009) state:

> The music is empowered in ways that in turn imbue its 'passive' recipients with forms of empowerment – or transubstantiation…Listening to recorded music was not predestined for the central place it eventually attained in modern life; but, in combination with cultural entrepreneurship, the increased reflexivity of modern life, and innovations in technology and distribution, it ended up being the normative mode of music enjoyment in industrialised societies. (p. 115)

Nonetheless, this is not to say that consumers' choices are entirely free from market control. In fact, choices are highly contingent on market availability (DiMaggio 1977; Turow 1997). Although consumers' final decision on what to purchase and their capricious taste has always been a concern for the recording industry, their choices were constrained by many factors in the pre-digital era. First, there was a considerable limitation on consumers' access to available records. The available products were restricted through a pre-selection process, and therefore, audiences' decision-making was, to a certain degree, influenced by the market control mechanism. Another layer of filtering was exercised in the ease of access. Small independent retail stores remained important for music aficionados who sought niche genres of music, while large chains such as HMV or Tower Records were more accessible options for music consumption for the majority of consumers. These large chains, by way of buying power, exerted tremendous influence over the records display and thus influenced the "construct" of consumers' choices. In other words, their general tendency to stock the top-selling records worked as part of the filtering mechanism in which consumers were exposed to what was already popular.

So far, I explored the conventional value networks operated in the pre-digital setting. In the next section, I move on to the discussion on how digital technology and the dominant discourses surrounding the digital recording industry have developed.

3.3 Digital Technology in the Recording Industry

The introduction of the compact disc (CD) in 1982 marked the beginning of the shift from the analogue to the digital era in the music industry. The disruptive nature that this technological advance has brought was realised only later. When the CD was initially introduced, the recording industry welcomed the huge popularity it gained during the 1980s, as it appeared to be an incremental innovation—simply a shift in the recording medium for music content—which worked perfectly within the existing business framework, generating a whole new revenue stream of selling back catalogues. The possibility of multiple copying without loss of signal quality did increase the possibility of unauthorised copying of music compared to previous recording technologies such as cassette players. However, this affected only a small share of the music trade. It was only when P2P file-sharing services arrived that the issue of technological innovation became particularly contentious (Ku 2002; Shirky 2001). The debut of Napster, a P2P-based digital file distribution technology, suggested the possibility of an imminent and radical transformation within the music industry.

Although Napster was the first widespread P2P file-sharing online music service, the cultural and technical framework predates Napster. In the wake of the computing industry's growth in the 1960s, the so-called hacker ethic was forged, providing a set of principles and values that represented the counterculture shared by the hacker community (Allen-Robertson 2013). At the heart of hacker ethics lies a firm belief that computers can be a vehicle for a better world by enabling us to achieve freedom of information and challenge authority (Levy 2001). With a strong connotation of libertarianism, hacker ethics are situated within a value proposition that hacker ethical codes could be used to emancipate the community from the constraints of capitalism (Himanen 2001). The alternative to capitalism, hackers believed, was their subcultural values: free distribution of information and collective altruistic intention with no commercial aspiration that would fulfil a wide array of social and cultural needs. These values became strongly associated with the subsequent development of P2P technology (Allen-Robertson 2013). They also influenced the formation of much of the academic and policy discussions on digital culture (Lessig 2001; Vaidhyanathan 2001; Benkler 2006). Their view is deeply rooted in the idea that unrestricted access to information and the subsequent changes in social practices of sharing should prevail in the digital communication environment. The radical idea that music, as information, should be free on the digital distribution network stood at sharp odds to the existing industry structure, where control and exploitation of information was of prime importance. Just as ideas of hacker ethics have been drawn into "a moral binary in which hackers are either lauded or denounced" (Coleman and Golub 2008, p. 256), Napster has become a conflated technological and social phenomenon, either hailed or vilified as the harbinger of the digital disruption to the prevailing structure of cultural industry. The next section explores how this dichotomous view of digital disruption in the music industry was formulated in the face of technological change.

3.3.1 Digital Disruption in the Recording Industry

3.3.1.1 Views on Dystopian Vision

Napster and later P2P file-sharing networks disrupted the economics of the recorded music business practices of granting exclusive rights to copy. As reflected by the accelerating pace of adoption, this change was desired by the public, but was perceived as a threat by recording companies, who had a vested interest in the legal and economic structures through which exploitation of copyright was institutionalised. Chief amongst the concerns was the duplication of perfect copies at a cost close to zero, which facilitated the large-scale distribution of free music through P2P file-sharing networks. The radical transformation and immediate demise of the industry were predicted. The primary evidence supporting this argument was the decline in record sales: the revenue from recording sales reached its peak in 2000 and plummeted until the growth of streaming services in 2008 (Lampel et al. 2006; IFPI 2009). Describing it as "digital piracy," the recording industry accused P2P file-sharing of being the primary cause of sales loss. The rhetoric of "piracy kills the industry" was highly publicised in a public campaign, in which P2P file-sharing activity was condemned as a crime of "music theft" (Siwek 2007). The notion of a terminal crisis of the recording industry was formulated. In 2000, IFPI released a special report on piracy named "IFPI Music Piracy Report 2000" and decried piracy as the threat to the fiscal soundness of the creative industries as a whole. The report said:

> The spread of piracy, both of CDs and on the internet, is the greatest threat to the legitimate music industry. The future of a dynamic creative sector, of artists' livelihoods and of hundreds of thousands of jobs are all

at stake. The need for governments worldwide to provide strong laws, effective enforcement and adequate deterrent penalties against piracy has never been greater. (IFPI 2000)

In addition, the decline of record sales was frequently equated with harm to artists, musical experience and cultural creativity. For example, the Recording Industry Association of America ("RIAA") asserted,

While downloading one song may not feel that serious of a crime, the accumulative impact of millions of songs downloaded illegally – and without any compensation to all the people who helped to create that song and bring it to fans – is devastating. (RIAA 2007)

In a speech endorsing HADOPI law,[2] Nicolas Sarkozy, President of France echoed this rhetoric:

We run the risk of witnessing a genuine destruction of culture...The internet must not become a high tech wild west, a lawless zone where outlaws can pillage works with abandon, or worse, trade in them in total impunity. And on whose backs? On artists' backs? (Reuters 2007)

IFPI has repeatedly reported a massive decline in sales. Up until very recently, this notion of a "digital crisis" has consistently been recited to describe the economic downturn of the recording industry (Rogers 2013; Hesmondhalgh 2009; Marshall et al. 2013). This rhetoric of irreversible decline has become a prevalent account in understanding the digital recording industry and has been used to lobby for strengthening copyright protection, shaping legal regulations and conducting litigations (Hesmondhalgh 2006). In addition, major labels escalated their efforts to maximise their revenue by developing "legitimate" digital music distribution systems, for example enforcing digital

[2]*Haute Autorité pour la Diffusion des œuvres et la Protection des droits d'auteur sur Internet*, also known as the three strikes law, is a legal means introduced to suspend Internet access when an Internet user is found to infringe copyright three times.

rights management ("DRM") technologies in the digital environment (Hesmondhalgh 2006; Burkart and McCourt 2006; Cummings 2010; Rogers 2014).

3.3.1.2 Views on Promising Vision

At the other end of the spectrum, views on the promising potential of digital technology produced a utopian vision of the industry. This idea was instigated by John Perry Barlow, who published the influential articles "The Economy of Ideas" (Barlow 1994) and "A Declaration of Independence in Cyberspace" (Barlow 1996). He proclaimed that information in cyberspace "wants to be free" from physical containers and is intrinsically free of the control of the existing legal framework, which is designed to regulate physical products. The distribution mechanism of Intellectual Property Law was to protect "the ability to deliver [ideas] into reality," not the ideas itself, he claimed, and hence, it was doomed to collapse on the Internet. The difficulty of applying the traditional legal regime gave rise to disputes over the controllability of cyberspace. Nicholas Negroponte, a celebrated guru of the information age, proclaimed that "[c]opyright law…is a Gutenburg artifact," becoming redundant in the Internet age, where it would "disintegrate," with everything capable of being digitalised being potentially "up for grabs" (Negroponte 1996, p. 58). He further contended that digitalisation would serve to flatten the organisational pyramid and decentralise control, therefore effectively levelling the mass media playing field (Negroponte 1996).

Other pundits and academics joined the discussion and proclaimed that digital technologies would serve to bring about an imminent restructuring and the demise of the recording industry. Their focus of attention was the fact that the development of cheap and easy means of music production and distribution enabled free exchange of music over the Internet and P2P file-sharing networks, and thus undermined the long-established legacy of the recording industry built around the physical artefact. Others pointed to the possibility of disintermediation "bypass[ing] the rats' nest of legal and technical problems that kept great music from busting out all over the World Wide Web," and stated that Napster had "changed the world" by "forc[ing] record companies to rethink their business models" (Greenfeld 2000). Described as "a tectonic upheaval in our commonwealth," the fundamentally different logic of the network-based economy was claimed to cause the demise of the old economy on which modern capitalism relied (Kelly 1998). That is, an economy based on plenitude and generosity—known as the gift economy—would enable artists to build their own career, with the help of fans who would provide economic support in exchange for the free digital music available on P2P file-sharing networks. One of the widely discussed cases of the successful adoption of this new mode of music distribution was the American rock band, The Grateful Dead, who distributed their music for free, bypassing middlemen (Alderman 2002). This revolutionary approach was conceived as a threat to the recording industry, but was hailed as a means of providing ultimate benefits for artists and fans in the digital age (Alderman 2002; McLeod 2005). From this viewpoint, the unparalleled opportunities of the digital age are something that should be embraced. Therefore, the recording industry's resistance to this new world of possibility, for example via legal measures against P2P file-sharing applications and their own fans, was criticised as "an appetite for self-destruction" that would lead to the restructuring or demise of the recording industry (Knopper 2009).

In a similar vein, Kusek et al. (2005) refute the recording industry's claim of the economic crisis in the digital age. They point out that the digital mobility which requires ubiquitous interoperability does not fit into the current value paradigms constructed to protect the physical product and that the obsession with control of the media oligopolies would lead to the outmoded business model that does not fit into the digital paradigm. They liken P2P file-sharing to cable television, which was once illegal but became legitimate via compulsory licensing to compensate the broadcasting companies. Proposing the vision of "music like water," they suggest the ubiquity of music should and could be cherished with a utility structure, charging people a monthly fee similar to the charge for water or cable bills.

Other scholars have paid a great deal of attention to the difficulty of control wrought by decentralised networks. Goldsmith and Wu (2006) offer a discussion of the initial vision of the borderless world of the Internet and the contingent issues of control. Ku (2002) goes further and claims that copyright is no longer needed to encourage distribution because consumers themselves could build and fund distribution channels for digital content. He contends that in this process of creative destruction, digital technology and the Internet strike at the foundation of copyright and the industries built upon copyright by eliminating the need for firms to distribute copyrighted works and for exclusive property rights to support creation. He therefore argues that:

> The economics of digital technology also suggests that exclusive rights created by copyright are inconsistent with society's interest in promoting the creation of new music and making music widely available to the public…When the rights of distributors are unbundled from the rights of creators, the case for protecting the rights of distributors cannot be supported. Under these circumstances, copyright serves no purpose other than to transfer wealth from the public and artists to distributors. In this case, the use of Napster is not theft – copyright is theft. (Ku 2002, p. 305)

In this context, new opportunities such as lowered barrier to entry, including cheaper and more powerful tools of music production and dissemination, are understood to level the playing field (Théberge 2001; Bakker 2005). Benkler (2006) states that digital technology and peer production offered an opportunity to reverse the long-lasting trend of the pre-Internet era typified as capital-intensive production and centralisation of information. He argues:

> The modern communications medium that expands its reach by decentralizing the capital structure of production and distribution of information, culture, and knowledge…[offers] the promise of a deep change in how we see the world around us, how we come to know about it and evaluate it, and how we are capable of communicating with others about what we know, believe, and plan. (Benkler 2006, pp. 33–34)

He stresses that the non-proprietary production enabled by digital technology offers the opportunity to shift our means of producing, distributing and consuming cultural works to a socially beneficial method. The new means of production, he continues, will increase productivity by removing exclusivity and diffusing the information "beyond the circles of the wealthiest nations and social groups" and, thus, will boost social welfare, justice and human development in general (Benkler 2006, p. 464).

This claim has resonance with Hippel (2005), whose main concern was the impact of innovation on democracy. He states that an open and distributed user-centred system contradicts the conventional structure of business, and a democratised and user-centric system is of crucial importance in the development of innovation. The radically different nature of digital technology would require a change in traditional policy, which has tended to favour the long-held business models. However, the welfare-enhancing values that innovation could bring, he stresses, make it worthwhile to strive for this, and the adapting to a user-centred system of innovation will ultimately contribute to a shift towards the democratisation of innovation. To Jenkins (2006), the quintessence of the innovation of digital technology is its crucial role in cultivating participatory culture. He defines the current culture as convergence culture, in that digital technology enables the media, producer and consumer to converge on multiple media platforms. He points out that this new culture offers the opportunity for us to avail ourselves of a more democratic and diverse society through more responsive media interactivity. Inspired by these opportunities, especially the ease of remixing by normal Internet users, Lessig (2008) proposes the necessity of building a cultural commons in the digital era. In his book, "Remix," he explains how digital technology has changed the culture from Reading Only (RO) to Read and Write (RW), which signifies the shift of consumers' role from passive receivers to active producers. He argues that this culture, empowered by digital technology, improves efficiency and diversity and is crucial in shaping the future. Zittrain (2007) agrees that, in contrast to the "walled garden" characterised by early networks, the future of the Internet lies with harnessing the power of "generativity" whose resilience to change operates better in the digitally networked environment.

For a brief period of time, this vision seemed to have been accepted as a cultural icon and social practice, when P2P file-sharing networks achieved enormous success owing to its easy-to-use application, immense and diverse catalogue and global content distribution network (Benkler 2006, p. 424). Particularly, the ubiquity of the music listening experience received significant attention, with Goldstein (1994) using the term "Celestial Jukebox." He describes it as:

> A technology-packed satellite orbiting thousands of miles above the Earth, awaiting a subscriber's order – like a nickel in the old jukebox, and the punch of a button – to connect him to any number of selections from a vast storehouse via a home or office receiver that combines the power of a television set, radio, CD player, VCR, telephone, fax, and personal computer. (Goldstein 1994, p. 22)

Goldstein (1994) diagnoses two significance of this practice: first, it is "perfecting the law's early aim of connecting authors to their audiences, free from interference" (Goldstein 1994, p. 216), and second, it is "the best prescription for connecting authors to their audiences is to extend rights into every corner" (Goldstein 1994, p. 216). The Celestial Jukebox, where music fans can enjoy an infinite number of music choices, aided with peer review and the opportunity to go viral on the Internet, would help fans discover hidden gems, building a culture where cultural diversity and creativity would thrive (Mann 2000; Pasquale et al. 2002).

3.3.2 P2P Technology

3.3.2.1 P2P File-Sharing and Record Sales

Many academic and media accounts portrayed major recording companies as bureaucratic behemoths, "struggling to maintain control and remain relevant in the face of digital satin" (Alderman 2002, p. 1). They pressed the need to embrace the radical changes that could fully materialise the potential of digital technology. Stating that "the genie is already out of the bottle," they conceived this change as an important and irresistible opportunity (Kusek et al. 2005; Benkler 2006; Cammaerts 2011). Benkler (2006), for example, stated,

> The genie of p2p technology and the social practice of sharing music, however, were already out of the bottle. First, it shows how institutional design can be a battleground over the conditions of cultural production in the digital environment. Second, it exposes the limits of the extent to which the institutional ecology can determine the ultimate structure of behaviour at a moment of significant and rapid technological and social perturbation. (Benkler 2006, p. 420)

As P2P file-sharing has been blamed for loss of sales by the recording industry, considerable attention has been paid to examining the relationship between these two aspects. Zentner (2005) uses a panel of European countries to examine country-level differences in broadband and its impact on music sales. The analysis, combined with individual surveys, demonstrates that P2P file-sharing led to a 30% decline in music consumption. Liebowitz (2006) is adamant that P2P was detrimental to the whole of the music industry, since it negatively affected music sales. He denies the derivative impacts that file-sharing could bring and argued that the network effect, if there was any, did not seem to be large enough to change the music market. He also raises doubts about the additional impact that file-sharing could generate when radio already provided unlimited free music listening.

Other scholars come to contrasting conclusions. Oberholzer-Gee and Strumpf (2007) analyse a large file-sharing data set in the USA and compared it to the concurrent USA weekly album sales data, proving that file-sharing had a negligible effect on music sales. Handke (2010) investigates the supply side of the business. He provides evidence that the number of albums released in the USA and Germany, as well as the number of new players in the label business in Germany, had not declined in the previous decade and argued that file-sharing had not interrupted supply in the creative production of the music industry. Blackburn (2004) observes a close correlation of CD sales and file-sharing: declining sales of CDs immediately following the appearance of file-sharing in the market, and an increase in CD sales when file-sharing declined. He acknowledges the negative impact that file-sharing had had on industry sales, but at the same time observes a beneficial effect on lesser-known artists. He demonstrates that greater exposure of music through file-sharing networks contributed to more sales of music for lesser-known artists, though it was the opposite for popular artists.

This discussion of the impact of P2P file-sharing on music sales treats the point of sale as the only point impinging upon music. This proposition is primarily predicated on the pre-digital music business structure built around physical artefacts such as CD or vinyl. Other scholars, therefore, proposed an alternative way of understanding P2P technology and music sales. Marshall (2005) stresses the beneficial impact that P2P technology brought to the industry. He denounces the claim that P2P is to blame for lost sales as exaggerated rhetoric, and stressed that P2P has proven to be conducive in building fan loyalty. Gayer and Shy (2006) demonstrate that copyright enforcement could have a different impact on publishers and artists. The widespread unauthorised sharing of music, they argue, might be a bane to publishers, but could be a boon to artists. In other words, the increased exposure of the music could lead to an increased demand for live performances, which is an important source of income for artists. Likewise, the elimination of illegal copies could reduce an artist's fan base, which would be detrimental. (Mortimer et al. 2012) analyse this influence on artists, paying special attention to live performances. They observed the changes in live performances since Napster. The data they provide have proved that file-sharing helped redistribute music to a wider audience. The increased awareness of artists led to an upswing in revenue from live concert performances. This was particularly stark in the case of lesser-known artists, though it had little impact for popular artists whose record sales have declined. This complementary impact enabled by digital technology, they suggest, should be interpreted as an indication that the losses illegal redistribution might have caused can be offset.

3.3.2.2 Debates on Piracy

Some of the criticisms were levelled at the unfair protection of IP tilted towards the recording industry. Ginsburg (2001) points out that legal decisions surrounding copyright have been interpreted in favour of giving control over the market to authors or artists. She contends that copyright control by authors should take into account the fact that unlicensed distribution of works could benefit the public by offering more and diverse creative works. Others question very notion of piracy. Litman (2001), for example, emphasises the need to distinguish "unauthorised" use from "illegal" use, in that unauthorised use can bring benefits to society by facilitating dissemination of cultural products and encouraging continued creation of new works. The content industry, she argues, has ascribed a moral value to the term "piracy" for their own benefit. A similar view was expressed by Marshall (2004), who argues that piracy is a value-laden term stigmatising all types of unauthorised use of copyrighted material. He contends that there are different types of variables in determining piracy; for example, counterfeiting, pirating, bootlegging, tape trading, CD burning/home-taping and file-sharing all have different impacts and values. He concludes that what is important to the industry is its rhetorical power, rather than the economic effects for which the term has been used and stated:

> To a certain extent, none of the above matters. In terms of the importance of piracy for the recording industry, what matters is not its economic effects but its rhetorical impact. We will never be able to ascertain the economic effects of piracy accurately, but piracy is not primarily an economic concept: it is an ideological one. Copyright protection is not a natural right, nor is it absolute: it is a socially mediated relationship between publishers, artists and the public. The particular rights granted and withheld by copyright at any particular time reflect wider power relations between these parties: 'copyright' is not a static thing, it is a constant struggle between competing interests. (Marshall 2004, p. 197)

Over time, the so-called war on piracy intensified; subsequently, the coverage and duration of copyright protection to reduce piracy were extended. The impact of legal measures on file-sharing users or file-sharing services proved to be limited affecting only locally (Lauinger et al. 2013), immediate but short-lived (Poort et al. 2014), or benefiting big corporations only (Danaher and Smith 2014). Some also raised concerns that these legal actions could stifle innovation and online sharing culture (Lemley and Reese 2004; Cammerts et al. 2013). Oram (2001) provides a more nuanced view of how P2P technology, as a disruptive technology, could be harnessed in a beneficial way. By bringing together experts with diverse backgrounds in P2P technology, his book discusses the potential way P2P technology could be used, practical examples of its usage and the obstacles that need to be overcome. Giblin (2011) traces the history of the court rulings on P2P technology-based services such as Napster, KaZaa, Grokster and BitTorrent. She raises questions about the applicability of two crucial grounds on which the court relied to determine the services as illegitimate: contributory and vicarious liability. She also demonstrates how the courts used an arbitrary interpretation of the liability, which, she argues, is based on the physical world and is therefore mistaken.

Various researches have investigated the determinants of P2P file-sharing activity. Eijk et al. (2010) examine the relevance of P2P file-sharing with legal, economic and cultural contexts. Watson et al. (2014) develop it to take account of six factors relevant to P2P file-sharing: financial and legal factor, experiential factor, technical factor, social factor, moral factor and demographics. Brown (2016) looks at psychological factors involved in file-sharing. No research so far has identified significant deterrent of P2P file-sharing except technical factor. What this suggests is that despite the widely perceived notion that digital music users want free music and that stronger legal protection will decrease music piracy, there was no strong indication from financial or legal factors that this deterred music piracy. The availability of free content on P2P file-sharing networks remains the main push towards P2P file-sharing activity.

The discussion on digital technology following the introduction of P2P technology has focused on the disruption of the existing market, with industry players expressing concerns about its impact on piracy. However, if we seek to understand how technological changes have affected the recording industry, we need a broader perspective. This should look at the whole system, including legal, social and technological dimensions, and, in particular, consumers' role in shaping the changes, which has rarely been discussed.

3.3.3 Technological Trajectory of P2P Networks

This section explores the development of P2P networks. Distinct from the prediction that they could be at the centre of digital music distribution, promotion and discovery, P2P networks evolved in a very different direction. This was in response to the court decisions of their precedent P2P technologies. The Ninth Circuit decision about Napster[3] ruled that it was responsible for copyright infringement based on the "actual knowledge" of users' infringing activities. The subsequent court rulings suggested that a greater degree of decentralisation would be more likely to make P2P networks legitimate. Following these roadmaps, P2P networks focused on developing a decentralised system (Nasir 2005), hence deviating from the initial predictions.

3.3.3.1 MyMp3.com and Napster

Before Napster, there was MyMp3, which was purely a client–server model.[4] Its web-based service uploaded a huge amount of albums and songs to its server and allowed users to listen to songs at the MyMp3.com website as long as the site recognised the legally purchased CDs uploaded by the users to their computers. In the case of UMG v. MyMp3.com,[5] the court ruled in favour of the record labels that MyMp3 had infringed copyright by using mechanical copies of

[3]A&M Records, Inc. v. Napster 239 F.3d 1004 (9th Cir. 2001).

[4]Distinct from "pure P2P network", a disintermediated application enabling direct communication amongst peers without gatekeepers, a client-server model is a hierarchical architecture which uses a server to initiate and control communication. For more discussion, see Wu (2003).

[5]*UMG Recordings, Inc. v. Mp3.com, Inc.* 92 F. Supp. 2d 349 (S.D.N.Y. 2000).

sound recordings without permission from copyright owners. Napster improved the model by combining a client–server model with a P2P network. This meant that users searched for files from an index located on a central server run by Napster, and exchanged the files with other users. The architecture was improved to facilitate the database search and mediate connections between peers. Although the legality of Napster was not a question from the outset, after a series of litigations, Napster's illegality became set in stone (Knopper 2009). The court ruled that Napster was held for a secondary liability: Napster did not commit copyright infringement directly, but was "aiding and abetting" copyright infringement. The two legal grounds of this decision are vicarious liability and contributory liability. Vicarious liability rests on the ability to control and potentially receive financial benefit, and contributory liability is applied based upon the knowledge of infringing activity.

The precedent decision Napster relied on was the so-called Betamax decision (Sony v. Universal Studios (1984)[6]). Based on the fact that substantial use of the new technology "Betamax" was for a non-infringing purpose, the court held that Betamax's recording capability to "time-shift" a broadcast programme so as to watch it at a more convenient time should be considered fair use. The court ruled that although Sony knew that the technology could be used for infringing purposes, it could "merely be capable of substantial non-infringing uses." This meant that Sony could not have specific knowledge about when and by whom the infringing use was taking place. Therefore, it did not constitute contributory infringement if the product could be widely used for legitimate purposes. The centralised database on Napster, however, meant that Napster did have actual knowledge of copyright infringement and therefore a capability to block the infringing conduct. Napster's case taught important lessons to future P2P developers in avoiding contributory liability (Giblin 2011). Subsequent P2P networks, therefore, became much more decentralised.

[6] *Sony Corporation of America et al. v. Universal City Studoios, Inc., et al.* 464 U.S. 417.

3.3.3.2 Aimster

Aimster was a file-sharing service used in conjunction with the AIM instant messaging ("IM") service. On this IM network, users could share files with nominated "buddies." Developed in August 2000, right after Napster's court case, Aimster "was blatantly coded with avoidance of the US secondary liability law in mind" (Giblin 2011, p. 47). Like Napster, it had a central server, but it used encryption technology to make it impossible to know exact information about the file-sharing and therefore keep Aimster immune from secondary liability. However, the court ruled that Aimster was liable for both contributory and vicarious liability. In the Aimster Copyright Litigation decision in 2003, the court held that Aimster's primary objective was to "influence and encourage" infringing uses, and therefore, it was not an "innocent enabler" like Sony.[7] Aimster was also ruled to be liable for vicarious liability for developing encrypted communication. The court's narrow interpretation of the Sony decision prompted much criticism that it was stifling innovation by forcing developers to "be concerned about whether non-infringing use of that technology will not only [be] 'substantial' but perhaps whether it will be the primary use, as well as whether she will be able to prove that substantial or primary use in court" (Lemley and Reese 2004, p. 1362).

3.3.3.3 Gnutella

Justin Frankel, a Winamp developer, and his colleague Tom Pepper wrote a brand new protocol to solve Napster's legal vulnerability. The end result was the Gnutella network, an Open Source-based project which radically decentralised the system and overcame the legal throttle that brought about Napster's downfall. Unlike Napster, Gnutella did not store the file directory on the central server, thus avoided the secondary liability that had brought down the preceding P2P networks

---

[7] *In re Aimster Copyright Litigation*, 334 F.3d 634 (7th Cir. 2003).

(Strahilevitz 2003). The removal of the central server, however, resulted in a few challenges. There was no place to initiate the network. To overcome this issue, the developers enabled all users' computers to bootstrap onto the network as mini servers. Once connected, clients communicated with one another, rather than the central server, in order to exchange files. Gnutella's radically decentralised network, enabling peer communication on P2P networks without any intermediation, took P2P technology to another level and successfully avoided legal liability.

3.3.3.4 FastTrack

A new class of P2P file-sharing network was born from Gnutella. Dutch programmers Niklas Zennstrom and Janus Friis developed a protocol called FastTrack; Kazaa was the client application for end-users to communicate with the FastTrack network. Instead of having a central index, it used supernodes as temporary index servers, which placed FastTrack in between the centralised Napster and the decentralised Gnutella (Giblin 2011). It improved Gnutella's bottleneck problems by distinguishing nodes (ordinary users) from supernodes (the best resourced users). By enabling users to communicate with the nearest supernodes, the system ensured that users could connect to the most powerful computers on the network. As FastTrack reached similar levels of popularity to Napster, the Dutch International Federation of the Phonographic Industry filed a suit against it. In January 2002, the hefty fines from the court ruling forced the developers to sell it to Sharman Networks (Drumm 2003). With regard to this development, Gibliin (2011) says:

> Gnutella and FastTrack were each deliberately and carefully engineered to exploit the physical world/software world divide by eliminating the control that was essential to liability under the post-Napster law. Their developers had carefully followed the Ninth Circuit's 'roadmap' by ensuring they did not provide any ongoing service or give their providers control over the networks. Their networks were so decentralized that they could and would continue operating regardless of the actions of the defendants. (p. 64)

3.3.3.5 Grokster and Morpheus

FastTrack had two other offspring; Grokster and StreamCast's Morpheus used Kazaa licenses. Grokster and Morpheus bore many similarities technically, but the latter left more of a mark legally. Grokster and Morpheus also did not maintain any central indices. There was no centralised control over the file-sharing activity on these platforms. Their platforms were decentralised to the extent that even if Grokster or StreamCast were closed down and all the computers within the control therefore deactivated, users could continue sharing files. In the case of MGM Studios Inc. v. Grokster Ltd.,[8] the Ninth Circuit rejected contributory liability and held that Groker and Morpheus could not be held liable since they did not provide the "site and facilities." They did not have actual knowledge of infringement and therefore could not stop particular infringements. Vicarious liability was also rejected due to the fact that the defendants could control the file-sharing networks. The US Supreme Court, however, soon reversed this decision. The Supreme Court created "a new theory of liability" and concluded that Grokster had "bad intent" to induce infringement (Giblin 2011). This decision was criticised, with claims that the decision offered innovators of dual-use P2P technologies substantially more protection against the danger of secondary liability for their users' acts of copyright infringement than did the Napster and Aimster decisions (Lemley and Reese 2004).

3.3.3.6 BitTorrent

BitTorrent was developed in 2002 by a programmer Bram Cohen. Initially, it was developed to solve the slow file-swapping problem that the Jamband community experienced when sharing large files at etree.org. Its efficiency was soon discovered by other Internet users who wanted to swap other types of large files. The essence of BitTorrent's efficiency lay in its re-allocation of bandwidth usage. The problem was

---

[8] *Metro-Goldwyn-Mayer Studios, Inc., et al. v. Grokster, Ltd., et al.* 545 U.S. 913 (2005).

that there were more users downloading than uploading, which slowed down the file-sharing process. Unlike previous P2P networks, which treated all users equally, BitTorrent distinguished between those who uploaded (seeds) and those who downloaded (leeches)—a group of seeds and leeches was called a "swarm." Once a file was uploaded, it was cut into many pieces. Everyone who shared the file was given a piece of the file, uploading and downloading simultaneously. This was to ensure that each swarm was committed to a distributing network and to minimise the bandwidth of the original seed. In this way, everyone who had a piece of the file associated with a particular torrent was sharing the file with one another, instead of downloading from a single source. BitTorrent gained a sudden peak of popularity after the Grokster decision in 2007. While efficiency had to be compromised by decentralisation in previous P2P networks, Cohen overcame this issue and ensured both high efficiency and liability resistance (Giblin 2011). With the court's ever-expanding provision of legal protection, BitTorrent could have been sued for inducement and authorisation (Giblin 2011). The "inducement" theory enacted in the Grokster case successfully closed down Limewire, a P2P files-haring website which once had 50 million monthly users, in October 2010.[9] The legal victory achieved by the recording industry was such that the mere threat of a cease and desist letter from RIAA was enough to shut down eDonkey, another popular P2P file-sharing website. However, the BitTorrent software providers have never been sued for copyright infringement, because suing companies like BitTorrent would have no impact on file-sharing. Underlying the problem was that the victory had been rather pyrrhic (Bridy 2009). The entertainment industry faced the dilemma that the very legal measures they lobbied for had become the bottleneck of controlling the problem they wanted to solve: legal precedents directed the P2P file-sharing networks to be decentralised to the extent that even their own legal measures were incapable of controlling them. That is, even if the client site is shut down, the legacy users still can swap files, new clients can easily be made, and the legal measures might have to

---

[9] *Arista Records LLC v. Lime Group LLC*, 715 F. Supp. 2d 481 (2010).

go too far to control the globally distributed files (Edwards 2011). As a result, the entertainment industry has sought different types of measures which involves "ISP co-operation" and the introduction of the "graduated response" or "three strikes" laws for ISPs that control access to the Internet,[10] or cutting off access to torrent sites or "cyber lockers[11,12]".

3.4 Concluding Remarks

From the early discussions of digital disruption in the music industry, we can extract three main themes that dominate the debates. First, digital technology will shorten the value chain in the music industry by diminishing the roles of intermediaries or rendering them redundant. Second, disintermediation will enable artists to connect their fans directly to digital distribution networks and retain legal rights over their own sound recordings. This will lead to the overturn of major labels' control, built through access to Intellectual Property Law. Third, the unbounded garden of musical choices, known as the Celestial Jukebox where music fans can enjoy infinite access to wide range of music choices, aided with peer review and the opportunity go viral on the Internet, would help fans discover hidden gems, building a culture where cultural diversity and creativity would thrive.

Despite the popularity of the topic, most scholarship has paid great attention to the potential opportunities or challenges suggested by digital distribution networks. With much emphasis on the legal impacts on the market, debates so far have fallen within the ambit of the dichotomy between utopian and dystopian understandings of the industry. This is manifested in the focus of existing studies so far, which has been on the sales loss of material products such as vinyl or CDs, with P2P

[10]Through ISP monitoring, users receive notifications in the case of alleged copyright infringement. In the third notification, users could be subject to the Internet connection suspension.

[11]Internet service hosting websites that provide file-storing or file-sharing service for media files and data.

[12]For a detailed discussion on the pros, cons and unintended consequences of "graduated response," see Edwards (2011).

technology heralding a sense of crisis. The focus on the point of sales, in conjunction with copyright protection, neglects the complex dynamics underlying technological development. An analysis of the divergent and often conflicting interests could help us move beyond technological determinism, which treats technological innovation as a simplistic and normative account. The underlying dynamics, in particular, are of great significance to understanding the way prevailing sets of values and disruptive beliefs are negotiated by a variety of players with different powers and interests. Most significantly, the complex, diverse and evolving requirements of users have rarely been taken into account in understanding the digital recording industry. In this context, the emerging changes in the digital recording industry, prompted by the growth of streaming services, are not just a response to legal regulations or the lineage of P2P technology. To fully understand the complicated dynamics emerging in the digital recording industry, this book will look into the system-wide changes, which include a wide array of realignments in the legal, technological and social infrastructures and a reworking of how music is valued.

References

Adorno, T.W. 1976. *Introduction to the Sociology of Music*. New York: Seabury Press.

Alderman, J. 2002. *Sonic Boom: Napster, MP3, and the New Pioneers of Music*. London: Four Estate.

Allen-Robertson, J. 2013. *Digital Culture Industry a History of Digital Distribution*. Basingstoke: Palgrave Macmillan.

Attali, J. 1985. *Noise: The Political Economy of Music*. Manchester: Manchester University Press.

Bakker, G. 2012. Adopting the Rights-Based Model: Music Multinationals and Local Music Industries Since 1945. *Popular Music History* 6 (3): 307–343.

Bakker, P. 2005. File-Sharing—Fight, Ignore or Compete: Paid Download Services vs. P2P-Networks. *Telematics and Informatics* 22 (1–2): 41–55.

Barlow, J.P. 1994. The Economy of Ideas [online]. *Wired*. Available from https://www.wired.com/1994/03/economy-ideas/. Accessed 31 May 2017.

Barlow, J.P. 1996. A Declaration of the Independence of Cyberspace [online]. *Electronic Frontier Foundation*. Available from https://projects.eff.org/~barlow/Declaration-Final.html. Accessed 19 Sept 2015.
Benkler, Y. 2006. *The Wealth of Networks: How Social Production Transforms Markets and Freedom*. New Haven, CT: Yale University Press.
Bently, L. 1994. Copyright and the Death of the Author in Literature and Law. *The Modern Law Review* 57 (6): 973–986.
Bently, L. 2008. *Intellectual Property Law*, 3rd ed. Oxford: Oxford University Press.
Bergh, A., and T. DeNora. 2009. From Wind-Up to iPod: Techno-Cultures of Listening. In *The Cambridge Companion to Recorded Music*, ed. N. Cook, E. Clarke, D. Leech-Wilkinson, and J. Rink, 102–115. Cambridge: Cambridge University Press.
Bettig, R.V. 1996. *Copyrighting Culture: The Political Economy of Intellectual Property*. Boulder, CO: Westview Press.
Blackburn, D. 2004. Does File Sharing Affect Record Sales. PhD Dissertation at Harvard University.
Boldrin, M., and D. Levine. 2002. The Case Against Intellectual Property. *American Economic Review* 92 (2): 209–212.
Boytha, G. 1993. The Intellectual Property Status of Sound Recordings. *Iic-International Review of Industrial Property and Copyright Law* 24 (3): 295–306.
Bridy, A. 2009. Why Pirates (Still) Won't Behave: Regulating P2P in the Decade After Napster. *Rutgers Law Journal* 40 (3): 565–611.
Brown, S.C. 2016. Where Do Beliefs About Music Piracy Come from and How Are They Shared? *International Journal of Cyber Criminology* 10 (1): 21–39.
Burkart, P., and T. McCourt. 2006. *Digital Music Wars: Ownership and Control of the Celestial Jukebox*. Lanham, MD: Rowman & Littlefield.
Burnett, R. 1993. The Popular Music Industry in Transition. *Popular Music and Society* 17 (1): 87–114.
Burnett, R. 1996. *The Global Jukebox: The International Music Industry*. London: Routledge.
Cammaerts, B. 2011. The Hegemonic Copyright Regime vs the Sharing Copyright Users of Music? *Media, Culture and Society* 33 (3): 491–502.
Cammerts, B., R. Mansell, and B. Meng. 2013. *Copyright & Creation: A Case for Promoting Inclusive Online Sharing*. The London School of Economics and Political Science, Department of Media and Communications. Media Policy Brief 9.

Caves, R.E. 2002. *Creative Industries: Contracts Between Art and Commerce*. Cambridge, MA: Harvard University Press.
Clair, W.S. 2004. *The Reading Nation in the Romantic Period*. Cambridge: Cambridge University Press.
Coleman, M. 2004. *Playback: From the Victrola to MP3, 100 Years of Music, Machines, and Money*. New York: Da Capo Press.
Coleman, E.G., and A. Golub. 2008. Hacker Practice: Moral Genres and the Cultural Articulation of Liberalism. *Anthropological Theory* 8 (3): 255–277.
Crisell, A. 2002. Radio: Public Service, Commercialism and the Paradox of Choice. In *The Media. An Introduction*, ed. A. Briggs and P. Cobley. Harlow: Longman.
Cummings, A.S. 2010. From Monopoly to Intellectual Property: Music Piracy and the Remaking of American Copyright, 1909–1971. *The Journal of American History* 97 (3): 659–681.
Cunningham, M. 1998. *Good Vibrations: A History of Record Production*. London, UK: Sanctuary Publishing.
Danaher, B., and M.D. Smith. 2014. Gone in 60 Seconds: The Impact of the Megaupload Shutdown on Movie Sales. *International Journal of Industrial Organization* 33: 1–8.
Davies, G. 1979. The Rome Convention 1961: A Brief Summary of Its Development and Prospect. *European Intellectual Property Review* 2: 154.
Deazley, R. 2003. The Myth of Copyright at Common Law. *The Cambridge Law Journal* 62 (1): 106–133.
Deazley, R. 2004. *On the Origin of the Right to Copy: Charting the Movement of Copyright Law in Eighteenth-Century Britain (1695–1775)*. Oxford: Hart.
Deazley, R. 2010. What's New About the Statute of Anne? In *Global Copyright: Three Hundred Years Since the Statute of Anne, from 1709 to Cyberspace*. Cheltenham: Edward Elgar.
DeNora, T. 2000. *Music in Everyday Life*. Cambridge, UK: Cambridge University Press.
DiMaggio, P. 1977. Market Structure, the Creative Process, and Popular Culture: Toward an Organizational Reinterpretation of Mass-Culture Theory. *The Journal of Popular Culture* 11 (2): 436–452.
Drumm, H.M. 2003. Life After Napster: Will Its Successors Share Its Fate? *Texas Review of Entertainment & Sports Law* 5: 157.
Edwards, L. 2011. *Role and Responsibility of the Internet Intermediaries in the Field of Copyright and Related Rights*. Geneva: WIPO. Available from http://www.wipo.int/meetings/en/doc_details.jsp?doc_id=170839.

Ehrlich, C. 1985. *The Music Profession in Britain Since the Eighteenth Century: A Social History*. Oxford: Clarendon Press.

Eijk, van, J.P. Poort, and P. Rutten. 2010. Legal, Economic and Cultural Aspects of File Sharing. *Communications & Strategies* 77 (1): 35–54.

Feather, J. 2006. *A History of British Publishing*. London and New York : Routledge.

Feather, J. 2007. Copyright and the Creation of Literary Property. In *A Companion to the History of the Book*, ed. S. Eliot and J. Rose. Malden, MA: Blackwell.

Frith, S. 1978. *The Sociology of Rock*. London: Constable.

Frith, S. 1981. *Sound Effects: Youth, Leisure, and the Politics of Rock'n'roll*. New York: Pantheon Books.

Frith, S. 1986. Art Versus Technology: The Strange Case of Popular Music. *Media, Culture and Society* 8 (3): 263–279.

Frith, S. 1987. The Industrialization of Popular Music. In *Popular Music and Communication*, ed. J. Lull. Newbury Park, Calif: Sage Publications, 53–77.

Frith, S. 1988. Copyright and the Music Business. *Popular Music* 7 (1): 57–75.

Frith, S. 1990. Picking up the Pieces. In *Facing the Music: Essays on Pop, Rock and Culture*, ed. S. Frith. London: Mandarin.

Frith, S. 2002. Music and Everyday Life. *Critical Quarterly* 44 (1): 35–48.

Garofalo, R. 1999. From Music Publishing to MP3: Music and Industry in the Twentieth Century. *American Music: A Quarterly Journal Devoted to All Aspects of American Music and Music in America* 17 (3): 318–353.

Gayer, A., and O. Shy. 2006. Publishers, Artists, and Copyright Enforcement. *Information Economics and Policy* 18 (4): 374–384.

Giblin, R. 2011. *Code Wars 10 Years of P2P Software Litigation*. Cheltenham: Edward Elgar.

Ginsburg, J.C. 2001. Copyright and Control Over New Technologies of Dissemination. *Columbia Law Review* 101 (7): 1613–1647.

Goldsmith, J.L., and T. Wu. 2006. *Who Controls the Internet?: Illusions of a Borderless World*. Oxford: Oxford University Press.

Goldstein, P. 1994. *Copyright's Highway: From Gutenberg to the Celestial Jukebox*. Stanford, CA: Stanford University Press.

Greenfeld, K.T. 2000. Meet the Napster. *Time*.

Gronow, P. 1983. The Record Industry: The Growth of a Mass Medium. *Popular Music* 3: 53–75.

Handke, C. 2010. The Creative Destruction of Copyright—Innovation in the Record Industry and Digital Copying. SSRN Working Paper Series.

Hardin, G.J. 1968. The Tragedy of the Commons. *Science* 162: 1243–1248.
Hennion, A. 1989. An Intermediary Between Production and Consumption: The Producer of Popular Music. *Science, Technology and Human Values* 14 (4): 400–424.
Hennion, A. 2001. Music Lovers: Taste as Performance. *Theory, Culture & Society* 18 (5): 1–22.
Hesmondhalgh, D. 1997. Post-Punk's Attempt to Democratise the Music Industry: The Success and Failure of Rough Trade. *Popular Music* 16 (3): 255–274.
Hesmondhalgh, D. 2006. Digitalisation, Copyright and the Music Industries. In *Unpacking Digital Dynamics: Participation, Control and Exclusion*, ed. P. Golding and G. Murdock. New York: Hampton Press.
Hesmondhalgh, D. 2009. The Digitalisation of Music. In *Creativity, Innovation and the Cultural Economy*, ed. A.C. Pratt and P. Jeffcutt. Hoboken: Taylor and Francis.
Himanen, P. 2001. *The Hacker Ethic: And the Spirit of the Information Age*. London: Secker & Warburg.
Hippel, E.V. 2005. *Democratizing Innovation*. Cambridge, MA: MIT Press.
Hirsch, P. 1969. *The Structure of the Popular Music Industry: An Examination of the Filtering Process by Which Records are Preselected for Public Consumption*. Ann Arbor, Mich.: Institute for Social Research, The University of Michigan.
Hirsch, P.M. 1972. Processing Fads and Fashions: An Organization-Set Analysis of Cultural Industry Systems. *American Journal of Sociology* 77 (4): 639–659.
Hirsch, P.M. 2000. Cultural Industries Revisited. *Organization Science* 11 (3): 356–361.
Hull, G.P. 2004. *The Recording Industry*. New York, NY: Routledge.
Hunter, D. 1986. Music Copyright in Britain to 1800. *Music & Letters* 67 (3): 269–282.
Huygens, M., C. Baden-Fuller, F.A.J. Van Den Bosch, and H.W. Volberda. 2001. Co-evolution of Firm Capabilities and Industry Competition: Investigating the Music Industry, 1877–1997. *Organization Studies (Walter de Gruyter GmbH & Co. KG.)* 22 (6): 971.
IFPI. 2000. IFPI Music Piracy Report 2000. Available from http://www.ifpi.org/content/library/Piracy2000.pdf.
IFPI. 2009. Digital Music Report 2009: New Business Models for a Changing Environment. Available from http://www.ifpi.org/content/library/DMR2009.pdf.

Jenkins, H. 2006. *Convergence Culture: Where Old and New Media Collide*. New York: New York University Press.

Jones, S. 1992. *Rock Formation: Music, Technology, and Mass Communication*. Newbury Park, CA: Sage.

Kaplan, B. 1966. *An Unhurried View of Copyright*. New York: Columbia University Press.

Katz, R.A., and R. Hepworth-Sawyer. 2009. *From Demo to Delivery: The Process of Production*. Boston: Elsevier/Focal Press.

Kelly, K. 1998. *New Rules for the New Economy: 10 Ways the Network Economy Is Changing Everything*. London: Fourth Estate.

Kernfeld, B. 2011. *Pop Song Piracy: Disobedient Music Distribution Since 1929*. Chicago: University of Chicago Press.

Knopper, S. 2009. *Appetite for Self-Destruction: The Spectacular Crash of the Record Industry in the Digital Age*. New York: Free Press.

Kretschmer, M. 2000. Intellectual Property in Music: A Historical Analysis of Rhetoric and Institutional Practices. *Studies in Cultures, Organizations & Societies* 6 (2): 197–223.

Kretschmer, M., G.M. Klimis, and R. Wallis. 1999. The Changing Location of Intellectual Property Rights in Music: A Study of Music Publishers, Collecting Societies and Media Conglomerates. *Prometheus* 17 (2): 163.

Kretschmer, M., G.M. Klimis, and R. Wallis. 2001. Music in Electronic Markets—An Empirical Study. *New Media & Society* 3 (4): 417–441.

Ku, R.S.R. 2002. The Creative Destruction of Copyright: Napster and the New Economics of Digital Technology. *The University of Chicago Law Review* 69 (1): 263–324.

Kusek, D., G. Leonhard, and S.G. Lindsay. 2005. *The Future of Music: Manifesto for the Digital Music Revolution*. Boston: Berklee Press.

Laing, D. 2004. Copyright, Politics and the International Music Industry. In *Music and Copyright*, ed. S. Frith and L. Marshall. Edinburgh: Edinburgh University Press.

Laing, D. 2013. The Recording Industry in the Twentieth Century. In *The International Recording Industries*, ed. L. Marshall. Milton Park: Routledge.

Lampel, J., A. Bhalla, and P. Jha. 2006. Back to the Digital Future: The Role of Copyrights in Sustaining Creativity and Diversity in the Music Industry. Project Report. Cass Business School.

Landes, W.M., and R.A. Posner. 1989. An Economic Analysis of Copyright Law. *Journal of Legal Studies (0047–2530)* 18 (2): 325.

Lathrop, T. 2007. *This Business of Global Music Marketing*. New York: Billboard Books.
Lauinger, T., M. Szydlowski, K. Onarlioglu, G. Wondracek, E. Kirda, and C. Kruegel. 2013. Clickonomics: Determining the Effect of Anti-piracy Measures for One-Click Hosting. NDSS Symposium.
Lee, S. 1995. Re-examining the Concept of the 'Independent' Record Company: The Case of Wax Trax! Records. *Popular Music* 14 (1): 13–31.
Lemley, M.A., and R.A. Reese. 2004. Reducing Digital Copyright Infringement Without Restricting Innovation. *Stanford Law Review* 56 (6): 1345–1434.
Lessig, L. 2001. *The Future of Ideas: The Fate of the Commons in a Connected World*. New York: Random House.
Lessig, L. 2008. *Remix*. New York: Penguin Press.
Levy, S. 2001. *Hackers: Heroes of the Computer Revolution*. New York: Penguin Press.
Leyshon, A. 2001. Time-Space (and Digital) Compression: Software Formats, Musical Networks, and the Reorganisation of the Music Industry. *Environment & Planning A* 33 (1): 49.
Liebowitz, S.J. 2006. File Sharing: Creative Destruction or Just Plain Destruction? *Journal of Law and Economics* 49 (1): 1–28.
Litman, J. 2001. *Digital Copyright: Protecting Intellectual Property on the Internet*. Amherst, NY: Prometheus Books.
Mann, C.C. 2000. The Heavenly Jukebox. *The Atlantic*.
Marshall, L. 2004. Infringers. In *Music and Copyright*, ed. S. Frith and L. Marshall. Edinburgh: Edinburgh University Press.
Marshall, L. 2005. *Bootlegging: Romanticism and Copyright in the Music Industry*. London: Sage.
Marshall, L., J. Williamson, and M. Cloonan (eds.). 2013. Contextualising the Contemporary Recording Industry. In *The International Recording Industries*. Milton Park: Routledge.
McLeod, K. 2005. MP3s Are Killing Home Taping: The Rise of Internet Distribution and Its Challenge to the Major Label Music Monopoly. *Popular Music and Society* 28 (4): 521–531.
Mortimer, J.H., C. Nosko, and A. Sorensen. 2012. Supply Responses to Digital Distribution: Recorded Music and Live Performances. *Information Economics and Policy* 24 (1): 3–14.
Napier-Bell, S. 2014. *Ta-ra-ra-boom-de-ay: The Business of Popular Music*. London: Unbound.

Nasir, C. 2005. Taming the Beast of File-Sharing—Legal and Technological Solutions to the Problem of Copyright Infringement Over the Internet. *Entertainment Law Review* 16 (4): 82–88.

Nathan, J. 1999. *Sony: The Private Life*. London: HarperCollins.

Negroponte, N. 1996. *Being Digital*. New York: Vintage Books.

Negus, K. 1992. *Producing Pop: Culture and Conflict in the Popular Music Industry*. London: Edward Arnold.

Oberholzer-Gee, F., and K. Strumpf. 2007. The Effect of File Sharing on Record Sales: An Empirical Analysis. *Journal of Political Economy* 115 (1): 1–42.

Oram, A. (ed.). 2001. *Peer-to-Peer: Harnessing the Power of Disruptive Technologies*. Beijing and Sebastopol, CA: O'Reilly Media.

Parker, N. 2004. *Music Business: Infrastructure, Practice and Law*. London: Sweet & Maxwell.

Pasquale III, F.A., K.G. Weatherall, and M.B. Fagin. 2002. Beyond Napster: Using Antitrust Law to Advance and Enhance Online Music Distribution. *Boston University Journal of Science & Technology Law* 8 (2): 451–573.

Passman, D.S. 2011. *All You Need to Know About the Music Business*. London: Penguin.

Patterson, L.R. 1968. *Copyright in Historical Perspective*. Nashville: Vanderbilt University Press.

Peacock, A.T., and R.B. Weir. 1975. *The Composer in the Market Place*. London: Faber Music.

Peterson, R.A. 1990. Why 1955? Explaining the Advent of Rock Music. *Popular Music* 9 (1): 97–116.

Peterson, R.A., and D.G. Berger. 1975. Cycles in Symbol Production: The Case of Popular Music. *American Sociological Review* 40 (2): 158–173.

Plumb, J.H. 1973. *The Commercialisation of Leisure in Eighteenth-Century England*. Reading: University of Reading.

Poort, J., J. Leenheer, J. van der Ham, and C. Dumitru. 2014. Baywatch: Two Approaches to Measure the Effects of Blocking Access to The Pirate Bay. *Telecommunications Policy* 38 (4): 383–392.

Porter, M.E. 1980. *Competitive Strategy: Techniques for Analyzing Industries and Competitors*. New York: Free Press.

Posner, R.A. 1998. *Economic Analysis of Law*, 5th ed. New York: Aspen Law & Business.

Rapaport, D.S. 2003. *A Music Business Primer*. Upper Saddle River, NJ: Prentice Hall.

Raven, J. 2007. *The Business of Books: Booksellers and the English Book Trade, 1450–1850*. New Haven: Yale University Press.

Reuters. 2007. French Pact Aims to Fight Unauthorized Downloading. *The New York Times*, November 24.

RIAA. 2007. Who Music Theft Hurts [online]. http://www.riaa.com. Available from http://www.riaa.com//physicalpiracy.php?content_selector=piracy_details_online. Accessed 22 Oct 2015.

Ricketson, S. 2006. *International Copyright and Neighbouring Rights: The Berne Convention and Beyond*, 2nd ed. Oxford: Oxford University Press.

Rogers, J. 2013. *The Death and Life of the Music Industry in the Digital Age*. London: Bloomsbury.

Rogers, J. 2014. Canary Down the Mine: Music and Copyright at the Digital Coalface. *Socialism and Democracy* 28 (1): 34–50.

Rose, M. 1993. *Authors and Owners: The Invention of Copyright*. Cambridge, MA: Harvard University Press.

Rosen, R.S. 2008. *Music and Copyright*. New York and Oxford: Oxford University Press.

Scherer, F.M. 2004. *Quarter Notes and Bank Notes: The Economics of Music Composition in the Eighteenth and Nineteenth Centuries*. Princeton: Princeton University Press.

Shirky, C. 2001. Where Napster Is Taking the Publishing World. *Harvard Business Review* 79 (2): 143–148.

Siwek, S.E. 2007. *The True Cost of Sound Recording Piracy to the U.S. Economy*. Policy Report, Institute for Policy Innovation.

Spellman, P. 1996. Creative Marketing: Making Media Waves: Creating a Scheduled Publicity Plan Music Business Insights [online]. Available from http://www.mbsolutions.com/biz/Info3.html#creative_marketing. Accessed 28 Feb 2016.

Strahilevitz, L.J. 2003. Charismatic Code, Social Norms, and the Emergence of Cooperation on the File-Swapping Networks. *Virginia Law Review* 89 (3): 505–595.

Teller, B. 1990. Toward Better Protection of Performers in the United States: A Comparative Look at Performers' Rights in the United States, Under the Rome Convention and in France. *Columbia Journal of Transnational Law* 28 (2): 775.

Théberge, P. 1997. *Any Sound You Can Imagine: Making Music/Consuming Technology*. Hanover, NH: Wesleyan University Press.

Théberge, P. 2001. 'Plugged in': Technology and Popular Music. In *The Cambridge Companion to Pop and Rock*, ed. S. Frith, W. Straw, and J. Street, 1–25. Cambridge: Cambridge University Press.

Thompson, E. 1986. Performers and Technological Change 25 Years After the Rome Convention. *International Labour Review* 125 (5): 575.
Towse, R. 1999. Copyright and Economic Incentives: An Application to Performers' Rights in the Music Industry. *Kyklos* 52 (3): 369–390.
Towse, R. 2001. *Creativity, Incentive, and Reward: An Economic Analysis of Copyright and Culture in the Information Age*. Cheltenham, UK: Edward Elgar.
Towse, R. 2004. Copyright and Economics. In *Music and Copyright*, ed. S. Frith and L. Marshall. New York: Routledge.
Towse, R. 2014. *Advanced Introduction to Cultural Economics*. Cheltenham, UK: Edward Elgar.
Toynbee, J. 2004. Musicians. In *Music and Copyright*, ed. S. Frith and L. Marshall. Edinburgh: Edinburgh University Press.
Tschmuck, P. 2012a. *Creativity and Innovation in the Music Industry*, 2nd ed. Berlin: Springer.
Tschmuck, P. 2012b. The Emergence of the Phonographic Industry Within the Music Industry. In *Creativity and Innovation in the Music Industry*, 225–251. Berlin: Springer.
Turow, J. 1997. The Organizational Underpinnings of Contemporary Media Conglomerates. In *The Political Economy of the Media. Volume 1*, ed. P. Golding and G. Murdock, 351–373. Elgar Reference Collection. International Library of Studies in Media and Culture, vol. 2.
Vaidhyanathan, S. 2001. *Copyrights and Copywrongs: The Rise of Intellectual Property and How It Threatens Creativity*. New York: New York University Press.
Wallis, R. 2006. The Changing Structure of the Music Industry: Threats to and Opportunities for Creativity. In *Music and Manipulation: On the Social Uses and Social Control of Music*, ed. S. Brown and U. Volgsten. New York: Berghahn.
Watson, S., D. Zizzo, and P. Fleming. 2014. Determinants and Welfare Implications of Unlawful File Sharing: A Scoping Review. *CREATe*.
Weissman, D. 2010. *Understanding the Music Business*. Upper Saddle River, NJ: Prentice Hall.
Wikström, P. 2013. *The Music Industry: Music in the Cloud*, 2nd ed. Cambridge, England: Polity.
Williamson, O.E. 1975. *Markets and Hierarchies: Analysis and Antitrust Implications; A Study in the Economics of Internal Organization*. New York: Free Press.
World Intellectual Property Organization. 1981. *Guide to the Rome Convention and to the Phonograms Convention*. Geneva: World Intellectual Property Organization.

Wu, T. 2003. When Code Isn't Law. *Virginia Law Review* 89 (4): 679–751.
Zentner, A. 2005. File Sharing and International Sales of Copyrighted Music: An Empirical Analysis with a Panel of Countries. *The BE Journal of Economic Analysis & Policy* 5 (1): 1–17.
Zittrain, J. 2007. *The Future of the Internet: And How to Stop it*. New Haven: Yale University Press.

4

Evolution of Digital Music Services

This chapter presents the detailed process of innovation involved in the evolution of digital music services. It describes the trials and errors that digital music firms experienced in trying to find a commercially viable business model in the digital era. This chapter is composed of four parts. Section 4.1 traces the early history of the digital music service building process after Napster was closed down. This period is characterised by the major labels' contradictory response to digital novelty. On the one hand, they resisted the change, but at the same time, they also sought to ensure that they were not displaced by new forms of digital distribution. This section discusses two major strategies they employed to sustain their position in new dynamics, which proved to be futile. Section 4.2 then discusses how Apple's iTunes service saved digital music business but could not be the ultimate solution, leaving a space for a new generation of experimentation in business models. This new experimentation is discussed with reference to two business models, YouTube and Last.fm, in Sect. 4.3. Section 4.4 discusses the process in which the anticipated P2P technology has declined, and instead, streaming services have emerged as a new form of digital music consumption platform.

H. Sun, *Digital Revolution Tamed*, https://doi.org/10.1007/978-3-319-93022-0_4

4.1 After the Wild West (1999–2001)

Napster was a pioneering P2P technology-based music file-sharing service developed by a 19-year-old college student named Shawn Fanning. Its simple and easy means of exchanging files of copyrighted materials drew 70 million users at its peak. In the landmark case of A&M Records, Inc. v. Napster, the court affirmed that Napster was liable for contributory and vicarious infringement of copyright. Following the court decision, the original model of Napster was shut down. Some efforts followed to make Napster legal by developing a subscription-based model with fingerprinting technology. In the process, the ownership of the company passed to Bertelsmann, a German media conglomerate, in 2002, then to Best Buy, a US electronic retailer, in 2008 and finally to Rhapsody in 2011. None of the measures brought Napster its original fame back. Opinions remain divided on how to interpret the downfall of Napster. A former employee at Napster thinks it was a negotiated outcome formulated by the elusive concept of intellectual property law at that time.

> One thing was only a matter of timing. The thing that was only a matter of timing was the fact that Napster was entirely from the beginning to the end illegal…The problem is society did not generally recognise the importance of one of the milestones of civilisation because it was kind of for specialists. So it's kind of esoteric, and that was intellectual property laws…If Napster could have lasted long enough to avoid the consequence of legal action, the legal action would have meant nothing. (Interview, name unrevealed at his/her request)

Shutting down Napster, however, did not solve the problems the recording industry had to face. One of the key challenges was to find ways to valorise music in the digitally networked environment. Having once tasted free access to the world's unlimited music library, digital music users would not easily go back to conventional music consumption. Instead of finding ways to meet digital music users' requirements, however, the recording industry tried to extend their existing control in the new environment. Significant efforts were made to persuade consumers of the significance of the illegality (Drahos 2002; Wu 2003; Hormann 2009; Jenkins 2006; Cummings 2010). The most intensive efforts were geared towards cracking down on piracy through diverse legal measures including public relations campaigns and litigation not only against the firms but also against individual users. They also employed technological protection measures (TPMs) so as to enforce the rights of copyright owners in digital networks. None of the measures proved to have any meaningful impact on P2P file-sharing activity (Akester 2005; Bakker 2005).

While resisting new forms of distribution and persisting to reassert prior forms of copyright protection, major labels also sought to ensure that they were not displaced by new forms of digital distribution. A wealth of literature has developed to discuss the implication of these defensive measures. For a discussion of the valorisation process on the digital music business, the discussion here will be focused on two of these early strategies the recording industry adopted: (1) attempts to set legal standards and (2) trials of their own legal digital music services. Both can be perceived as efforts to extend the industry's long-established business structure by fitting the accompanying infrastructure to the edifice of the existing model.

4.1.1 Legal Standards

4.1.1.1 The RIO

The history of setting legal standards dates back before Napster, in October 1998, when the Recording Industry Association of America (RIAA) filed a suit against Diamond Multimedia Systems, the manufacture of the first MP3 player, RIO. The RIAA alleged that the RIO violated the Audio Home Recording Act (AHRA), an act legislated in 1992 to impose restrictions on digital recording devices and prevent the mass reproduction of digital files (Webb 2000). The RIAA claimed that the RIO failed to incorporate the serial copy management system (SCMS), a mandatory copyright protection technology for digital audio recording devices under AHRA, and thus facilitated the unauthorised copying of copyrighted digital audio files. The Ninth Circuit, however, denied the RIAA's claim on the grounds that "the Rio cannot make copies from transmissions, but instead, can only make copies from a computer hard drive."[1] Based on the fact that RIO only enables "space-shift" to use the copies users already own, the court dismissed the RIAA's argument that MP3 file usage on the RIO violated AHRA, and recognised its legitimacy.

4.1.1.2 Secure Digital Music Initiative (SDMI)

As the effort to stamp out the proliferation of unauthorised use of copyrighted digital audio files had failed, the RIAA decided to take on their own project of securing technological control over the burgeoning digital recording device market. The RIAA forged a coalition of recording companies, consumer electronics and IT companies and launched a project called "the Secure Digital Music Initiative (SDMI)" in July 1999. The main objective of the project was to set a technological standard that manufacturers can use in developing new portable devices (Quan 1999). To achieve this goal, the plan required all digital music devices to affix an SDMI-compliant label and a rights management system consisting of digital watermarking (Pollack 1999). In other words, the plan was designed to prevent any use of MP3s not approved by SDMI. The coalition, however, failed to meet the release date, most likely because of the technical difficulties (Levy 2000). The plan to build an infrastructure from scratch simply was not feasible within the time period targeted (Knopper 2009).

Gordon Rintoul, currently working at INgrooves' Client services and former employee of Napster's legalisation project, provides a glimpse of the lack of accompanying infrastructure for the digital music business at that time.

---

[1] *Recording Industry Association of America, et al. v. Diamond Multimedia Systems, Inc.*, 180 F.3d at 1076.

> Eventually, we did a lot of work. We got a thousand direct deals and started digitalising them. Storage was a big problem at that time. Not like today when we have 300 to 400 GBs, or a terabyte drives, at that time, one gigabyte drive was a big, big drive. So we had to figure out certain things like storage, and we had to figure out how to transfer all this content, from the UK to the US, which was a bit complicated, because most of them were over by CDs in boxes. Then we started a different process, where we put in the drives. We hadn't dealt too much with Napster, because Napster ended up basically getting caught. (Gordon Rintoul, Interview)

An additional and even more difficult obstacle to overcome was to persuade all the parties involved in the project. As retailers had continued to be the main destination for music consumption, for the project to safely launch, it was imperative to have retailers' cooperation in place. However, retailers were not convinced by the major labels' efforts to create a novel distribution system without retailers as part of their business structure (Levy 2000). A former member of the SDMI reveals that the conflicting interests of diverse players involved in the project caused it to fail.

> That was a colossal waste of time. This was a time to create rules and formats that could support a wide variety of future services, and at the same time provide a copy protection to minimise the ease with which music could be consumed from the beginning to the end of the chain. So there was this computer Internet service people (who thought people) could stream but not steal the stream, and then the other piece of it was consumer electronics device makers who had to implement the hardware side. Then there are computer makers who didn't want to risk anything, their world is 'hey as long as you buy this, you can do pretty much do anything you want.' So we had these brightest people from three different industry areas and three different industries and a lot of meetings and a lot of places, we ended up not very good. (Interview, name unrevealed at his/her request)

Eventually, SDMI has become regarded as an impediment of innovation, slackening the expansion of legitimate use of MP3s (Levy 2000). In October 1999, Scheirer, a digital music analyst for Forrester Research, released an article titled "The end of SDMI" and proclaimed that the near monopoly the recording industry had aimed to achieve had failed. Eventually, Leonardo Chiariglione, the executive director of SDMI, also admitted that it was a futile effort to stop an unstoppable flow (Twohey 2000).

> We realized it was impossible to create a dam to stop this [MP3] phenomenon. (Twohey (2000), sampled 15 February 2016)

4.1.2 Legal Digital Music Services

The ambition to enforce an industry-wide technological measure to prevent unauthorised use of digital audio files had failed. The recording industry would not easily give up the control they enjoyed. This time, they changed their plan and decided to build their own digital music services. PressPlay and MusicNet were two digital music services set up by the major labels. PressPlay was initiated by Sony and Universal, while MusicNet was led by the other majors, Warner, EMI and Bertelsman. Two other digital music services, Rhapsody and EMusic, were run independent of the major record labels.

PressPlay and MusicNet had the advantages of providing top-selling catalogues owned by major labels.[2] However the price was "set artificially high" and had "cumbersome digital rights management restrictions" (Sheffner 2011). Rhapsody and EMusic were run independently of the major labels and had less strict usages in terms of streaming. However, the major labels "collectively agreed not to do business with potential licensees" (Sheffner 2011), so these services' incomplete catalogues could not sufficiently meet digital music users' demands for a wide breadth of catalogue. An industry expert says this was a futile effort by major labels to extend their control, which did not fit very well with the new regime.

> Major labels had a strong desire to control the future digital business. And that included the desire to operate the streaming service…so that they took the retail share of the value chain as well. That obviously didn't sit very well. (Interview, name unrevealed at his/her request)

[2] See Hiatt (2002) or Hill (2018) for more information on each of the four services.

This attempt to extend their control was particularly out of tune with the public's widespread hostility towards the music industry. Alison Wenham, Chairman and CEO of the Association of Independent Music (AIM),[3] experienced first-hand the way it had become a social phenomenon not to pay for music when she was teaching at a university.

> When I first started lecturing at the Warwick University, MA in 2001, I walked into a room where the attitude of my students was clearly hostile. I was the music industry and they were the new generation of file shares. They had decided to break away, 'stick it to the man', they were going to show the industry that it was very fashionable not to pay. It was very fashionable to be making a statement about the new choices that consumers can make. (Alison Wenham, Interview)

On the whole, the subscription business model afforded a limited number of streams, and restricted usage was not enough to bridge the gulf between market affordances and digital music users' demands for new digital music consumption. Its complete failure to take into account of digital music users' requirements subjected the services to landing at the number nine on the "25 Worst Tech Products of All Time" list by PC World (Tynan 2006).

4.2 Apple to the Rescue (2001–2003)

4.2.1 How iTunes Saved the Digital Recording Industry

The relentless tide of P2P file-sharing seemed unstoppable, and the CD sales continued to plummet. When the change happened, as often seems to have been the case in the history of the recording industry, the key breakthrough was not led by a music company but by a technology

[3]A non-profit organisation established in 1998 in the UK to represent the independent record labels' interests. The American Association of Independent Music ("A2IM") is a sister organisation in the USA.

firm, in this case Apple. It was major labels who first approached Apple, which at that time had only a 2% market share in the PC industry (Pham 2013a). But iPod, their newly developed portable media player, was growing fast, and iTunes, a media management application for iPod, needed contents. From Sony's Walkman experience, major labels learned that the integration of music catalogue and music device could bring a great synergy effect. Andrew Lack, CEO at Sony Music, said:

> My point was that the iPod was empty without the music…I felt strongly that without a dual revenue stream, music was going to struggle. If they'd stuck together, there was a chance they could have gotten somewhere. It's my greatest regret. (Pham (2013a), sampled 15 February 2016)

With this idea in mind, executives from Warner and Sony approached Steve Jobs to ask Apple to take part in a consortium to develop a music device interoperable with a standard in January 2002. The discussion did not go far, but led to a different momentum for the digital music industry. Two months later, Steve Jobs went back to Warner with his own vision for a music business. Apple built an infrastructure for a new business plan that it formulated with Warner (Pham 2013a). From the very beginning, Steve Jobs strove to make sure that they had all the major catalogues. In an interview with Rolling Stone in 2003, he said,

> At first, they (majors) kicked us out. But we kept going back again and again. (Goodell (2003), sampled 15 February 2016)

Steve Jobs' approach was conceived apt to the problems the recording companies have wrestled with since Napster and eventually convinced three major labels to license their catalogues on iTunes before its launch. Sony was included later, presumably because Apple perceived Sony, which was running PressPlay at that time, as a potential competitor (Pham 2013a).

The iTunes store debuted in April 2003 and, within a week, sold one million tracks. iTunes' remarkable success can be attributed to various factors. First, it was the first legal alternative with a wide breadth of catalogues, including all four major labels and independent labels at a reasonable price. Steve Jobs had a clear vision that giving users a better experience was a better solution than suppression of piracy (Goodell 2003). He said:

> To tell them that they should stop being thieves – without a legal alternative that offers those same benefits – rings hollow. We said, 'We don't see how you convince people to stop being thieves unless you can offer them a carrot – not just a stick. We're gonna offer you a better experience…and it's only gonna cost you a dollar a song'. (Goodell (2003), sampled 15 February 2016)

Not only does suppression not suffice, Apple noticed, but there clearly was a room for innovation. The solution they adopted was a better experience than P2P file-sharing download. Steve Jobs continued:

> The other thing we told the record companies was that if you go to Kazaa to download a song, the experience is not very good. You type in a song name, you don't get back a song – you get a hundred, on a hundred different computers. You try to download one, and, you know, the person has a slow connection, and it craps out. And after two or three have crapped out, you finally download a song, and four seconds are cut off, because it was encoded by a ten-year-old. By the time you get your song, it's taken fifteen minutes. So that means you can download four an hour. Now some people are willing to do that. But a lot of people aren't. (Goodell (2003), sampled 15 February 2016)

Scott Cohen, co-founder of The Orchard, an independent music distributor, thinks iTunes' success owes to the attention it paid to consumers' requirements by refining the technology.

> What Apple understood was the interface, the consumer experience. When you plugged your iPod into your computer, it makes basic assumptions that you probably want to transfer music on your computer to your other device. And it just did it. Before the iPod, it was a difficult process to get the music to your computer and to your digital music player.

> The computer was like going to the C drive, under this, find this. It wasn't really a drag and drop world that we know now. It was much more challenging. Apple changed that. You just plug it into your computer. They began a level of trust with the consumers. And the device proliferated and reached the critical mass of enough digital players. Then when they launched the store, it was like, 'Hey! If you have the iPod then you can just get the music on it.' Why buy a CD when you can just get it there and play it on your device? (Scott Cohen, Interview)

In addition, its a-la-carte option was breaking unprecedented industry ground; bundling had long been a method of maximising profit for the recording industry by forcing consumers to purchase an entire album (Zhu and Macquarrie 2003). Since the commodification of music, music had been turned into a rival good in which artificial scarcity was crucial to uphold the consumer price. Breaking this down was not easy as Paul Vidich, former executive at Warner Music, says, "We knew we needed to alter consumer behavior in a big way. Below $1 was an emotional threshold for people. It became an acceptable impulse purchase" (quoted in Goodell 2003).

It didn't take long until Apple became one of the largest sellers of musical content in the USA (Wingfield and Smith 2007). By 2007, as a medium to experience music differently, iPod became the dominant digital music player with a market share in excess of 70% (Levy 2006). Up until recently, iTunes remained the most successful legitimate digital music service (Bell 2014). Its influence in the industry is far-reaching; it was perceived to have "created a commercial superhighway that connected the artist to the consumer and rescued the industry…[and Steve Jobs] showed the music industry how to capture the value that was quickly being eroded by old-world ideals" (Nash 2011).

4.2.2 Limitations

As an alternative digital music commercialisation platform, iTunes allowed labels to generate revenue from digital music, enabled users to consume music legitimately at a reasonable price and gave more opportunity to independent musicians to distribute their music online.

Crucially, iTunes has brought a larger proportion of digital music users to a legal platform, making a significant contribution to the recovery of the digital music sales that has been spiralling downward since Napster (Koh et al. 2014).

However, iTunes' success attracted as much criticism as acclamation. Many criticisms were centred on the issues surrounding the DRM restrictions that iTunes initially put in place. Jobs expressed that the decision to use the DRM system was an inevitable choice in order to comply with the contractual obligations that major labels required (Jobs 2007).

Nevertheless, FairPlay, the DRM system created by Apple, is often perceived to be fair only to the labels, not to the consumers. Sharpe and Arewa (2006) argued that iTunes' DRM was a destructive stranglehold for the industry in that the market dominance through network effects created a barrier for competition and thus eventually restricted consumers' choices. Apple's failure to meet consumers' expectations, they insisted, would make Apple "a victim of its own success" (Sharpe and Arewa 2006, p. 350). As criticisms and complaints ensued, the DRM restrictions were loosened over time. It started with EMI, the major player with the least market share, announcing that they would make their entire catalogue DRM-free on iTunes (Apple Press 2007). In 2009, Apple extended the DRM-free scheme to 80% of its repertoire (Apple Press 2009).

In addition, its inclination to have legitimate digital music catalogues came at the price of consolidating the existing power relationship (Wikström 2013). Arditi (2014) also argued that iTunes is a system built to be favourable to major labels, at the expense of not fully tapping into the potential of disintermediation. Although it is possible for artists to distribute their music by themselves, he argued, iTunes allowed major labels to maintain the traditional network effects that stem from marketing and promotion. iTunes eventually "len[t] itself to concentrating power in the major record labels. The walls that digital distribution broke down have been replaced by distribution barriers in the form of iTunes" (Arditi 2014, p. 422).

As a PC manufacturing company, Apple was able to weather the small amount of money it made through digital music sales, because the ultimate goal was to create significant profits by selling Apple products.

Its preoccupation with creating loyalty to its products, however, came at the expense of limiting interoperability between iTunes Music Store and non-iPod players (Sharpe and Arewa 2006). The network effects that Apple enjoyed through its dominant market power were criticised to be "in large part wedded to its exercise of proprietary strategies that include a significant exercise of intellectual property rights" (Blankenhorn 2006, p. 348). Apple's closed system, albeit optimal for Apple consumers, left many non-Apple consumers unenthusiastic (Medford 2008). While iTunes arose as an alternative to piracy by giving an option to consume music on legitimately, the deliberately restricted consumers' choices left piracy unabated (Medford 2008). Eventually, it provided leeway for other services to spring up.

4.3 Emergence of New Models (2004–2007)

4.3.1 Last.fm

4.3.1.1 Beginning

Last.fm is the joint firm of Last.fm and Audioscrobbler. Audioscrobbler began when Richard Jones started his project in computer science at the University of Southampton in the UK. The project was to build a software program to recommend new music and connect with people who have similar music taste (BBC News 2003). He invented "Audioscrobbler," a plug-in that could collect data on the music to which its users listened, and shared the application with his friends. The service gained popularity very quickly. Last.fm, meanwhile, was founded in 2002 as an Internet radio station and music community website, designed as an avenue for unsigned bands to have their music heard. Upon reading a newspaper article about Audioscrobbler, the founders of Last.fm met with Richard Jones. In 2005, the two companies were merged and became the current Last.fm.

Scrobbling, which stores people's music listening history, became Last.fm's unique business model. It helps users to explore new music and listen to tracks from their favourite artists and enables diverse social networking functionalities such as finding out which friends have similar tastes. It keeps track of what a given user listens to (the tracks are "scrobbled," a reference to the original website's name, Audioscrobbler.com), building a user profile of how many times and when the user listened to a particular track. That profile is then compared with everyone else's profile to generate basic associations such as users who like Bob Dylan tend to listen to The Band, Neil Young and Leonard Cohen. Last.fm's user base was growing very fast through which a big network of users made Last.fm's recommendations more relevant to users (McCarthy 2007). Its innovative approach brought last.fm Digital Music Award in 2006 (TechRadar 2006). This success led to the acquisition by CBS, which ultimately brought a great change in the direction of business development.

4.3.1.2 CBS Acquisition

In 2007, CBS, one of the biggest radio broadcasting companies, acquired Last.fm at £140 million, the largest ever UK Web 2.0 acquisition at the time. Last.fm, at that time, was "one of the most well established, fastest growing online community networks" with around 20 million active users (Kiss 2007). It is known that Last.fm's strength in building music communities through music syndicating technology and appeal to the younger generation was enticing to CBS, who were losing audiences to Internet media (*The New York Times* 2007).

The immediate change of the acquisition was the approach to copyright issues. Since its acquisition by CBS, Last.fm has become much more compliant with copyright laws. It used to take the approach of playing the music as much as possible until it was challenged legally. An employee at Last.fm describes the approach Last.fm used to take before the acquisition as a "relaxed" one:

> Before we were run by CBS, and before the legality of the streaming of music was defined, Last.fm was more relaxed about playing music… before Last.fm was owned by CBS, Last.fm was more relaxed about some of these practices, essentially they would wait for the challenge. They could do until they were challenged. That's no longer the case. We're always compliant. (Interview, name unrevealed at his/her request)

As an international company, CBS took a more serious approach to the copyright licensing scheme. In February 2007, Warner Music signed a deal with Last.fm to allow its entire catalogue to be played on the service (Holton 2007). In 2008, CBS announced a plan to provide tracks from all four major labels. On 23 January 2008, Last.fm announced a "free the music" initiative, which would allow users to play music for free up to three times (Last.fm blog 2008). The catalogue included music from all four major labels, and artists were remunerated each time their tracks were played. And it was welcomed by many users (Buskirk 2008).

CBS also intensified their efforts to making the business profitable and made a few changes to the business strategy. On 12 April 2010, Last.fm withdrew its free play-on-demand service and experienced a significant drop in number of users. The expensive royalties paid to the major labels are known to be the reason for this change. An employee at Last.fm explains:

> The difference is the on-demand-streaming service was turned off after the acquisition. And the reason for that was basically it was too expensive. So my understanding, I'm not a lawyer, but my understanding is that for on-demand streaming services, the royalty payment is much higher. You understand we have a radio product and the radio product has to comply with an American copyright act called DMCA (Digital Millennium Copyright Act).[4] DMCA requires tracks which are played…they made a threshold of unpredictability, which means anything we allow our users to choose what they're listening to, we have to be very careful about. So the immediate consequence of the acquisition by CBS was that the free on-demand service was removed. Free on-demand service has literally been on up until 2008. Until then, users could find a song on Last.fm, and play it on-demand for free. And this was obviously a very expensive service to support. So that was turned off. (Interview, name unrevealed at his/her request)

[4]Digital Millennium Copyright Act is a US copyright law signed in 1998. It amended the previous copyright law, Digital Performance Right in Sound Recordings Act of 1995 (DPRA) and included webcasting as part of sound performance licensing scheme (Craft 2001; Delchin 2004; Lane 2011).

In 2007, Warner Music signed a deal to allow its entire catalogue to be played on Last.fm, but withdrew the deal in 2008. This approach caused enormous overhead both bureaucratically and technically. The complicated nature of copyright required a significant amount of negotiation and technical operation. A Last.fm employee continues:

> In terms of attaining catalogue, that's a really complicated business. It creates enormous bureaucratic overhead and enormous amount of time negotiating. And because we're an international company, we're an Internet company, people can have an access to the site anywhere in the world, we have services in 12 languages, and we have a global audience, copyright law which applies in national level, which it does, is extremely complicated to negotiate both bureaucratically and technically: bureaucratically because we have to negotiate separately for every territory, for abroad territories, and technically because we have to have means of identifying somebody's location in order to determine what is allowed to listen to. (Interview, name unrevealed at his/her request)

Two years later in 2009, Last.fm announced another change in relation to the free streaming policy. From then on, users in areas other than the USA, UK and Germany would be required to pay €3.00 per month to listen to the radio on Last.fm (Last.fm blog 2009). The licensing costs would be covered through advertisement revenue in those three countries. For other countries, where advertising revenue was not enough to cover the licensing cost, the subscription fee would make up the difference (BBC News 2009). As a result, Last.fm became profitable immediately. However, this measure left many users disappointed; many stopped using the service or switched to Spotify, which was an emerging service at that time (BBC News 2009). A blog poster, StudleyUK, commented,

> A word of the wise: if this charge ever comes to the UK, I'll be ditching my subscription immediately. Right now, you're just making Spotify look more and more attractive. (BBC News (2009), sampled 15 February 2016)

A series of restrictive measures followed. On 12 April 2010, Last.fm removed the feature to preview entire tracks. Users who wanted to preview entire tracks were redirected to other sites such as Spotify, Hype

Machine or Mog, where Last.fm's scrobbling is integrated. On 17 November 2010, custom radio stations, also known as "loved tracks radio," was removed for licensing issues (Last.fm blog 2010). A Last.fm employee shares the frustration she/he experienced from not being able to offer the service users want due to licensing issues.

> For the business, the obstacle that I think we face is the fact that we can't offer play-on-demand. I mean, my job is to design services and products, in the music service you can't just listen to the music? It's very complicated. We have an enormous amount of catalogue. If you look at the website, we have millions and millions of artists and track pages, we can provide cover art from an album, but we can't play the album, because the price of on-demand service is high. But that's the problem from my point of view. (Interview, name unrevealed at his/her request)

Last.fm experimented a few new features attractive users. In January 2014, Last.fm's on-demand streaming was integrated with Spotify. Its scrobbling plug-in is provided for many other services including iTunes, Spotify, Deezer and other music services on Linux OS. Cooperation with these companies helps Last.fm to attract new users and to acquire more scrobbling information from these users, which could serve well both for the Last.fm users and the partnering companies. On 28 April 2014, Last.fm stopped providing streaming radio service, and in 2015, Last.fm released a subscriber-exclusive service. However, its incomplete features, as well as some technical glitches, caused some users to stop subscribing.

In summary, the innovative business model that combined free streaming of immense catalogues with music recommendation and sharing mechanism gained Last.fm a fast-growing user base. Following the acquisition by CBS, the business experienced a series of changes. The most notable change was manifested in strict copyright compliance policies, which led to the falling popularity of the service. Copyright licensing issues were not the only factor that influenced the decline of the business—there were also internal conflicts between the large corporation and the "upstart" Internet company. However, the company's strategy for coping with the challenges of the copyright licensing issue resulted in compromised user experiences and hence contributed to the downturn of the business.

4.3.2 YouTube

4.3.2.1 Evolution of the Business

YouTube began as a video-sharing website created by three former PayPal employees, Chad Hurley, Steve Chen and Jawed Karim, in February 2005. Two different origin stories exist for the business: the widely known version is that Hurley and Chen developed the service after they struggled to share some videos at a dinner party at Chen's apartment, while Karim believes that it was instigated by his difficulties in finding two hotly discussed videos in 2004—Janet Jackson's "wardrobe malfunction," in which her breast was accidentally revealed by Justin Timberlake during the performance at the Super Bowl show, and the Asian tsunami (Hopkins 2006). Regardless, the explosive response to this service reflected the impending need for such a service: in less than a year after the official launch of the service in July 2006, 65,000 new videos were uploaded and 100 million videos were viewed per day (Reuters 2006).

The essence of the business lies in allowing users to upload and share videos through which advertisements are tied to generate revenue. Whereas YouTube is not the only or the first service of this kind, YouTube gained exponential popularity due to its ease of use: instant, free and unlimited access to global catalogues, simple upload of videos in any format and easy sharing (O'Brien and Fitzgerald 2006).

YouTube's legal ordeals are well known. The company has been sued in three major media content consuming countries, the USA (Viacom), the UK (PRS for Music) and Germany (GEMA). YouTube, however, wasn't always embroiled with copyright issues. During the early days, a significant portion of YouTube videos featured user-generated content. The original, thus legal, contents kept YouTube free from concerns about copyright infringements (Breen 2007). The concept of the service's legitimacy was not solid in the beginning. This began to change as YouTube's user base increased, obliging the service to be more alert to the concept of legitimacy. First, the increased number of users brought increased copyright infringement. Increasing number of videos was simple uploads of TV programmes or music videos—oftentimes without permission from the rights owners—than "user-generated" videos. Secondly, the explosive growth of the user base meant a new revenue-generating avenue. This was something that YouTube did not consider in the beginning. An employee at YouTube describes it as something that happened "all of a sudden."

> We got this possibility of monetising content you originally didn't plan for to get there, but you see the value of it. (Interview, name unrevealed at his/her request)

Pressured by media companies, YouTube took a few new measures to enhance the legitimacy of the service. In August 2006, they unveiled a new advertising plan providing content providers with more control over YouTube as a revenue stream. Brand Channels were created to cater for advertisers who wished to present video contents on YouTube with a consistent look and feel with their brand imagery, with Paris Hilton's channel as the first case (McCarthy 2006). In September 2006, the deal between YouTube and Warner marked the beginning of YouTube's official move to reify the legitimacy of its business (YouTube 2006). Under the revenue-sharing agreement, YouTube allowed Warner to identify the use of their recordings and to share the revenue generated from advertisements appearing alongside the video clips with the copyright owner (Leeds 2006). This agreement hinges on a technology that compares "audio uploaded to the site to unique attributes of copyrighted content it already knows" (Delaney and Smith 2006). Also known as "fingerprinting," this technology resembles an audio-identification system that Shawn Fanning presented at Snocap Inc., a company set up after Napster (Delaney and Smith 2006).

Defining YouTube's business model as a compromise over copyright issues, Delaney and Smith (2006) argued that this was "a move that could defuse the threat of legal action against it, (YouTube) is racing to overhaul the way media and entertainment companies view unlicensed online use of their content." Nonetheless, this measure was well greeted in the market. In October 2006, Google announced that it had acquired YouTube for $1.65 billion (Google 2006). It is alleged that Google's acquisition accelerated YouTube's transition to a legitimate service, leading with measures to include advertisements on as many pages as possible (von Lohmann 2006). Google also tried to sign deals with as many media companies as possible. Companies such as CBS, MTV2 and Sony BMG joined the partnership in order to use YouTube as a revenue-sharing platform.

Nevertheless, a more pernicious legal battle has yet to come. On 13 March 2007, Viacom filed suit against YouTube. Accusing YouTube's business model of "massive copyright infringement," Viacom sought $1 billion in damages (Helft and Fabrikant 2007). Viacom's argument was that YouTube relied heavily on copyrighted materials but "has deliberately chosen not to take reasonable precautions to deter the rampant infringement on its site."[5] The evidence Viacom provided was that the uploaded videos "are not identified by copyright owner or registration number but rather by the uploader's idiosyncratic choice of descriptive terms to describe the content of the video – tags making it extremely impractical to identify plaintiff's copyrighted works" (Reed 2006). YouTube has "Terms of Use" which inhibits users from uploading illegal content and allows YouTube to remove content that infringes on copyright or does not comply with the terms. The nature of the service, which relies on users' uploads, has subjected YouTube to potential legal litigation; not only is the automated process of users' voluntary "flagging" highly arbitrary and unreliable, but it is nearly impossible to expect someone to constantly police potential infringement (Hormann 2009).

In legal circles, DMCA's "safe harbour" provision has not proven to protect services like Napster, Grokster and Aimster, which are akin to YouTube in that the essence of business rests on contents uploaded by

[5] Complaint for Declaratory and Injunctive Relief and Damages ||2,10, Viacom Int'l, Inc. v. YouTube, Inc., No. 1:08-cv-02103 (LLS), 2007 WL 775611 (S.D.N.Y. 13 March 2007).

users. There is a legal dispute about whether YouTube as an Internet service provider (ISP) is subject to the protection of "safe harbour" provisions under DMCA. In order to qualify for immunity from liability for contributory infringement, an ISP must prove that it had neither actual knowledge nor awareness of facts or circumstances of infringement and must take down infringing materials once it acquires knowledge of the infringement. The US Congress created a "red flag" test designed to investigate whether an ISP has apparent knowledge of infringement; the debate on this "red flag" test dragged on for seven years. During this long battle, Google twice got the upper hand in the courts, in 2010 and in 2012. The summary judgement in the 2nd Circuit stated, "The burden of showing that YouTube knew or was aware of the specific infringements of the works in suit cannot be shifted to YouTube to disprove" (Gardner 2014a). After the judgment, Viacom was to appeal the verdict, but a resolution between the two parties was announced on 18 March 2014 (Gardner 2014a).

The long-run lawsuit left Viacom with expensive legal bills, not the billions of dollars for damages which Viacom filed for in the first place. However, the strife did have some impact. Corynne McSherry, Intellectual Property Director at the Electronic Frontier Foundation, says, "For one thing, the case arguably pushed YouTube and others online towards copyright detection technology. The world has changed quite a bit since the lawsuit was filed. YouTube's practices have changed quite a bit in adopting Content ID" (Gardner 2014b). The full implication of its legal battle remains to be seen. At the very least, this legal battle ended with a settlement that "reflects the growing collaborative dialogue…on important opportunities," as the settlement announcement stated (Viacom Newsroom 2014).

4.3.2.2 Controversies and Limitations

Without a doubt, YouTube's success is phenomenal, leaving numerous impacts on the market. Much of it owes much to the emergence of user-generated content, which was not possible in the pre-digital era. By enabling users to upload videos, it became a platform where anyone can share their videos. By breaking the barrier to entry, it facilitated "participatory culture," in which the traditional distinction between producer and consumer becomes blurred (Jenkins 2006). As a platform for "vernacular creativity," YouTube allowed grassroots culture to surface from marginal to the mainstream. Viewed as a platform for the democratisation of cultural production and amateurship (Benkler 2006), YouTube is often perceived to have valorised "digital utopianism" (Turner 2006). TIME's acknowledgement of the power of the collective "You" signifies the role of YouTube as a "million-channel people's network" that empowers users' ability to change the way information is produced and distributed (Grossman 2006).

This change culminated in the services' new role as a platform for viral hits. Chris Brown's song "Forever" was featured in the viral video "JK Wedding Entrance Dance," which became the third most watched video on YouTube in 2009, with 60 million views. The song came out more than a year before the wedding occurred but had long fallen off the chart by that time (*JK Wedding Entrance Dance* 2009). In the wake of the video being posted, the song had a second life commercially, and once again turned into a bestseller: it rose to number four on iTunes' chart due to this video (*Fred von Lohmann 'Copyright and Innovation Policy'* 2012) Bon Jovi's "Living On A Prayer," the 1987 classic rock hit, also got a second life due to a YouTube video of basketball fan Jeremy Fry dancing to the song at a Boston Celtics basketball game (*Jeremy Fry—Celtics Fan Dancing to Bon Jovi Living on a Prayer at a Celtics game* 2009). The viral effect on YouTube and Facebook subsequently caused Bon Jovi's song to re-chart in the Billboard Hot 100, 26 years after its last appearance in the chart. A more recent example is Soko's song "We Might be Dead Tomorrow." It was used in the video "First Kiss," where 20 strangers were asked to kiss for the first time (*First Kiss* 2014). The huge popularity of the video earned Soko a lot of money for the synchronisation fee.

Underneath the viral impact, however, there was an ever-increasing encroachment of the power from the conventional media. Burgess (2009) pays a closer attention to this and stresses the converging aspects of YouTube, where both "user-created" content and videos by "traditional media" co-exist. Contrary to the weight given to the contribution of user-created content to YouTube, she points out, these videos take up only a very small proportion of "popular" YouTube videos, while content from traditional media counts for the majority of the videos in the "Most Viewed" and "Most Favourited" sections. Underpinning this uneven distribution of value is the mechanism by which certain works rise to the top. Although YouTube is widely epitomised as the incarnation of Web 2.0, the evolution of the business, which has been as much driven by its users as by traditional media, suggests that YouTube is not immune from contested power relations between users and corporation.

A good manifestation of it is its partnership with Vevo, a music video and entertainment platform. Overshadowing the diversity and enormity of the catalogues on YouTube, Vevo channel has been the number one channel on the service, generating over 2.6 billion views (Sandoval 2008). The service was borne out of an idea that Doug Morris, Universal's chairman and CEO, had to launch a "Hulu-like" standalone music video service, in an effort to generate more revenue out of this popular channel. Established as a joint venture between Sony and Universal, YouTube's partnership with Vevo gives YouTube enhanced legitimacy and more high-end advertisers, by attracting advertisers to YouTube better than user-generated content does (Sandoval 2008). The British band Bastille's debut single "Pompeii" typified the significance of Vevo as a platform for breakout artists. After being featured on the service's home page, the song attracted 46 million views and 386,000 sales on the band's Vevo channel (Pham 2013b) and eventually became the most streamed song of all time (Lane 2014). More recently, Despacito's record of 1 billion views on Vevo music video raised a concern on its role as a hit-generating machine (Mulligan 2017a).

Another controversy arose in relation to the power relations between YouTube and independent labels. On 12 November 2015, YouTube launched an on-demand streaming service called YouTube Music. In preparing the service, YouTube became embroiled in ferocious rows with independent labels. YouTube sent out a "template contract" giving indie labels two choices: take it or leave it. The terms were non-negotiable, and undervalued independent labels and associated entities responded with tremendous frustration (Dredge 2014). Independent labels argue that this uproar is less about the actual money than about YouTube's unequal approach to labels (Dredge 2014). The typical contract that YouTube sent out to the labels included terms and clauses such as "most-favored nation," which would entitle YouTube to reduce the rate for independent labels if major labels agree to a lower rate. While YouTube argues that this clause was included so as not to affect independent labels disproportionately, independent labels regard the asymmetry in power as inevitably leading the contract to work more favourably for major labels than for independent ones. In other words, major labels would be able to negotiate a third option for payment, either a non-recoupable advance or a per-stream minimum rate on top of a percentage of revenue or a minimum per subscriber. Independent labels' lack of negotiation power for a third option, meanwhile, would force independent labels to accept the lowered rate chosen by majors. Independent labels are also infuriated that they did not get the minimum-guarantee payment that the major labels allegedly did (Christman 2014). A complaint to the European Commission, filed by the Independent Music Companies Association (IMPALA), followed (Christman 2014). YouTube eventually announced its plan to re-negotiate the terms with independent labels (Flanagan 2014). The independent labels' furore, however, was not to be easily appeased. They responded with the "Fair Digital Deals Declaration." Under the flag of the Worldwide Independent Network (WIN), more than 700 indie labels joined the initiative to voice their impending request to ensure fair treatment for indies which, they argue, will eventually help remunerate artists better (Minsker 2014). This invocation of independents' appeal for fairer treatment itself might serve as an indication of the increasing power of independent labels.

4.3.2.3 Limitations

YouTube's business model manifests much of the potential digital technology presented: it is free, easy to share, and has an immense number of music catalogues. Notwithstanding the immense popularity of the service, particularly amongst young generation, the service did not serve to solve the industry's quagmires: piracy and the declining sales.[6] The appeal of free and unlimited access to music itself, although is important, proved to attract only certain type of digital music users. YouTube is a predominant avenue of music listening particularly for the younger generation of 18- to 25-year-olds to whom free access is significant. While this age group can account for crucial music aficionados, it does not represent the overall music consumption crowd. As far as music consumption is concerned, it takes more than free of charge access and a large number of catalogues. One of the factors that count as significant—if not more—as free is the quality of service. As a result of the copyright compliance policy, YouTube compromised a few of the features. For example, the ten-minute time limit imposed on video uploads and the poor video quality made YouTube inferior to contents distributed on P2P networks, whose compression technology supports content of far superior quality. Although its impact on music might not be as big as it is on film, this restriction led users to continue to use P2P file-sharing as a "venue" for digital music experience. The increasing uptake of smartphones rendered the endless supply of music that comes with video subject to running up data charges. Overall, the abundance of free content could not prevail over the limitations of YouTube such as the inconsistent quality of sound and the annoyance of advertisements (Jarrett 2008), and left a room for a new innovation.[7]

[6]Lately, this has become subject of debate around "the value gap" in which YouTube's low royalty payout is considered problematic as it does not increase in proportion to the stream rate (UK Music 2016; IFPI 2017).

[7]Google introduced paid services with Google Play in 2013, and YouTube Red in 2015. Google Play Music featuring podcast streaming and online music locker and YouTube Red is a subscription-based music service enabling subscribers to listen to music without the interruption of the advertisements and data charges. Despite the vast user base, the number of paid users even when subscribers of the two services combined still is far behind its market leaders such as Spotify and Apple Music (Gensler 2017).

4.4 The Rise of Streaming Services (2008–Present)

4.4.1 The Decline of P2P File-Sharing

Before we discuss the significant changes that streaming services are making in the contemporary digital recording industry, this section briefly looks at the decline of P2P file-sharing. In 2013, Peter Sunde, co-founder of Pirate Bay, prophesised the "imminent death" of the peer-to-peer system (Solon 2013). Later in 2015, he stated that "the death of [the] pirate movement" had occurred (Sunde 2015). The same year, International Federation of Phonographic Industry (IFPI), an organisation representing the interests of the recording industry, condemned P2P networks as "the biggest source of online copyright theft," admitting a considerable decline in P2P file-sharing, with website blocking being the most effective measure (IFPI 2015). Since 2016, there is no mention of piracy in IFPI's reports[8]: instead, the growth of the streaming business replaced the space.

While P2P file-sharing's popularity owed much to its convenience and free access to the unlimited music catalogue, this changed over time for a few reasons. As discussed in Chapter 3, Sect. 3.3, P2P file-sharing application developers became more preoccupied with ensuring that systems were resilient against legal allegations than meeting digital music users' needs. In other words, user experience on P2P file-sharing could not be a matter of priority for P2P file-sharing service developers. In tandem, people's perception of P2P file-sharing changed over time from something justifiable or even desirable to the activity degraded into something more dubious over time. From a business perspective, P2P file-sharing application providers rely heavily on advertisement for their revenue source. The illegality of P2P technology made it increasingly difficult to attract decent advertisement, leaving pornography as almost the only option (interview with Rasmus Fleischer, co-founder of

[8]Piracy is briefly mentioned in IFPI (2017) report to discuss the changing climate of digital music business in China where piracy is declining with the increasing growth of the legal music business.

Piratbyrån). In addition, labels distributed fake files on P2P file-sharing networks, which left many P2P downloaders frustrated with failed attempts to download files (DeVoss and Porter 2006). While P2P technology has become decentralised following the "roadmap" of the court decisions of the precedent P2P technologies, this development had unexpected consequences. The intensified takedown online measures subjected P2P networks' resilience to a perfect avenue for malware distribution (Rossow et al. 2013), and hence became a significant concern for P2P network users. Along with these changes, the superior legal offerings instigated by Spotify were increasingly perceived to be a main driving force against piracy (Page 2013; Aguiar and Waldfogel 2015; IFPI 2015; Wlömert and Papies 2016). The next section looks at the developments in this field.

4.4.2 The Rise of Streaming Services

With varying degrees of failure, nonc of the measures sufficiently addressed the recording industry's struggle to reduce piracy and regain economic growth in digital music networks. Things began to change significantly in 2008, marking the beginning of what Samuel (2014) called a "new world of music," dominated by online streaming services.[9] Central to the change was on-demand streaming services.[10] As shown in Table 4.1, revenue from streaming services has continued to grow since their inception. In 2017, IFPI reported streaming "as the most prevalent and significant format in the modern music industry, fuelling growth in almost all major markets and starting to unlock the phenomenal potential within developing territories (IFPI 2017, p. 16)." At the time of this writing, revenues from streaming account for more

[9]Samuel (2014) distinguishes the history of recorded music into four phases grouped by the unique features of each phase. Phase I (up to 1983) is Physical Analogue with cassettes, LPs, singles and 8-tracks; Phase II (1984–2003) is Physical Digital with CDs; moving into the "New World of Music", Phase III (2004–2007) is Online Downloads, i.e. downloads from the Internet; and Phase IV (2008 onwards) is Online Streaming.

[10]Marshall (2015) groups current digital music services into three types: streaming radio (webcasting), locker services and on-demand streaming.

Table 4.1 The growth of streaming music revenue and subscribers

Year	2009	2010	2011	2012	2013	2014	2015	2016	2017
Streaming revenue ($bn)	0.4	0.4	0.6	1.0	1.4	1.9	2.8	4.7	6.6
Number of paying subscribers (m)	6	8	13	20	28	41	68	97	176

(*Source* Author, compiled from IFPI Global Music Reports from 2010–2018)

than half (56%) of digital revenue, with near 100 million paying users globally (IFPI 2017). A closer look at how streaming services brought the wind of change in the unyielding tide of piracy will be discussed with a case study of Spotify in the next chapter. In this chapter, I will provide a brief discussion of the streaming music market's current status quo by looking at four major streaming services providers, Spotify, Apple Music, Amazon Music and Deezer (Fig. 4.1).[11]

4.4.2.1 Spotify[12]

Spotify, as the most popular streaming service as of 2017, arose to provide an alternative to piracy. Its basic concept is to provide free access to a wide breadth of legal catalogues and to cause users to become "hooked" so that they will subscribe to a premium service, featuring an ad-free "offline" mode. By achieving a critical mass in Sweden where the company originated, Spotify offered a solution to market entrenchment: large-scale access at low cost. It was the result of an alignment between the two biggest players in the recording industry with conflicting interests: digital music users and labels. Spotify's freemium-based music service, with its "legal and superior quality" to P2P file-sharing, as well as its immense number of legal catalogues, have proved to be enticing enough to attract 60 million paid users as of July 2017 (Spotify 2017).

[11]The four companies were chosen based Mulligan (2017a)'s streaming market share analysis.

[12]A detailed analysis of Spotify's business development is discussed in Chapter 5.

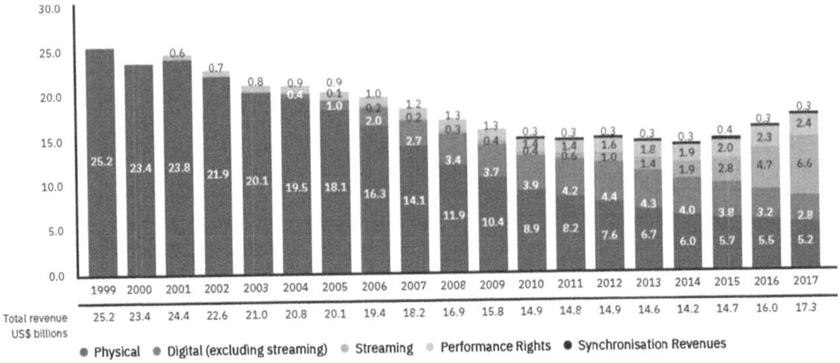

Fig. 4.1 Global recorded music industry revenues 1999–2017 ($bn) (IFPI 2018) (*Source* IFPI. See IFPI's Global Music Report 2018)

4.4.2.2 Apple Music

While Apple appeared to remain "the last defender" of the download music business, it was becoming increasingly clear that "streaming services like Spotify will overturn the music ownership model that Jobs fought to preserve" (Weinman 2011). Prompted by this change, Apple launched a music streaming service called Apple Music on 30 June 2015. Early in 2014, Apple Music purchased Beats Music, which had originally arisen as a competing streaming music service to Spotify named Daisy. Beats Music aimed to challenge its competitors by providing a solution to "a problem that most music fans may not realize they have: deciding what to listen to" (Sisario 2014). Apple Music uses Beats Music for personal music recommendations in its live radio station, a feature distinguishable from Spotify. Apple Music hired BBC Radio 1 DJ Zane Lowe as a music curator (Thorpe 2015). After three months' free trial, 40 per cent of users cancelled their subscription, leaving 6.5 million paying subscribers, a drop from 11 million (McIntyre 2015). Despite Apple Music's emphasis on new music discovery, Spotify is credited to be superior for new sounds, while Apple tends to feed listeners popular and familiar sounds (Mitroff 2015). As of 2017, Apple music has 30 million paid users, which is half of its competitor Spotify (Sparks 2017). Still, uncertainty abounds as to the future of digital music services: the majority of users might prefer to stay in their music comfort zone; music discovery might not be as crucial as music service providers assume; or new forms of service will overtake the current streaming service model.

4.4.2.3 Amazon Music Unlimited

Amazon Music is another streaming service run by a tech giant, along with Apple Music. Backed up by its massive existing number of user base, Amazon rose to the third largest streaming services, switching 35% of Amazon Prime subscribers to Amazon streaming music services including Amazon Prime Music and Amazon Prime Music Unlimited (Mulligan 2017b). Historically Amazon Music has provided download music service under Amazon MP3. Prompted by the sweeping growth of streaming services, Amazon added an advertising-free access-based music service called Amazon Unlimited in 2016 (Hern 2016). Amazon's vantage point lies with its existing suite of services including Amazon Echo, smart speaker, and Amazon Prime which gives more benefit for existing Amazon customers (Fitzpatrick 2016). Amidst the increasing popularity of smart speakers for early adopters (Dredge 2018), it remains to be seen whether Amazon can bring changes to streaming business sphere.

4.4.2.4 Deezer

Deezer is another major on-demand digital music streaming service provider, headquartered in Paris, France. As of 2017, it has 12 million active users and 9 million subscribers (Sassard 2017). The service started as a free streaming music service on a website called Blogmusik in 2006. The growing popularity of the service, however, drew attention from record labels. Daniel Marhely, who first developed Deezer, had to stop the service until he signed agreements with SACEM, a collecting society in France (Rozat 2011). Re-launched with proper agreements in place, Deezer attracted a large number of customers, positioning as the largest music service in France (Aguiar 2017) and the 4th biggest streaming music service provider in the world after Spotify, Apple Music and Amazon Music (Mulligan 2017a; Sassard 2017). From early on, Deezer paid a special attention to helping their users discover new music so as to offer a distinct experience (Interview with an employee at Deezer). Its success owes much to its partnership with Orange, the largest telecom company in France, which helped its exposure to young users greatly. Deezer strategically placed more on global market where Spotify is not available, to target markets with high mobile phone uptakes, which the company perceives as the largest attraction for streaming services (interview with an employee at Deezer).

4.5 Concluding Remarks

This chapter has discussed the actual process of innovation involved in building a commercially viable business model in the recording industry, as well as the post-Napster early trials, characterised by major labels' resistance to digital novelty and independent players' efforts to embrace the change. Neither of the approaches proved to be effective in solving market entrenchment. A technology firm, in this case Apple, provided a new approach of pay-per-track download at a fairly low price for a wide breadth of legal catalogues. Although it was successful to a certain degree, piracy continued unabated. This left a space for new experimentation. Through the cases of Last.fm and YouTube, we observed how companies with more or less the same business model, in this case an advertising-based free music service with unlimited access, experienced different fates as they coped with challenges differently. As Spotify's freemium-based streaming service began to make a significant change in the market, other services such as Apple Music, Amazon Music and Deezer are making inroads to offer better experiences to digital music users. Although these services are increasingly perceived to signal a recovery of economic growth for the recording industry as a whole, many other issues remain to question its sustainability. More discussion will continue in the next chapter.

References

Aguiar, L. 2017. Let the Music Play? Free Streaming and Its Effects on Digital Music Consumption. *Information Economics and Policy* 41: 1–14.

Aguiar, L., and J. Waldfogel. 2015. Streaming Reaches Flood Stage: Does Spotify Stimulate or Depress Music Sales? Working Paper No. 21653, National Bureau of Economic Research.

Akester, P. 2005. Copyright and the P2P Challenge. *European Intellectual Property Review* 27 (3): 106.

Apple Press. 2007. Apple Unveils Higher Quality DRM-Free Music on the iTunes Store [online]. *Apple Press*. Available from https://www.apple.com/uk/pr/library/2007/04/02Apple-Unveils-Higher-Quality-DRM-Free-Music-on-the-iTunes-Store.html. Accessed 2 Aug 2014.

Apple Press. 2009. Changes Coming to the iTunes Store [online]. *Apple Press Info*. Available from https://www.apple.com/uk/pr/library/2009/01/06Changes-Coming-to-the-iTunes-Store.html. Accessed 2 Aug 2014.

Arditi, D. 2014. iTunes: Breaking Barriers and Building Walls. *Popular Music and Society* 37 (4): 408–424.

Bakker, P. 2005. File-Sharing—Fight, Ignore or Compete: Paid Download Services vs. P2P-Networks. *Telematics and Informatics* 22 (1–2): 41–55.

BBC News. 2003. Website Offers New View of Music. *BBC*, March 27.

BBC News. 2009. Last.fm to Charge for Streaming. *BBC*, March 25.

Bell, K. 2014. Spotify Now Generates More Royalties Than iTunes In Europe [online]. Business Insider. Available from http://uk.businessinsider.com/spotify-royalties-itunes-europe-2014-11 Accessed 6 July 2018.

Benkler, Y. 2006. *The Wealth of Networks: How Social Production Transforms Markets and Freedom*. New Haven, CT: Yale University Press.

Blankenhorn, D. 2006. Dana Blankenhorn: How Much Further Can Apple Go? [online]. Available from http://www.danablankenhorn.com/2006/12/how_much_furthe.html. Accessed 7 Aug 2014.

Breen, J.C. 2007. YouTube or YouLose: Can YouTube Survive a Copyright Infringement Lawsuit? *Texas Intellectual Property Law Journal* 16 (1): 151–182.

Burgess, J. 2009. *YouTube: Online Video and Participatory Culture*. Cambridge: Polity.

Buskirk, E.V. 2008. Free Music Boosts Last.fm's Traffic 58 Percent [online]. *Wired*. Available from http://www.wired.com/2008/02/free-music-boos/. Accessed 10 Feb 2016.

Christman, E. 2014. IMPALA Files Complaint Against YouTube with European Commission [online]. *Billboard*. Available from http://www.

billboard.com/biz/articles/news/global/6141020/impala-files-complaint-against-youtube-with-european-commission. Accessed 25 July 2014.

Craft, K.L. 2001. The Webcasting Music Revolution Is Ready to Begin, as Soon as We Figure Out the Copyright Law: The Story of the Music Industry at War with Itself. *Hastings Communications and Entertainment Law Journal* 24: 1.

Cummings, A.S. 2010. From Monopoly to Intellectual Property: Music Piracy and the Remaking of American Copyright, 1909–1971. *The Journal of American History* 97 (3): 659–681.

Delaney, K.J., and E. Smith. 2006. YouTube Model Is Compromise Over Copyrights. *Wall Street Journal*, September 19.

Delchin, R.J. 2004. Musical Copyright Law: Past, Present and Future of Online Music Distribution. *Cardozo Arts & Entertainment Law Journal* 22: 343.

DeVoss, D.N., and J.E. Porter. 2006. Why Napster Matters to Writing: Filesharing as a New Ethic of Digital Delivery. *Computers and Composition: An International Journal for Teachers of Writing* 23 (2): 178–210.

Drahos, P. 2002. *Information Feudalism: Who Owns the Knowledge Economy?* London: Earthscan.

Dredge, S. 2014. Musician Zoe Keating Reveals iTunes, Spotify and YouTube Payouts for 2013. *The Guardian*, February 24.

Dredge, S., 2018. What do smart speakers like Amazon Echo, Google Home and Apple HomePod mean for music? *Medium*. Available from https://medium.com/@stuartdredge/what-do-smart-speakers-like-amazon-echo-google-home-and-apple-homepod-mean-for-music-5da4589dbdc6.

First Kiss. 2014. Available at https://www.youtube.com/watch?v=IpbDHxCV29A.

Fitzpatrick, A. 2016. Streaming Showdown: Amazon Music Unlimited vs. Spotify [online]. *Time*. Available from http://time.com/4533923/amazon-music-unlimited-spotify/. Accessed 5 Feb 2018.

Flanagan, A. 2014. YouTube Re-negotiating with Indies Following Outcry [online]. *Billboard*. Available from http://www.billboard.com/biz/articles/news/digital-and-mobile/6150292/youtube-re-negotiating-with-indies-following-outcry. Accessed 12 July 2014.

Fred von Lohmann 'Copyright and Innovation Policy'. 2012. Available at https://www.youtube.com/watch?v=kd4BprytFFk.

Gardner, E. 2014a. Viacom, Google Settle Long-Running YouTube Copyright Lawsuit [online]. *The Hollywood Reporter*. Available from http://www.hollywoodreporter.com/thr-esq/viacom-google-settle-long-running-689291. Accessed 7 Aug 2014.

Gardner, E. 2014b. What Viacom Has to Show for Seven Years of Pursuing YouTube [online]. *Billboard.* Available from http://www.billboard.com/biz/articles/news/legal-and-management/5937673/what-viacom-has-to-show-for-seven-years-of-pursuing. Accessed 16 July 2014.

Gensler, A. 2017. Lyor Cohen on the Streaming Business, Combining YouTube Red and Google Play, and SoundCloud's 'Sad Experience' [online]. *Billboard.* Available from http://www.billboard.com/articles/business/7881753/lyor-cohen-streaming-business-youtube-red-google-play-soundcloud. Accessed 31 Oct 2017.

Goodell, J. 2003. Steve Jobs: Rolling Stone's 2003 Interview [online]. *Rolling Stone.* Available from http://www.rollingstone.com/music/news/steve-jobs-rolling-stones-2003-interview-20111006. Accessed 31 July 2014.

Google. 2006. Google to Acquire YouTube for $1.65 Billion in Stock [online]. *Google News.* Available from http://googlepress.blogspot.co.uk/2006/10/google-to-acquire-youtube-for-165_09.html. Accessed 10 Feb 2016.

Grossman, L. 2006. You—Yes, You—Are TIME's Person of the Year. *Time.*

Helft, M., and G. Fabrikant. 2007. WhoseTube? Viacom Sues Google Over Video Clips. *The New York Times,* March 14.

Hern, A. 2016. Amazon Launches Spotify and Apple Music Competitor [online]. *The Guardian.* Available from http://www.theguardian.com/technology/2016/oct/12/amazon-music-unlimited-launch-spotify-apple-streaming-competitor-echo. Accessed 5 Feb 2018.

Hiatt, B. 2002. Which Online Music Service Is Worth Paying for? [online]. *Entertainment Weekly.* Available from http://ew.com/article/2002/08/28/which-online-music-service-worth-paying/. Accessed 16 Apr 2018.

Hill, B. 2018. The Digital Songstream: Mastering the World of Digital Music (Paperback)—Routledge [online]. *Routledge.com.* Available from https://www.routledge.com/The-Digital-Songstream-Mastering-the-World-of-Digital-Music/Hill/p/book/9780415942034. Accessed 17 Apr 2018.

Holton, K. 2007. Warner Music Announces Last.fm Content Deal [online]. *Reuters.* Available from http://uk.reuters.com/article/industry-warner-last-fm-dc-idUKL0662451720070207. Accessed 10 Feb 2016.

Hopkins, J. 2006. Surprise! There's a Third YouTube Co-founder [online]. *USA Today.* Available from http://usatoday30.usatoday.com/tech/news/2006-10-11-youtube-karim_x.htm?csp=34. Accessed 28 Feb 2016.

Hormann, K.C. 2009. The Death of the DMCA? How Viacom v. Youtube May Define the Future of Digital Content. *Houston Law Review* 46 (4): 1345–1377.

IFPI. 2015. Digital Music Report 2015: Charting the Path to Sustainable Growth. Available from http://www.ifpi.org/downloads/Digital-Music-Report-2015.pdf.
IFPI. 2017. IFPI Global Music Report 2017: Annual State of the Industry. Available from http://www.ifpi.org/news/IFPI-GLOBAL-MUSIC-REPORT-2017.
IFPI. 2018. Global Music Report 2015: Annual State of the Industry. Available from http://www.ifpi.org/downloads/GMR2018.pdf.
Jarrett, K. 2008. Beyond Broadcast Yourself™: The Future of Youtube. *Media International Australia* 126 (1): 132–144.
Jenkins, H. 2006. *Convergence Culture: Where Old and New Media Collide*. New York: New York University Press.
Jeremy Fry—Celtics Fan Dancing to Bon Jovi Living on a Prayer at a Celtics Game. 2009. Available from https://www.youtube.com/watch?v=mOHkRk00iI8.
JK Wedding Entrance Dance. 2009. Available from https://www.youtube.com/watch?v=4-94JhLEiN0.
Jobs, S. 2007. Apple—Thoughts on Music [online]. Available from http://web.archive.org/web/20080517114107/; http://www.apple.com/hotnews/thoughtsonmusic. Accessed 31 July 2014.
Kiss, J. 2007. Last.fm Fetches $280m. *The Guardian*, May, 30.
Knopper, S. 2009. *Appetite for Self-Destruction: The Spectacular Crash of the Record Industry in the Digital Age*. New York: Free Press.
Koh, B., B.P.S. Murthi, and S. Raghunathan. 2014. Shifting Demand: Online Music Piracy, Physical Music Sales, and Digital Music Sales. *Journal of Organizational Computing and Electronic Commerce* 24 (4): 366–387.
Lane, D. 2014. The Top 10 Most Streamed Songs and Artists of All Time Revealed! [online]. Available from http://www.officialcharts.com/chart-news/the-top-10-most-streamed-songs-and-artists-of-all-time-revealed-3107/. Accessed 24 July 2014.
Lane, M.A. 2011. 'Interactive Services' and the Future of Internet Radio Broadcasts. *Alabama Law Review* 62: 459.
Last.fm Blog. 2008. Free the Music [online]. *Last.fm Blog*. Available from http://blog.last.fm/2008/01/23/free-the-music. Accessed 10 Feb 2016.
Last.fm Blog. 2009. Last.fm Radio Announcement [online]. Available from http://blog.last.fm/2009/03/24/lastfm-radio-announcement. Accessed 11 Feb 2016.
Last.fm Blog. 2010. April 12 Site Update—Track Page Beta, Streaming Changes—Feedback and Ideas [online]. *Last.fm*. Available from http://www.last.fm/forum/21717/_/617074. Accessed 11 Feb 2016.

Leeds, J. 2006. Warner Music Makes Licensing Deal with YouTube [online]. *New York Times*. Available from http://www.nytimes.com/2006/09/19/business/media/19tube.html. Accessed 28 Feb 2016.

Levy, N.N. 2000. Method to Their Madness: The Secure Digital Music Initiative, a Law and Economics Perspective. *Virginia Journal of Law and Technology* 5: 1.

Levy, S. 2006. *The Perfect Thing: How the iPod Shuffles Commerce, Culture, and Coolness*. New York: Simon and Schuster.

von Lohmann, F. 2006. Thoughts on Google, YouTube [online]. *Electronic Frontier Foundation*. Available from https://www.eff.org/deeplinks/2006/10/thoughts-google-youtube. Accessed 10 Feb 2016.

Marshall, L. 2015. 'Let's Keep Music Special. F—Spotify': On-Demand Streaming and the Controversy Over Artist Royalties. *Creative Industries Journal* 8 (2): 177–189.

McCarthy, C. 2006. Paris Hilton Showcases YouTube's New ad Concepts [online]. *CNET*. Available from http://www.cnet.com/uk/news/paris-hilton-showcases-youtubes-new-ad-concepts/. Accessed 29 Feb 2016.

McCarthy, C. 2007. What Does CBS Want with Last.fm? [online]. *CNET*. Available from http://www.cnet.com/news/what-does-cbs-want-with-last-fm/. Accessed 25 Feb 2016.

McIntyre, H. 2015. Apple Music Has Lost 40% of Users After Its Free Trial—Forbes [online]. *Forbes*. Available from http://www.forbes.com/sites/hughmcintyre/2015/10/20/apple-music-has-lost-40-of-users-after-its-free-trial/#7e4e6d041c1c. Accessed 9 Feb 2016.

Medford, C. 2008. Report: Apple Killed Music Industry. *Red Herring*, 2–2.

Minsker, E. 2014. Indie Labels Unite to Launch 'Fair Digital Deals Declaration' Initiative [online]. *Pitchfork*. Available from http://pitchfork.com/news/55909-indie-labels-unite-to-launch-fair-digital-deals-declaration-initiative/. Accessed 25 July 2014.

Mitroff, S. 2015. Apple Music vs Spotify: What's the Difference? [online]. *CNET*. Available from http://www.cnet.com/uk/news/apple-music-vs-spotify-whats-the-difference/. Accessed 9 Feb 2016.

Mulligan, M. 2017a. Announcing MIDiA's Streaming Services Market Shares Report. *Music Industry Blog*.

Mulligan, M. 2017b. Amazon Is Now the 3rd Biggest Music Subscription Service. *Music Industry Blog*.

Nash, E. 2011. How Steve Jobs Saved the Music Industry. *Wall Street Journal*, October 21.

O'Brien, D.S., and B.F. Fitzgerald. 2006. Mashups, Remixes and Copyright Law. *Internet Law Bulletin* 9 (2): 17–19.

Page, W. 2013. Adventures in the Netherlands: New Spotify Study Sees Encouraging Downwards Trend in Music Piracy in the Netherlands. *Spotify Press*.

Pham, A. 2013a. The Evolution of iTunes: The Birth of a Colossus: The Creation of the World's Biggest Music Retailer Seemed to Happen Almost in spite of the Record Labels, but They Knew a Good Thing When Steve Jobs Showed It to Them. *Billboard* 125 (17): 24.

Pham, A. 2013b. Vevo Pumps Up the Volume with More Than 1 Billion Monthly Views on Mulitple Platforms, Vevo Has Become Crucial. *Billboard* 125 (45): 36.

Pollack, W.M. 1999. Tuning In: The Future of Copyright Protection for Online Music in the Digital Millennium. *Fordham Law Review* 68: 2445.

Quan, M. 1999. SDMI Releases Portable-Player Spec [online]. *EETimes*. Available from http://www.eetimes.com/document.asp?doc_id=1139861. Accessed 28 Feb 2016.

Reed, M. 2006. Publishers vs. YouTube: Does Either Side Win? [online]. *USC Annenberg Online Journalism Review*. Available from http://www.ojr.org/?s=Publishers+vs.+YouTube%3A+Does+Either+Side+Win. Accessed 22 Feb 2016.

Reuters. 2006. YouTube Serves Up 100 Million Videos a Day Online [online]. *USA Today*. Available from http://usatoday30.usatoday.com/tech/news/2006-07-16-youtube-views_x.htm. Accessed 7 Aug 2014.

Rossow, C., D. Andriesse, T. Werner, B. Stone-Gross, D. Plohmann, C.J. Dietrich, and H. Bos. 2013. SoK: P2PWNED—Modeling and Evaluating the Resilience of Peer-to-Peer Botnets. In *2013 IEEE Symposium on Security and Privacy*. Presented at the 2013 IEEE Symposium on Security and Privacy, 97–111.

Rozat, P. 2011. Deezer: Profitability Down the Line? [online]. *InaGlobal*. Available from http://www.inaglobal.fr/en/music/article/deezer-profitability-down-line. Accessed 1 Feb 2018.

Samuel, M.C. 2014. Winds of Change. Journey of UK Music from the Old World to the New World. *Review of Economic Research on Copyright Issues* 11 (2): 27.

Sandoval, G. 2008. Source: Universal Music Group Plans 'Hulu-Like' Site [online]. *CNET*. Available from http://www.cnet.com/uk/news/source-universal-music-group-plans-hulu-like-site/. Accessed 24 July 2014.

Sassard, S. 2017. The French Music Streaming Service Taking on Spotify, Apple and Amazon [online]. *The Independent*. Available from http://

www.independent.co.uk/news/business/analysis-and-features/deezer-music-streaming-spotify-amazon-apple-subscritpiton-hans-holger-albrecht-len-blavatnik-a7940896.html. Accessed 1 Feb 2018.

Sharpe, N.F., and O.B. Arewa. 2006. Is Apple Playing Fair—Navigating the iPod FairPlay DRM Controversy. *Northwestern Journal of Technology and Intellectual Property* 5: 332.

Sheffner, B. 2011. The Antitrust Case Against Major Record Labels, in Perspective [online]. *Billboard*. Available from http://www.billboard.com/biz/articles/news/1179723/the-antitrust-case-against-major-record-labels-in-perspective. Accessed 5 Aug 2014.

Sisario, B. 2014. Beats Music Enters Online Streaming Market—The New York Times [online]. Available from http://www.nytimes.com/2014/01/12/arts/music/beats-music-enters-online-streaming-market.html. Accessed 28 Feb 2016.

Solon, O. 2013. Pirate Bay Interview: You Can't Beat Politics with Technology Says Peter Sunde [online]. *Wired UK*. Available from http://www.wired.co.uk/news/archive/2013-11/18/peter-sunde-hemlis-political-apathy. Accessed 7 Feb 2016.

Sparks, D. 2017. Apple Music Subscribers Hit 30 Million, but It's Not as Impressive as It Sounds [online]. *Business Insider*. Available from http://www.businessinsider.com/apple-music-subscribers-30-million-2017-9. Accessed 15 Dec 2017.

Spotify. 2017. Fast Facts—Spotify. *Spotify Press*.

Sunde, P. 2015. The 'Pirate Movement' Is Dead. *TorrentFreak*.

TechRadar. 2006. Digital Music Award Winners Announced [online]. *TechRadar*. Available from http://www.techradar.com/news/portable-devices/other-devices/phone-and-communications/mobile-phones/internet/web/audio/portable-audio/digital-music-award-winners-announced-159274. Accessed 23 Feb 2016.

The New York Times. 2007. CBS Buys Last.FM, an Online Radio Site. *The New York Times*, May 31.

Thorpe, V. 2015. Zane Lowe to leave BBC Radio 1 for Apple. *The Guardian*, February 15.

Turner, F. 2006. *From Counterculture to Cyberculture: Stewart Brand, the Whole Earth Network, and the Rise of Digital Utopianism*. Chicago: University of Chicago Press.

Twohey, M. 2000. Land of the Free and MP3. *National Journal* 32 (3): 182–183.

Tynan, D. 2006. The 25 Worst Tech Products of All Time [online]. *PCWorld*. Available from http://www.pcworld.com/article/125772/worst_products_ever.html. Accessed 10 Feb 2016.
UK Music. 2016. *Measuring Music 2016*. London: UK Music. Available from https://www.ukmusic.org/assets/general/measuring-music-2016.pdf.
Viacom Newsroom. 2014. Viacom and Google Resolve Copyright Lawsuit [online]. Available from http://news.viacom.com/press-release/legal/viacom-and-google-resolve-copyright-lawsuit. Accessed 8 Aug 2014.
Webb, S.W. 2000. RIAA v Diamond Multimedia Systems: The Recording Industry Attempts to Slow the MP3 Revolution-Taking Aim at the Jogger Friendly Diamond Rio. *Richmond Journal of Law & Technology* 7: 5–34.
Weinman, J.J. 2011. How Jobs Rescued Old Media: Music Was Free Online, Until He Showed That People Still Wanted to Pay. *Maclean's* 124 (41): 48.
Wikström, P. 2013. *The Music Industry: Music in the Cloud*, 2nd ed. Cambridge, England: Polity.
Wingfield, N., and E. Smith. 2007. Music's New Gatekeeper. *Wall Street Journal*, March 9.
Wlömert, N., and D. Papies. 2016. On-Demand Streaming Services and Music Industry Revenues—Insights from Spotify's Market Entry. *International Journal of Research in Marketing* 33 (2): 314–327.
Wu, T. 2003. When Code Isn't Law. *Virginia Law Review* 89 (4): 679–751.
YouTube. 2006. YouTube Unveils New Advertising Concepts [online]. *YouTube News Room*. Available from http://www.marketwired.com/press-release/youtube-unveils-new-advertising-concepts-697771.htm. Accessed 29 Feb 2016.
Zhu, K., and B. Macquarrie. 2003. The Economics of Digital Bundling: The Impact of Digitization and Bundling on the Music Industry. *Communications of the ACM* 46 (9): 264–270.

5
Case Study—Spotify

This chapter provides an in-depth analysis of how Spotify found a solution to the digital recording industry's financial woe persisted since Napster. It examines how this successful legitimate digital music service innovation could arise in the least likely place, Sweden, the hotbed of piracy, and addresses major attributes that brought victory to Spotify over then seemingly unflinching popularity of P2P file-sharing. I continue the discussion on the changing dynamics brought by Spotify and some of the concerns emerging on this new digital music consuming platform.

5.1 Background

5.1.1 Early History

Spotify was established in 2006 by two founders, Daniel Ek and Martin Lorentzon, in Stockholm, Sweden. Daniel Ek is a former CTO

H. Sun, *Digital Revolution Tamed*, https://doi.org/10.1007/978-3-319-93022-0_5

of Stardoll[1] and former CEO of µTorrent, one of the most popular BitTorrent clients. Martin Lorentzon is a co-founder of Tradedoubler, an advertising networking company based in Stockholm, Sweden.

Ek first met Martin Lorentzon when he was asked to develop a program for Tradedoubler and earned a lot of money through this project. Later, Ek met Lorentzon again, who had since become a millionaire by listing Tradedoubler on the Swedish stock market. They shared a vision to reinvigorate a declining music industry, and so Spotify was born. Ek realised Lorentzon's determination to work with him when, in addition to the million Euros of seed money deposited in his bank account, he read the press release that Lorentzon had resigned as the chairman of Tradedoubler within the week-long deadline set by Ek. The company name "Spotify," which will forever be etched in the music history, was born from a mistake. Ek misheard something from Lorentzon, who was sitting in another room making suggestions for a company name. The name had no hits on a search engine and its domain name was soon registered for an advertisement-based music company.

5.1.2 Muddling Through Piracy

Spotify emerged as an answer to piracy following many experiments and trials with different business models since Napster. Whilst iTunes and YouTube grew, piracy continued and the monetary contribution from iTunes, YouTube and everything else put together fell far short of the peak of music sales in the 1980s. The voices of the diverse parties involved describe the change and the internal conflict that the music industry was undergoing.

Since the advent of Napster, music businesses' profits had been on a downhill trajectory; moreover, digital music services seldom proved to be reliable money-makers. The lack of a proven record gave rise to widespread suspicion, hesitance and even hostility towards new services from

[1] A game company that allows users to dress up dolls online.

record labels. Simon Wheeler, Director of Digital at Beggars Group, is familiar with this phase of music history.

> I think the whole industry has been burned by a lot of companies over the years, who have come in and promised the earth but deliver nothing. And in the meantime made a lot of value for themselves. (Simon Wheeler, Interview)

The paucity of digital music sales has been a considerable concern. Most digital music services failed to gain significant popularity. Even those that did become popular rarely became profitable avenues. Simon Wheeler gives Last.fm as an example that did not fulfil the promise of generating revenue on digital music platforms.

> Last.fm is a great example. They never paid me licence fees. They were always talking about how great they were for the industry and they were working something out and they got sold for 288 million dollars. They never had any licences. Service which purely at the back of music which never had any licences, which promised to deliver over a year, yeah, we have sold some advertisements, we will give you a share of it. Nothing really materialised. (Simon Wheeler, Interview) §

Up until the end of 2008, multinational entertainment companies were striving to reduce P2P file-sharing activities by any means possible. Not only did these measures prove to be ineffective in abating piracy, their aggressiveness—even going so far as to sue the very people who comprised their largest consuming demographic—sowed the seeds of hostility towards anti-piracy measures. The repugnance of these measures culminated in pro-piracy activities. Alison Wenham, Chairman of AIM, thinks that this pro-piracy sentiment was used by many users to justify their P2P file-sharing activities.

> I think consumers were justifying their attitude by reference to the behaviour of the major record companies. It's easy not to like the music industry. 'You (music industry) have ripped off your artists, you have not treated your artists well, you ripped me off during the '80s and '90s with

> inflated CD prices, so you deserve it'. There was a certain, some would say justifiable anger in the way that the public perceived us. However, it may not have been as complicated as that, I think people did it because it was easy and it was fashionable. (Alison Wenham, Interview)

However, the recording industry was not likely to change that easily and was mired in a seemingly endless dark tunnel. None of the industry's attempts to quash the rising tide of piracy proved effective, and new strategies were not immediately apparent. Will Page, Director of Economics at Spotify, clearly remembers this dark phase of uncertainty and doubt when a better torrent technology seemed to be the answer.

> I met the maker of that documentary [TPB AFK: The Pirate Bay Away From Keyboard] and he just said something to me which had made hair stand up on the back of my head, which was 'Do you understand what it was in Sweden in 2005, 2006, 2007, 2008?' There were some incredible engineers building torrent tools that nobody could have imagined. So powerful. μTorrent was another one, Kazaa was developed by engineers in Sweden. They were all there determined to build the best torrent pirate facility. They could. (Will Page, Interview)

5.1.3 Sweden, the Kingdom of Piracy

In the midst of piracy's golden era, Daniel Ek wanted to produce a breakthrough solution, but not the best torrent technology. Ek decided to build a digital music service, legal and superior to piracy. The birthplace of this company, Spotify, was ironically Sweden, once the Kingdom of Piracy. To discuss this further, it would be helpful to understand the particular conditions Sweden was in for the piracy to flourish. First, Sweden had a good infrastructure of high-speed Internet early on. The Swedish government initiated a plan called "Home PC Reform" in 1998, which enabled households to purchase their home computers through a monthly, tax-free paycheque deduction; 1.7 million people became equipped with new personal computers, all of which had CD players, allowing people to rip their CDs (Buskirk

2013). The civic disposition for Internet use prompted Sweden to act fast in building fibre-based broadband, which led to a much better Internet user environment than in many other countries such as the UK and USA, where ADSL or dial-up was predominant. Based on this infrastructure, Sweden's cold weather facilitated IT innovations even further (Buskirk 2013).

The enormous popularity of P2P in Sweden also meant there was little room for the growth of iTunes. An employee at Spotify, explains this:

> Piracy was quite rampant in Sweden. Anyone could download music with very little risk of being prosecuted. So it was the de facto way of getting music - just downloading it from Pirate Bay or other P2P sites. iTunes wasn't as prominent in Sweden at that time, people wouldn't buy singles or albums. They would download music from Pirate Bay and they would put it into iTunes. So, people were using iTunes as a music player but they weren't buying music. (Interview, name unrevealed at his/her request)

Culturally, Sweden was in conflict with the IP regime. As a country that embraced capitalism only at the end of the twentieth century, the Swedish people's perception of intellectual property was a result of conflicting ideas between indigenous culture and the normativity reinforced by IP export countries. As Burkitt (2001) pointed out, the "assimilation, justified by Western countries on the premise that intellectual property represents an absolute moral value and irrefutable economic logic is not borne out by the history of copyright in Europe and America (p.186)." A good example of this "lack of conceptual cohesion" (Burkitt 2001, p. 174) in Sweden is that "it has a long tradition of private imports of goods, home brewing, and tax evasion…there is (also) an element of looking up to more culturally resonant countries, such as the United States" (Schwarz 2014, p. 124). Whereas the popularity of cultural products is largely dependent on fads, making timing essential, the unavailability of some materials through legal channels prompted and perhaps even justified the act of P2P file-sharing (Schwarz 2014).

5.1.3.1 Kingdom of Piracy

Sparked by Napster, the fight against P2P file-sharing has been an uphill battle for the recording industry. Up until 2008, IFPI reported declining sales, including the decline of global music sales from $33.7 billion in 2001 to $18.4 billion in 2008 and P2P file-sharing has been blamed for this loss. Sweden gained international attention for its role in facilitating piracy. According to the 2005 IFPI press release, Sweden was one of the top five countries, alongside Finland, France, Spain and South Korea, that had been "drastically hit by internet piracy" (IFPI 2015). Sweden was reported to have "the largest number of DirectConnect hubs [P2P facilitators] and the most DirectConnect users in the world" (International Intellectual Property Alliance 2006, p. 495). The country's "notoriety as a piracy safe haven" (International Intellectual Property Alliance 2006, p. 495) owes much to two high-profile organisations that originated in Sweden: The Pirate Bay and the Pirate Party. The organisation that inspired the birth of these two entities was Piratbyrån (The Piracy Bureau), established in 2003 to discuss issues related to copyright policy.

Later, the Pirate Bay became "the world's largest index site for BitTorrent files" (Poort et al. 2014, p. 383). On 31 May 2006, the world observed arguably the most dramatic incident in the history of P2P file-sharing. The Swedish police raided The Pirate Bay's office and took away its web servers, presumably pressured by the Motion Picture Association of America ("MPAA") (King 2007). Following a series of lawsuits, four people involved in running the Pirate Bay—Peter Sunde, Fredrik Neij, Gottfrid Svartholm and Carl Lundström—were found guilty of assisting copyright infringement and sentenced to a one-year prison sentence. They were fined approximately £2.8 million within nine days of the trial. In 2014, Frederik Neij closed the door for arrest of all four members (Jozuka 2014). Despite the Swedish government's drastic measures and the staggering size of fines, piracy was not easily abated; in fact, it had the opposite effect. The Pirate Bay flourished, with over a million unique visitors a day in February 2007 following the crackdown (Lewen 2008). The persecution, rather than acting as a deterrent to would-be pirates, galvanised opposition to the establishment and gave birth to a new, politically minded offspring. Piratpartiet (the Swedish Pirate Party; SPP) was founded later in 2006—and what was once a niche movement became a populist-rallying cry.

In 2006, Rickard Falkvinge established the paratpartiet.se website, garnering many new followers in the process; within 24 hours, he collected the 1500 signatures required to register a political party in Sweden. The SPP is considered to be the world's first Pirate Party, inspiring people to establish pirate parties in a number of countries and US states (Pirate Parties International was founded in April 2010). Some of these national branches have won local council seats, and the German Pirate Party (GPP) now has seats in the Berlin state legislature. In 2009, at the European Parliament elections, the Pirate Party won 7.13% of the vote and gained one seat in the European Parliament (later expanded to two seats as part of EU parliamentary reform).

5.2 In Search of an Answer to Piracy

Growing up in the piracy safe haven as a young IT-talented man, Daniel Ek was himself a fan of Napster. Struck by an attraction to P2P file-sharing, he founded µTorrent, one of the most successful BitTorrent trackers.

> It was so obvious to me after getting Napster and Kazaa and all the services that this is the way that people want to consume music. And the more I started researching it, it actually turned out that there was half a billion people that consumed music that way. (Stanford's Entrepreneurship Corner (2014), sampled 15 February 2016)

He was startled by the fact that illegitimate use was better and easier than the legitimate options and there was no legal digital music service accommodating consumer desires without sacrificing financial legitimacy. Ek continues:

> Musicians were struggling and they can't make money out of music anymore…When we started Spotify in 2006, iTunes still sold DRM tracks…

> they were copyright protected songs, [yet] you couldn't play them anywhere. The quality was 160 Kilobits. And at the same time I could go to Pirate Bay or Kazaa and download the same song pretty much as fast in lossless quality and with no protection whatsoever. So it was obvious to me that for the first time in history, the pirated product was actually a lot better than the one you could buy. (Stanford's Entrepreneurship Corner (2014), sampled 15 February 2016)

The end result was the "disconnect" between the way consumers behave online and the way copyright has historically been regulated. That is, the clash between online behaviour and compliance with legal regulation was conflated with the mismatch between socio-technological change and the legal path (Ginsburg 2001; Vaidhyanathan 2001; Lessig 2004; Larsson 2011). The battlefield of music was in a stalemate where neither side was ready for a compromise or surrender. Will Page thinks this is better understood as an unmet supply than a rampant illegal activity needing to be condemned.

> Music consumption has never been higher, but music monetisation has never been lower. Is piracy kids ignoring intellectual property and undermining copyright laws, or is it demand not being met by supply? That's quite a taboo question to ask, but it's worth taking the second view. (Will Page, Interview)

Spotify began its search for the answer to digital music industry's impasse: piracy. The following section looks at four major factors attributable to Spotify's success: (1) P2P heritage, (2) free, (3) easy to use, and (4) legality.

5.2.1 P2P Heritage

Ironically, a vestige of P2P heritage dominates the narrative in Spotify's early business endeavours. With a notable contribution from Ludvig Strigeus, a former employee of µTorrent, Spotify's system is modelled after the BitTorrent client system (Palmås et al. 2014), which it continued to use until early 2014 (Flanagan 2014). The working knowledge of running µTorrent proved crucial in building cutting edge streaming technology. For seamless playback, Spotify had to reduce the latency, as the delay in playback was the biggest bottleneck in attaining popularity for streaming services before Spotify. Knowing that the P2P network was very efficient for fast and seamless searching and downloading, Spotify integrated a P2P network in pre-fetching the data and thus resolved this issue (Kreitz and Niemela 2010).

The P2P network was also useful when Spotify needed contents for their beta version of the service. An indie band in Sweden released an album, the band put it out only on The Pirate Bay. One member of the band experimented with the beta version of Spotify. As most musicians would do, he searched for his band's album. Surprised to find that the album was indeed on Spotify, she/he contacted the company and asked how they had acquired the catalogue. The response from Spotify was simply that they liked the music and wanted to distribute it through Spotify (interview, name unrevealed).

5.2.2 Free

Amongst all the disruptions Napster brought to the music industry, one of the biggest impacts was left on users' perception of the value of music. Once exposed to free digital music, users were not easily convinced to go back. The recording industry waged a constant battle against "free" music. The depreciated value of the copyright and the consequent loss of royalties to the artists, the industry claimed, stifled innovation and hurt cultural creativity. This rhetoric continues up until very recently. IFPI Digital Music Report 2013 states:

> It is the 'free-to-use' appeal of illegal file-sharing that creates its unfair advantage over legitimate music services, whose cost base, including payments to artists and copyright holders, cannot compete with the free illegal alternative. This, more than any other factor, explains why the growth of an innovative and entrepreneurial legitimate music sector is being stunted in the absence of an effective response to digital piracy. (IFPI 2013)

Despite this assiduous appeal, no digital music service managed to put the genie back in the bottle. iTunes perhaps came the closest, but left many users continue to resort to P2P file-sharing.[2] As an alternative to piracy, Spotify provides a free service with an option for an upgrade, known as Freemium.[3] Sung-Kyu Choi, Head of Global Content Operation at Spotify, explains this background.

> It's free, and that's where the main audiences are consuming the music. We see our challenge is to get them into the legal environment. So if you're in an environment where you don't pay to get all the songs in the world, and someone tells you 'Hey, you can get the same song, but you have to pay $1 per track', then a lot of people would say, 'No I actually like it here where it's free'. So what we had to offer was to provide two products, which is the uniqueness of Spotify. We have the free and the paid. (Sung-Kyu Choi, Interview)

However, this was not an easy sell to record companies. As a new company, Spotify did not have enough proof to show that the model would work. Sung-Kyu Choi continues:

> We want to compete with piracy, the vast majority of new users want to try out. So they go to the free service. And the free service needs to have ads to generate revenues. You go to the media service and say, 'Hey, we want you to buy our service on our platform.' 'So what's your reach? How many users do you reach?' And then in the beginning 100? 100,000? Because you were new, you didn't get to have many advertisements. So in the beginning you're in a very challenging situation, where you're having a lot of people in the free service. (Sung-Kyu Choi, Interview)

It was a struggle to get users to make sense of this new model, as well. Spotify had a hard time convincing people to pay for music when there were free options. Spotify's plan for persuading people to convert to

---

[2]For more discussion on this, see this chapter, Sect. 5.2.2.

[3]"Freemium," a word combining "free" and "premium," had been around since the 1980s but became popular due to Chris Anderson's (2009) book "Free: The Future of a Radical Price," signifying an alternative to the free digital economy.

premium was to hook users on the service so that they would switch to the paid model. Sung-Kyu Choi explains the concept:

> We want consumers to finally transition to paying users. But to make them become paying users, we have to attract them to our free service below the level. Free service is a mass-market service, apparently because you don't have to pay anything. (Sung-Kyu Choi, Interview)

5.2.3 Easy to Use

Being equal is not enough to win a game. In addition to providing a "free" option, Spotify had to offer something better than piracy. Although "free" was the strongest reason why people are attracted to P2P file-sharing activity,[4] it is not the only reason. To Daniel Ek, it was clear that the primary cause of widespread non-compliance was the far greater ease of use on P2P services compared to their legal substitutes; thus, he felt imperative to bridge this gap. Spotify's answer was to shorten the route to acquiring music by getting rid of the need to download the music.

> We created Spotify to be an alternative to piracy. So what we looked at and what we benchmark ourselves against [were] other services out there, like Pirate Bay and Kazaa…We actually look at ease-of-use as the biggest single competitive advantage. It was the shortest period from point A to point B that wins. So what we're focusing on with Spotify, it's just making sure that as you go on to the Spotify service, that the shortest point from you getting your music, you being able to share your music with your friends, and you being able to discover music. And if we just solve those three problems, we're in a really good place. (Stanford's Entrepreneurship Corner (2014), sampled 15 February 2016)

---

[4]IFPI's Digital Music Report (2009) cites "[a] study by Entertainment Media Research in the UK," which discovered that 71% of those who admitted they increased their file-sharing activity in 2008 did so "because it's free." According to a recent research, convenience has overtaken free for the main reason for infringement, as well as being the main reason why people consume on the legal platform (UK IPO 2017).

Scott Cohen, CEO at The Orchard, affirms that one of the major contributions that Spotify has made is a great user experience.

> Before Spotify we used to have this thing called buffering. The streaming services sucked. You click on it, it would start to play and ten seconds later it would stop and the wheel would start spinning. With Spotify, we never got that. They developed some really sophisticated technology underneath it. So that moment when you clicked, it plays and it never buffers ever. Just like the user experience with the iPod and the iTunes was brilliant, it was the user experience of the technology of Spotify that was the game changer. They were not the first streaming services. They were not the first subscription service. They were just the first one that worked so seamlessly. (Scott Cohen, Interview)

Cohen thinks that the significance of Spotify should be viewed in the context of the way technology evolves. He emphasises that technology rarely follows radical ideas but evolves once it has taken on board the many steps of consumers' learning process.

> It was Napster that just took it to another level. [But] people were highly resistant to that. Then you'd begin to get the business models in early 2000. But most of those were kind of Web 1.0 models, which were just like the old world replicated online. It might not be a good business model, but consumers need to be taken through the steps. The early adopters need to take one, two, three steps. You can't just leap from them. Ideas can be revolutionary but change is evolutionary. We might have had revolutionary ideas but to get people to actually do it, they have to go through steps to get there. (Scott Cohen, Interview)

Cohen proceeds to explain that the crucial element to get to the next level is critical mass, which is what Spotify achieved.

> Once you get enough consumers into the 'new' world, then all the new ones can leapfrog and go from listening to a cassette and radio into a fully immersive digital experience where you don't buy anything and everything is on…Everyone follows it. It just goes right into the 'New Thing'. You need to get to whatever that critical mass is which most

people would say is around 15% adoption rate. Once you get the 15% population to do something, adopt a new technology, a new device, and a new way of purchasing and consuming, you now have enough critical mass that it's just a matter of time before everyone else comes on forward. And they don't have to go through the steps that the first 15% went through. (Scott Cohen, Interview)

5.2.4 Legality

Whereas findings about the motivations behind piracy are bound to vary,[5] few would dispute the idea that the general public prefers legal to illegal options. Having witnessed many companies collapsing due to not following the major labels' code, Daniel Ek envisioned that Spotify must be legal (Pollack 2010). In an interview with Wired magazine, he says:

> The reason I started Spotify was not because of my love of music. It was because I saw an opportunity to create something that made it easier for people to do the stuff that they were already doing, but legally. (Pollack (2010), sampled 15 February 2016)

What might appear obvious now was not always so, even just a few years ago. Will Page, Director of Economics at Spotify, emphasises the significance of this shift of attention.

> This one guy said, 'I am going to build the best of all and I am going to get a license.' It just reminds you for all the bitching and criticism we sometimes receive. Could someone tell me what's so good about the music industry in 2008? Could someone raise their hand and explain that point clearly to me? Because this one guy says I am going down this road and build Spotify and that's a true story. When you watch the video [TPB AFK: The Pirate Bay Away From Keyboard] and you watch the mentality of these engineers, to have somebody who says actually I am going

[5] For debates on piracy, see Chapter 3, Sect. 3.2.

> to climb the mountain of licensing, get this thing a ticket. It's huge and I don't want the history of that chapter to get lost. (Will Page, Interview)

One of the crucial elements to Spotify's successful innovation is its efforts to make its technology relevant and attractive to digital music users. Sung-Kyu Choi, Global Head of Content Operation at Spotify, explains Spotify's efforts to find and match what users want.

> We filled the gap for the consumers. They've been shouting about it. In Sweden, for instance, everyone said I download it illegally, but I want it to be legal, but I don't have any good alternative. (Sung-Kyu Choi, Interview)

However, acquiring licensing deals from labels was no easy task for this unknown music company. It was perhaps Daniel Ek's naivety that drove him to get started, but it would not have gone further without his ruthless persistence. Neither countless rejections nor outright animosity came close to dampening his determination. He spent many sleepless nights on the street in front of major labels' offices (Stanford's Entrepreneurship Corner 2014). It soon became clear that these difficulties were only the first stage in what would prove to be a very long path. Looking back at the early days of his negotiations with labels, Ek explains how difficult it was to convince major labels to give away their music when the recording industry was still caught up in measures to protect their digital property using DRM technology.

> We started negotiating around early 2007 and we launched in October 2008. So it took us more than one year to get that done. What was so complex at the time was there was really no one that had the type of execution. This was going into the record labels at the time when they still had DRM on iTunes, and telling them to give away all their music for free, against in the future making more money. It's a kind of tough sell. I don't really think that anyone of you should go to a record label with that. (Stanford's Entrepreneurship Corner (2014), sampled 15 February 2016)

A breakthrough came from the crisis. In 2008, the music industry's overall sales were half of what they were in the halcyon years of the 1980s. In piracy-stricken Sweden, the picture was even grimmer. However, this ghastly impasse caused by the failed copyright policy in Sweden became the very seed to open windows of opportunity for Spotify. Since there was nothing much to lose, there was a room for new experimentation. Per Sundin, Chairman and CEO of Universal Music Sweden, recalls the time when the downturn of the business had forced him to lay off 200 employees, and the Swedish election debate in 2006 was heated over whether to endorse piracy (Lynskey 2013). The debate convinced Sundin's mother to urge him to make a career change (Lynskey 2013). It certainly was not the peak of his career. He says, "It was terrible. All the newspapers were laughing at us" (quoted in Lynskey 2013). Spotify's technical superiority and willingness to license, which was a rare combination back then, were good enough to convince Sundin to give it a try. After trying Spotify's demo, Sundin urged his team to venture into this model.

> This is Jesus coming to town! If this fucks up, we're going to be dead. So let's go all in. (Lynskey (2013), sampled 15 February, 2016)

Still there were many other obstacles to overcome. To Daniel Ek, there were two major issues: first, the industry's monolithic structure, which is not necessarily conducive to nimble decision-making, and second—closely related to the first—the industry's entrenched infrastructure built around physical artefacts.

> What is really unique about a record label is it's rarely one person who decides. It's a group of 20, 25 people, and you can imagine going into a meeting, as Rob [Rob Wells, President of Global Digital Music at Universal Music Group] did, and say, hey, we're going to start giving away our music for free, where there were record label presidents who might have been 60-70 years old, that have all their life sold physical discs and have just got around the idea to selling it on iTunes for $0.99 a piece. So it was a tough sell, but we eventually got there. (Stanford's Entrepreneurship Corner (2014), sampled 15 February 2016)

How Spotify "eventually got there" is something Spotify has not clearly stated. AK Swedish IT magazine, Computer Sweden, detected hints from a document that Spotify submitted to the Register of Luxembourg for incorporation of the company. Given the fact that the four large majors at that time, as well as Merlin, an independent music licensing agency, already had 18% of shares in Spotify when it was incorporated, the article suggests that Spotify's licensing deals were traded with the company's equity for a meagre amount from the labels (Jerräng 2009). The labels' ownership in Spotify raised a serious concern that this signified the usurpation of majors' control in the digital music business (Teague 2012; Barr 2013). Although wedding with major labels perhaps was a sine qua non, its consequence deserves close attention.

5.3 Remedying the Digital Recording Industry

In 2008, Spotify's official version finally got off the ground in eight countries in Europe—the UK, Germany, France, Italy, Spain, Finland, Norway and Sweden. Spotify had only just begun, but it already had comprehensive catalogues from both major and independent labels—Universal, Sony, EMI, Warner, Merlin and The Orchard, offering users instant access to a wide range of music choices. Unlike today, where users are swamped with "Tyranny of Choice" (Mulligan 2014), this was a time when the number of catalogues held by a digital music service mattered to users.

The user base grew exponentially in Sweden as well as in other markets. In the UK, Spotify successfully enticed two million users within the first year (Bradshaw et al. 2009). After a two-and-a-half-year's struggle, Spotify launched in the biggest music market, the USA, in 2012. Soon enough, Spotify proved they could change the culture of "for the first time in the music industry, it was better to steal than to buy" into a place where people paid for digital music on a large scale for the first time in the digital era. Spotify has made and continues to make dramatic changes in the digital music industry. Two points are worth mentioning in detail: (1) reduced piracy, (2) increasing number of people paying for music.

5.3.1 Reduced Piracy

First and foremost, the streaming-based subscription service Spotify is increasingly perceived to be a solution to the digital recording industry's problems in dealing with and eliminating piracy. Increasing research is being develop to evince the correlation between growth of streaming services and the reduced piracy (Page 2013; Aguiar and Waldfogel 2015; Wlömert and Papies 2016; IFPI 2017). IFPI also acknowledged that "music access" is seen as a compelling legitimate alternative to piracy. Music is bundled with services and devices or offered at no cost to the consumer on an advertising-supported basis. This low "average revenue per user" and high volume approach is seen as one of many hybrid revenue models rather than a single model for the future (IFPI 2010, p. 5).

Will Page probes whether Spotify contributed to reduced piracy and finds a strong correlation between decreased piracy and increased Spotify use in the Netherlands (Page 2013). He stresses the significance of this change taking place in the Netherlands: a country synonymous with freedom that treats P2P file-sharing similarly to the use of cannabis.

> The interesting thing in Holland is that they've got a very encouraging trend of piracy down, Spotify up, which continues to this day, but piracy is not even illegal in Holland. Their copyright infringement rules are as relaxed as like as cannabis' laws. It's lawful to take a file from an unlicensed site. So we move people from Kickass Torrent to Spotify, not because it is legally or morally wrong, but just because we are better. That's something we didn't prove in that study, but it is a fascinating fact. There's nothing legally saying we should stop doing that. (Will Page, Interview)

For Page, the significance of this change is the making of a legal digital music consuming platform as THE venue. He continues:

> Eric Garland from BigChampagne, when he did the Radiohead work, called the Internet a venue. So what is your venue? Yours might be

> Mininova, or a Pirate Bay as where I go I get stuff. It's like a pub, if you've had a bad day at university, you are going to go to a bar in Edinburgh, have a drink, you will text your friends and then you will go home. Nobody bothers you, it's your business and you leave. That's what venues are like on the Internet. It's your business, it's your space. (Will Page, Interview)

Another employee agrees with this view and says that Spotify not only helps reduce piracy, but even prevents future events.

> If you look at recent reports that are coming out of Sweden, for every year less and less people have tried piracy. So today a lot of youngsters who were the primary perpetrator before the piracy, that generation, the new generation's youngsters, they haven't even tried out piracy. They go to YouTube or Spotify to find music and video. (Interview, name unrevealed at his/her request)

5.3.2 Increasing Number of People Paying for Music

Another important acclamation with which Spotify is accredited is its contribution to the shift from the so-called digital crisis to optimism for the future. This optimism has grown out of consumers' ever-increasing attraction to paid music services. There existed a plethora of digital music services before Spotify whose business was based on freemium. With its impressive 20% conversion rate, Spotify became the first that actually proved it worked in the music business. This is a distinct phenomenon that many entrepreneurs have willingly embraced. Simon Wheeler, Director of Digital at Beggars Group, has seen waves of digital music changes first-hand right from the outset and is impressed by Spotify's outstanding conversion rate.

> They have got a conversion rate of around 20% which is absolutely staggering in today's terms. Before Spotify come along if anyone had conversion rate above 1%, we were shouting from the rooftop. But for someone to come in and get a little bit of scale, it has got bit of scale now and 20% conversion is, frankly incredible. (Simon Wheeler, Interview)

In 2009, just one year after Spotify's official launch, IFPI announced that the streaming-based business model propagated by Spotify was "the single most important development" (IFPI 2009, p. 4). In 2009, "for the first time, more than one quarter of record companies' revenues came from digital channels" (IFPI 2010, p. 19), but "the increase in the music industry's digital sales" was reported as "not offsetting the sharp decline in sales of physical formats" (IFPI 2010, p. 10). The year 2012 was heralded as the music industry's "best year-on-year performance since 1998" (IFPI 2013). As the fastest growing access-based music service provider, Spotify began creating buzz around "ownership replaced by access." This marked the overturning of the decade-old predominance of a-la-carte download, which had remained the largest revenue source.

Central to this shift lays the freemium model that Spotify was able to successfully convert free users to the premium service. The premium service features on Spotify have evolved over the years, but the two most obvious differences are advertisement and offline-mode functions. That is, the premium service frees users from the annoyance of a sudden high-pitched advertisement in the middle of music immersion. The most enticing feature of all is the offline mode. This is reflected by the increasing uptake of mobile devices; Spotify paid attention to consumers who would pay for premium mobile use. Halmenschlager and Waelbroeck (2014) call this "fighting piracy with free" in which the principal target was segmented to the consumers who were exposed of free music with more willingness to pay. This is a stark superiority that Spotify presented in comparison with P2P. It dramatically reduced the friction in downloading and transferring the files to mobile devices. In conjunction with a reasonable price, this feature proved to be a good incentive for people to convert to premium. This well evidences why the partnership with Telecom companies has been very efficient for conversion. A Spotify employee explains:

> We, Spotify and other companies in the streaming business, have seen that partnerships with Telecoms is very efficient. Up till now you have paid for access to music on your phone. So it has made sense to bundle music service with the phone and phone contract and the Telecoms

> are usually very aggressive when it comes to marketing. They are good at marketing, being there where the customers are. So it has made a lot of sense for us to work closely with Telecoms. (Interview, name unrevealed at his/her request)

The significance of appeal to smartphone users precipitated Spotify to extend its free listening on mobile phone with limited features in December 2013 (Katz 2013). A recent study of users' perception of the freemium service on Spotify has confirmed that the ubiquity of music listening is one of the most important features that premium users appreciate (Mäntymäki and Islam 2015). A Spotify employee confirms that music ubiquity enabled by Spotify is the most appealing way to convert people to the premium service.

> The most effective mechanic that we have is our product itself. And we have a very good free offering that is fantastic which is also now works on mobile. But in the long run, users find out that they love music and they love Spotify. They decided that they want to be able to listen on demand anywhere, they want offline music and they want to get rid of the ads. And that effectively converts them to be paid users instead of being free users. So we have a tremendous belief in our model, how it works. (Interview, name unrevealed at his/her request)

5.4 From Streaming to Mainstreaming

With 60 million paid user as of July 2017 (Spotify 2017), Spotify is well established as the most popular streaming service. The increased number of users meant diverse segments of users getting on board. And Spotify configured their services in response to users' evolving requirements. Faced with freshly emerging demands from the expanded users, Spotify is morphing from a mere music library to a medium for the mass market. This evolution may be best described through the developments in Spotify's music sharing and discovery features.

5.4.1 Search and Social Sharing

As discussed in Sect. 5.2.1 of this chapter, Spotify's beta version was modelled after P2P file-sharing websites and its distinctive footprint could be found in the search feature. Just like all P2P websites' interfaces, the only function provided on Spotify was a basic keyword search function. It was based on the assumption that Spotify users already knew which tracks they wanted to hear, just as P2P file-sharing users had a general idea of what they wanted to download on file-sharing websites. A Spotify employee explains this background:

> When Spotify started out, what it had was really a search box where you could input your search query and you could find any music in the whole world. At that time, that was what made Spotify successful, because it was a huge experience superior to what piracy would offer and also embedded in iTunes. You could search for anything, and you didn't always search for songs in your library. That became a huge success especially in Sweden where people were very used to Pirate Bay, where people were used to having music in the computer and searching for it. You could create a playlist which was the concept people was used to. (Interview, name unrevealed at his/her request)

For music discovery, Spotify relied on peer-sharing. Describing sharing as "the golden path" (Bendz 2008), Spotify released "collaborative playlists" in January 2008, enabling users to share playlists with other people. The early Spotify, concerned mostly with winning the hearts of P2P users, had not yet tapped the mass market. Spotify assumed that its targeting audience already knew what they wanted to hear, and that the organic mechanism of sharing music with their peers would be enough to quench people's music discovery thirst. This assumption is well manifested in Daniel Ek's interview with *The Guardian* (Dredge 2012).

> Spotify is great when I know what I want to listen to, but not so great when I don't. (Dredge (2012), sampled 15 February 2016)

5.4.2 Music Recommendation and Third-Party Apps

Soon after Spotify's official launch, its user base grew meteorically. More than just P2P users began using the service. The number of catalogues also increased as an increasing number of labels and artists joined together to put their albums into this new avenue of digital music consumption. The expanded user base and exponential music library prompted Spotify to make technological advancements in music discovery. Under the name of "Discover", Spotify began to offer personalised recommendations based on previous tracks to which a consumer has listened and to which other people with similar tastes listen.

Its algorithm-based music recommendation was still rudimentary which was more or less machine-like and therefore was not sufficient to comprehend people's complicated taste in music. Spotify decided to resort to existing expertise in this field. On 30 November 2011, the company presented a new plan to enhance music discovery by providing a platform where third-party developers could build music applications and integrate them with Spotify (Ek 2011). By bringing together important music discovery media, such as Guardian, Pitchfork, Rolling Stones, Last.fm and concert management services such as Songkick within its platform, Spotify removed many layers of steps involved in finding new music and adding it to a collection. Instead of buying a magazine or finding an article online, searching the catalogue on music websites and purchasing or downloading it, all Spotify users have to do is drag and drop. Later in 2014, Spotify stopped adding new apps due to the difficulty of the monetisation of third-party apps (Constine 2014).

5.4.3 Browse (Playlist) and Spotlight

5.4.3.1 Browse (Playlist)

Soon, Spotify took on the role previously held by third parties. The change was partly sparked by "Daisy," a streaming music service with a curatorial focus and urban lifestyle aesthetic, which had emerged as a competitor to Spotify. It caught the attention of Dr Dre, an American record producer and rapper, who staked a significant investment in the fledgling service and renamed Daisy "Beats Music" to capitalise on the already well-established branding of his wildly successful Beats headphones. Beats Music aimed to challenge its competitors by providing a solution to "a problem that most music fans may not realize they have: deciding what to listen to" (Sisario 2014), a refined music discovery platform based on the combination of algorithm and expert music suggestions. This novel approach indicated the digital recording industry's transition from music accessibility to music curation as a means to increase both consumption and brand loyalty. As other digital music service providers joined forces to provide a large number of catalogues, Spotify's exhaustive database was losing its uniqueness. Beats Music has chosen a timely moment to distinguish itself as a trusted tastemaker.

A more important push for a change came from within. The success of Spotify enabled it to expand across countries and generations. The service's popularity was well on its way to mass market. Becoming a "Mainstream Music Player" means courting the majority of the consumers, and most people are not "music omnivores" (Peterson and Kern 1996) who appreciate the diverse choice of music. A Spotify employee describes most people as "passive listeners" who like their choices to be made for them rather than seeking out their own music choices.

> Most people in the world are passive listeners. They don't actively seek new music. They do not read music blogs. They hardly listen to radio. They don't read music magazines. They don't share music and they like being spoon-fed. What they are listening to just so happens because they are listening to it with their mom on their way drive home and then they are like, 'Oh, I like that song.' (Interview, name unrevealed at his/her request)

As its user base grew, Spotify realised that most users wanted their music choices to be presented to them. A Spotify employee explains:

> As the market is growing and more mainstream users, if that's what you call [them] are coming into streaming, into Spotify and they don't have

> the same drive to search music. They want it to be presented to them, with less friction and at least that's one hypothesis that we have. So then we felt that we needed to create, we have to reduce friction while still increasing the quality of music recommendations that you get. (Interview, name unrevealed at his/her request)

The product development team took note that playlists play a vital role in building an emotional connection with the service. Spotify set out to provide playlists curated for different genres and moods. A Spotify employee says the popularity of this service, labelled "Browse", underpins that this is what the users wanted.

> It was very quickly apparent that it was something that the users really liked and they want to be able to find music quickly that suits a specific mood for example. And with 'Browse' they know that Spotify curators have spent a lot of time to make sure that it is the right mix and that it is quality music. And it has become a service that [you] can't even imagine Spotify without today. (Interview, name unrevealed at his/her request)

Behind these improvements in music discovery was the realisation that infinite access does not diminish the need for tastemakers and gatekeepers. Unlimited access to music can bring tremendous benefits for digital music users who seek out diversity in music choices. However, it is often at odds with the average consumer's reality of limited time and attention. Spotify sought ways to understand better what users want. Through data analytics, combined with qualitative analysis of users' listening behaviours, Spotify came to the realisation that not many of its consumers were tapping into the great potential of the Celestial Jukebox. Furthermore, peer-sharing was not as widely used as expected. One explanation of this is most people's tendency to listen to familiar songs.[6] Donovan Sung, project manager of Discover at Spotify, says that most Spotify users are not "power users" who want to explore diverse music choices (Smith 2014). Although music discovery is not exclusively for lean-back listeners, so far, they are the best beneficiaries.

---

[6]This was observed in the development of Top40 playlist (Frith 2002).

> We've actually found that a lot of music discovery sessions aren't about listening to new music; they're actually about familiar music or things you've played recently. Music discovery, in the case of discovering new things, is not a super main use case for most users; those are the power users who want to hear every indie band they haven't discovered yet. There are ways for them to do that beyond Discover. (Smith (2014), sampled 15 February 2016)

While it is increasingly clear that accessibility does not autonomously produce diversity, it would be equally misleading to deny the impact of increased access on the music listening experience. Spotify's diverse playlists help people discover unknown music as well.[7] A Spotify employee says:

> We create lists that contain the top hits and those lists are so immensely popular because people recognise that music but we also have playlists containing music that no one has heard about and which people still love. [As of June 2014] 'Your Favourite Coffee House' is the most popular playlist on Spotify [and] almost becomes its own brand. So people trust that and people know that the music that is coming out of this playlist is something that I will enjoy. (Interview, name unrevealed at his/her request)

Be they familiar tunes or new ballads, what this change attests to is Spotify's new role as a facilitator to guide and shape people's music choices and tastes. A Spotify employee explains:

> We are able to drive, we are able to make music that no one has heard about. We have been able to make that music very popular. So people subscribe to that list and they listen to it and they really love what they are hearing. (Interview, name unrevealed at his/her request)

[7]According to a recent research, curated playlist is creating a culture of lean-back listening, as well as cultivating music diversity particularly cross-border music choices (Mulligan 2016).

Armed with top-notch editors, meticulous attention to data and a spectacular user base, Spotify can be a crucial part of the mechanism of a song rising above the noise. Then on what criteria does Spotify rely when creating playlists? Reflecting on the lessons they learned from algorithm-only music recommendation, Spotify now combines both tastemakers' experts and the data. A Spotify employee explains:

> We use our curators' own knowledge of music and their own gut feeling. And we combine that with our internal data. Our music is tagged using different criteria. So combining those two has shown to be very successful and we can see that in a playlist. Users skip a certain song or if they don't want that in it, then we can make adjustments to the playlist. And we can even make it better. (Interview, name unrevealed at his/her request)

5.4.3.2 Spotlight

Spotify's position as a new breed of gatekeeper is even more enhanced through its acquisition of a music intelligence platform company, The Echo Nest (Spotify 2014). Founded in 2005, The Echo Nest was based on the PhD dissertation of Tristan Jehn and Briaan Whitman, who studied at MIT. Its basic mechanism is derived from algorithm-based music recommendation, yet its system is designed to go beyond simple recommendation and to provide music catering for each individual, combining all the information that consumers put into the music service.

This acquisition has improved the quality of playlists greatly. A more significant result, perhaps, is Spotify's newfound position as a hitmaker. Lorde, a 16-year-old New Zealand singer-songwriter, is one of those who rose to stardom overnight through Spotify. Will Page explains how Sean Parker's[8] playlist on Spotify brought Lorde this instant stardom.

---

[8] Co-founder of Napster. He negotiated licensing deals with Warner and Universal on behalf of Spotify for its launch in the USA and now serves as a board member for Spotify.

> Here's the streams from Spotify from 19th of March to 16th of April… What happens on the 2nd of April? So this is not a radio plugger or PDs, promotion department, this is just drinking a coffee, like that song, put it on my playlist and he [Sean Parker] has 850,000 followers to that playlist. Pretty mad, no? So much so that by the 2nd week, she got to number two in the US viral chart. Crazy, for a 16-year-old girl in New Zealand. (Will Page, Interview)

Spotify, as a platform for breaking artists, has in fact already experimented in the market through a service called "Spotlight": a feature designed to break emerging artists and help users discover new music (Katz 2013). Spotlight, however, is not without criticism. Some have pointed out that possible influence from the labels contrasts with Spotify's aim to help break unknown artists (Dredge 2013a, Peoples 2013). Considering that being featured on Spotify's Spotlight is almost analogous to "winning a lottery" (Peoples 2013), Spotify is increasingly positioned as a launching pad for certain songs or artists chosen by Spotify's own purview. The full implication of whether this will serve to break new talent or to feed vested interests is yet to be seen.

Spotify has continued to experiment with ways to improve personalised playlists and offered features such as Discover Weekly, Daily Mix, Release Radar and Autoplay. Aided with massive database and enhanced analytics, the playlists now have become sophisticated to the extent that human curation assists data processing (Pelly 2017). While this improved digital music discovery features were designed for people to discover diverse music, the cultivation of lean-back listening paradoxically could lead to creating a culture of lowest common denominator fed by industry interests (Sun, forthcoming).

5.5 Puzzles Created by Spotify

5.5.1 Artists' Earnings and the Value of Digital Music

Although Spotify managed to win the favour of both consumers and labels, resistance still persists from the artists' side. One of the crucial issues at the heart of the artists' resistance is the insignificant amount of artists' earnings generated from this new digital music consumption platform. The concerns were fuelled by a few celebrities' public criticisms. Thom Yorke, a member of Radiohead, denounced Spotify as "the last desperate fart of the dying corpse" and removed his album "Atoms for Peace" from the service in July 2013 (Dredge 2013b). David Byrne, lead singer of the American band Talking Heads, raised a more fundamental question: the sustainability of the model. His argument was that if the current cheap streaming music service continues to be the prevailing mode of music consumption, it will lead to inappropriate compensation for artists. Therefore, "[t]he inevitable result would seem to be that the Internet will suck the creative content out of the whole world until nothing is left" (Byrne 2013). Zoe Keating, an unsigned cellist, emphasised this point by publishing her income (Dredge 2014). In the spreadsheet she shared, she reported 92% sales from streaming service, out of which Apple's iTunes earned her most of her revenue; this confirmed a miniscule pay-per-stream $0.0044 payout from Spotify.

When all these criticisms were directed at streaming services, especially Spotify, artists from Sweden, the birthplace of Spotify, pointed their fingers somewhere else: at record labels. The Swedish Musicians' Union claimed that record labels, while benefiting from the new surge of revenue from digital music services, had not distributed a fair share of the royalties to artists. Agreement came from Billy Bragg, a British musician. He argued, "Artists have identified that the problem lies with the major record labels rather [than] the streaming service and are taking action to get royalty rates that better reflect the costs involved in digital production and distribution. UK artists would be smart to follow suit" (Dredge 2013c).

Spotify responded with a detailed description of the way they distribute their revenue to rights holders (Spotify 2013). In essence, Spotify's position is that their service created a fertile ground to generate revenue from a digital music business that had been plummeting since the advent of Napster; 70% of their total revenue goes to the rights holders. Spotify argues that however miniscule they might be at the moment, artists earnings are very likely to increase, considering that the streaming business has only just begun and has great potential for further growth.

Despite the continuous rise in the total sum of royalties that Spotify pays out, the clashes between Spotify and some artists persisted. Through a so-called "windowing" strategy, some artists who are not happy with the new mode of royalty distribution have pulled their albums from Spotify. Taylor Swift is one of them. The American singer-songwriter withheld her 2014 album "1989" from Spotify, arguing that Spotify's meagre payout was not enough for her work of art (Dickey 2014). After a few games of tug of war, including the one with iTunes (Bajarin 2015), she finally changed her mind and put her albums back on all streaming services (Nicolaou 2017).

"Windowing" is not a digital phenomenon. Its history traces back to the 1920s, when musicians' unions held back their music as an act of "boycott" of the "free use" of their music in what was at that time a novel medium, radio broadcasting (Peacock and Weir 1975, p. 71). As the increased significance of radio as a medium for songs' discovery and popularity dispensed the windowing, Spotify's rising to the stature of radio appears to follow its suit.

The issue of artists' earnings on Spotify provoked something more significant for digital music consumption: the value of digital music. The way we value music has evolved in the light of various factors such as social, economic, industrial and legal settings (Sun 2018). From a longitudinal perspective, the issue of digital music value signals a transition from the previous way we valued music to a new one that streaming service model has enabled. That is, the pay-per-unit value established in the course of developing physical artefacts onto sounds, crumbled in the face of digital piracy, and market entrenchment persisted until Spotify came up with a solution of large access to music at a low cost. It successfully answered the most vexing issue of how to make people pay for music as an interplay of the negotiation between two major players in the music industry: major labels and consumers. The sheer lack of consideration for artists in the negotiation process, however, left the issue of digital music value in constant flux.

One of the manifestations of the unresolved issue on digital music value is the "unfair" distribution (Erickson 2015) in which major labels are the major beneficiary of the growing digital music revenue (Tschmuck 2015). The lack of transparency for important issues, such as terms of contracts between artists and labels and the details on the revenue distribution from the labels, has long impeded correcting the problem (Hirschhorn 2015; Rethink Music 2015)

The appeal to build a digital music value chain where artists could be fairly compensated (Lalonde 2014; ECSA 2015; Rethink Music 2015; Music Managers Forum 2016), henceforth, is gaining a particular prominence. The key point is that digital technology brought about the potential to enable an efficient and transparent data transaction and therefore an infrastructure tapping into this potential will revitalise digital music market, ultimately compensating artists better (Ghafele 2014). The growing interest was reflected in an independent review of the creative industries by Sir Peter Bazalgette in the UK which made recommendations to improve data transparency and rejuvenate revenue streams on the digitally networked creative industries (Bazalgette 2017). Further research on ways to address the issues entangled in digital music valorisation will help us understand how best we can value music on this hard-won digital music consumption platform.

5.5.2 The Paradox of Celestial Jukebox

The quintessence of Spotify's reputation, hailed as "the future of the music industry"(Roberts 2011), lies in its solution to the industry's struggle to make people pay for music. Spotify's answer to the industry's financial ailments was large-scale access at low cost. Despite its great success, the subsequent growth has provoked some to question its sustainability. The Celestial Jukebox we have now came at the expense of decreased pay-per-person music consumption. To make the current model sustainable, the scale of economy has become the key. Faced with this challenge, the contemporary music industry is preoccupied with generating more revenue by increasing the number of paid users. The challenge here is that there is an inverse correlation between the expanding volume of available content and the attention span of its potential audience. Combined with the majority users' inaptitude to enjoy diverse music (Rogers 2013, p. 174), the existing market players' inclination to control musical taste is bringing a resurgence of market control (Sun, forthcoming). However, the key to building a sustainable musical economy is ultimately interlinked to cultivating an environment where diverse music could flourish. In addition, music consumers' ability to tap into the musical diversity is a vital element of the cultural capital (Tepper and Hargittai 2009). While the Celestial Jukebox is generally regarded as a boon to world culture, the ever-increasing encroachment of the commercial interest in this new digital music consuming platform not only would not serve the long-term sustainability of the digital music economy, but also will stifle the cultural creativity and diversity, the celebrated culture of Celestial Jukebox has promised.

References

Aguiar, L., and J. Waldfogel. 2015. Streaming Reaches Flood Stage: Does Spotify Stimulate or Depress Music Sales? Working Paper No. 21653, National Bureau of Economic Research.

Anderson, C. 2009. *Free: The Future of a Radical Price*. New York: Hyperion.

Bajarin, T. 2015. How Taylor Swift Saved Apple Music. *Time*.

Barr, K. 2013. Theorizing Music Streaming: Preliminary Investigations. *Scottish Music Review* 3 (2). Available from http://www.scottishmusicreview.org/index.php/SMR/article/view/40.

Bazalgette, P. 2017. *Independent Review of the Creative Industries*. GOV.UK.

Bendz, S. 2008. Collaborative Playlists [online]. *Spotify News*. Available from https://news.spotify.com/uk/2008/01/30/collaborative-playlists/. Accessed 27 Feb 2016.

Bradshaw, T., A. Edgecliffe-Johnson, and Tim Mitchell. 2009. Spotify Wins High-Profile Backing to Expand iTunes Challenge in US. *Financial Times*, August 4.

Burkitt, D. 2001. Copyrighting Culture-The History and Cultural Specificity of the Western Model of Copyright. *Intellectual Property Quarterly* 2: 146–186.

Buskirk, E.V. 2013. What Is It About Sweden and Digital Music? We Ask Some Swedes. *Evolver.fm*.

Byrne, D. 2013. The Internet Will Suck All Creative Content Out of the World [online]. *The Guardian*. Available from https://www.theguardian.com/music/2013/oct/11/david-byrne-internet-content-world. Accessed 31 May 2017.

Constine, J. 2014. Inside the Spotify—Echo Nest Skunkworks. *TechCrunch*.
Dickey, J. 2014. Taylor Swift Talks Business. *Time*.
Dredge, S. 2012. Spotify's Daniel Ek: 'We Want Artists to Be Able to Afford to Create the Music They Want to Create'. *The Guardian*, December 6.
Dredge, S. 2013a. Spotify Launches Artist Spotlight Feature with Haim and Lorde [online]. *Musically*. Available from http://musically.com/2013/10/01/spotify-launches-artist-spotlight-feature-with-haim-and-lorde/. Accessed 18 Feb 2016.
Dredge, S. 2013b. Thom Yorke Calls Spotify 'the Last Desperate Fart of a Dying Corpse'. *The Guardian*, October 7.
Dredge, S. 2013c. Billy Bragg: Labels Not Spotify Deserve Streaming Music Payouts Scrutiny. *The Guardian*, November 7.
Dredge, S. 2014. Musician Zoe Keating Reveals iTunes, Spotify and YouTube Payouts for 2013. *The Guardian*, February 24.
ECSA. 2015. ECSA Position Paper—What Music Creators Want—ECSA-Composer Alliance [online]. *European Composer & Songwriter Alliance*. Available from http://composeralliance.org/ecsa-position-paper-what-music-creators-want/. Accessed 25 Aug 2015.
Ek, D. 2011. Say Hello to Spotify Apps. *Spotify News*.
Erickson, K. 2015. Five Things to Understand About That Spotify Contract Leak [online]. *Future of Music Coalition*. Available from http://www.futureofmusic.org/blog/2015/05/27/five-things-understand-about-spotify-contract-leak. Accessed 25 Aug 2015.
Flanagan, A. 2014. YouTube Re-negotiating with Indies Following Outcry [online]. *Billboard*. Available from http://www.billboard.com/biz/articles/news/digital-and-mobile/6150292/youtube-re-negotiating-with-indies-following-outcry. Accessed 12 July 2014.
Frith, S. 2002. Music and Everyday Life. *Critical Quarterly* 44 (1): 35–48.
Ghafele, R. 2014. Europe's Lost Royalty Opportunity: A Comparison of Potential and Existing Digital Music Royalty Markets in Ten Different EU Member States. *Review of Economic Research on Copyright Issues* 11 (2): 60–91.
Ginsburg, J.C. 2001. Copyright and Control Over New Technologies of Dissemination. *Columbia Law Review* 101 (7): 1613–1647.
Halmenschlager, C., and P. Waelbroeck. 2014. Fighting Free with Free: Freemium vs. Piracy. Available from SSRN https://ssrn.com/abstract=2475641 or http://dx.doi.org/10.2139/ssrn.2475641.
Hirschhorn, J. 2015. Less Money, Mo' Music & Lots of Problems: A Look at the Music Biz [online]. Available from https://www.linkedin.com/pulse/less-money-mo-music-lots-problems-look-biz-jason-hirschhorn. Accessed 22 Jun 2017.

IFPI. 2009. Digital Music Report 2009: New Business Models for a Changing Environment. Available from http://www.ifpi.org/content/library/DMR2009.pdf.

IFPI. 2010. Digital Music Report 2010: Music How, When, and Where You Want It. Available from http://www.ifpi.org/content/library/DMR2010.pdf.

IFPI. 2013. Digital Music Report 2013: Engine of a Digital World. Available from http://www.ifpi.org/downloads/dmr2013-full-report_english.pdf.

IFPI. 2015. Digital Music Report 2015: Charting the Path to Sustainable Growth. Available from http://www.ifpi.org/downloads/Digital-Music-Report-2015.pdf.

IFPI. 2017. IFPI Global Music Report 2017: Annual State of the Industry. Available from http://www.ifpi.org/news/IFPI-GLOBAL-MUSIC-REPORT-2017.

International Intellectual Property Alliance. 2006. *International Intellectual Property Alliance 2006 Special 301 Special Mention Sweden*. International Intellectual Property Alliance.

Jerräng, M. 2009. Documents Reveal Major Labels Own Part of Spotify [online]. *Computer Sweden*. Available from http://computersweden.idg.se/2.2683/1.240046/documents-reveal-major-labels-own-part-of-spotify. Accessed 28 Feb 2016.

Jozuka, E. 2014. Last Fugitive Pirate Bay Member Arrested [online]. *Wired UK*. Available from http://www.wired.co.uk/news/archive/2014-11/04/last-fugitive-member-of-pirate-bay-arrested. Accessed 14 Nov 2014.

Katz, C. 2013. Music for Everyone. Now Free on Your Mobile. *Spotify Blog*. December 11.

King, J. 2007. *Steal This Film*. Artefact Films.

Kreitz, G., and F. Niemela. 2010. Spotify–Large Scale, Low Latency, P2P Music-on-Demand Streaming. 2010 IEEE Tenth International Conference on Peer-to-Peer Computing (P2P), 1–10.

Lalonde, P.-E. 2014. Study Concerning Fair Compensation for Music Creators in the Digital Age [online]. *CIAM*. Available from http://www.songwriters.ca/studyconcerningfaircompensation2014.aspx. Accessed 2 Aug 2015.

Larsson, S. 2011. The Path Dependence of European Copyright. *SCRIPT-ed* 8 (1): 8–31.

Lessig, L. 2004. *Free Culture: How Big Media Uses Technology and the Law to Lock Down Culture and Control Creativity*. New York: Penguin Press.

Lewen, Ulric M. 2008. Internet File-sharing: Swedish Pirates Challenge the U.S. *Cardozo Journal of International & Comparative Law* 16 (1): 173–206.

Lynskey, D. 2013. Is Daniel Ek, Spotify Founder, Going to Save the Music Industry … or Destroy It? [online]. *The Observer*. Available from http://www.theguardian.com/technology/2013/nov/10/daniel-ek-spotify-streaming-music. Accessed 27 Jan 2016.
Mäntymäki, M., and A.K.M.N. Islam. 2015. Gratifications from Using Freemium Music Streaming Services: Differences Between Basic and Premium Users. In *ICIS 2015 Proceedings*.
Mulligan, M. 2014. Tyranny of Choice. *Music Industry Blog*.
Mulligan, M. 2016. Cross Border Listening: Borderless Hits and Curated Playlists. *MIDiA Research*.
Music Managers Forum. 2016. *Dissecting The Digital Dollar*. CMU Insights.
Nicolaou, A. 2017. Taylor Swift Changes Her Tune and Returns to Spotify. *Financial Times*, June 9.
Page, W. 2013. Adventures in the Netherlands: New Spotify Study Sees Encouraging Downwards Trend in Music Piracy in the Netherlands. *Spotify Press*.
Palmås, K., J. Andersson Schwarz, and S. Larsson. 2014. The Liability of Politicalness: Legitimacy and Legality in Piracy-Proximate Entrepreneurship. *International Journal of Entrepreneurship and Small Business* 22 (4): 408–425.
Peacock, A.T., and R.B. Weir. 1975. *The Composer in the Market Place*. London: Faber Music.
Pelly, L. 2017. The Secret Lives of Playlists [online]. *WATT*. Available from https://watt.cashmusic.org/writing/thesecretlivesofplaylists. Accessed 24 Aug 2017.
Peoples, G. 2013. Spotify Throws Its Weight Behind Artist Marketing [online]. *Billboard*. Available from http://www.billboard.com/biz/articles/news/digital-and-mobile/5740703/spotify-throws-its-weight-behind-artist-marketing. Accessed 18 Feb 2016.
Peterson, R.A., and R.M. Kern. 1996. Changing Highbrow Taste: From Snob to Omnivore. *American Sociological Review* 61 (5): 900–907.
Pollack, N. 2010. Spotify Is the Coolest Music Service You Can't Use. *Wired*.
Poort, J., J. Leenheer, J. van der Ham, and C. Dumitru. 2014. Baywatch: Two Approaches to Measure the Effects of Blocking Access to The Pirate Bay. *Telecommunications Policy* 38 (4): 383–392.
Rethink Music. 2015. Fair Music: Transparency and Payment Flows in the Music Industry [online]. *Rethink Music*. Available from http://www.rethink-music.com/research/fair-music-transparency-and-payment-flows-in-the-music-industry. Accessed 15 Aug 2015.

Roberts, R. 2011. Critic's Notebook: With Spotify, the Future of Music Is Here. *LA Times Blogs—Pop & Hiss*.

Rogers, J. 2013. *The Death and Life of the Music Industry in the Digital Age*. London: Bloomsbury.

Schwarz, J.A. 2014. *Online File Sharing Innovations in Media Consumption*. New York: Routledge.

Sisario, B. 2014. Beats Music Enters Online Streaming Market—The New York Times [online]. Available from http://www.nytimes.com/2014/01/12/arts/music/beats-music-enters-online-streaming-market.html. Accessed 28 Feb 2016.

Smith, C. 2014. How Spotify, Netflix and Amazon Control Your Online Habits [online]. *TechRadar*. Available from http://www.techradar.com/us/news/internet/how-spotify-netflix-and-amazon-s-powerful-discovery-tools-control-our-habits-1216211. Accessed 18 Feb 2016.

Spotify. 2013. Spotify Explained [online]. *Spotify for Artists*. Available from http://www.spotifyartists.com/spotify-explained/. Accessed 28 Feb 2016.

Spotify. 2014. Spotify Acquires the Echo Nest. *Spotify Press*.

Spotify. 2017. Fast Facts—Spotify. *Spotify Press*.

Stanford's Entrepreneurship Corner. 2014. *Stanford's Entrepreneurship Corner: Daniel Ek, Spotify*. Available from http://ecorner.stanford.edu/authorMaterialInfo.html?mid=2964. Accessed 28 June 2018.

Sun, H. 2018. The Times They Are a-Changin': Digital Music Value in Transition from Piracy to Streaming. In *Digital Piracy: A Global, Multidisciplinary Account*, ed. S.C. Brown and T.J. Holt. Arbington, Oxon and New York.

Sun, H. Forthcoming. *Creative Industries Journal (Under Review)*. Resurgence of Market Control.

Teague, E.J. 2012. Saving the Spotify Revolution: Recalibrating the Power Imbalance in Digital Copyright. *Case Western Reserve Journal of Law Technology & Internet* 4: 207.

Tepper, S.J., and E. Hargittai. 2009. Pathways to Music Exploration in a Digital Age. *Poetics* 37 (3): 227–249.

Tschmuck, P. 2015. Music Streaming Revisited—The Problem of Income Distribution [online]. *Music Business Research*. Available from https://musicbusinessresearch.wordpress.com/2015/07/18/music-streaming-revisited-the-problem-of-income-distribution/. Accessed 21 Jun 2017.

UK Intellectual Property Office. 2017. Online Copyright Infringement Tracker Survey (7th Wave)—GOV.UK [online]. Available from https://www.gov.uk/government/publications/online-copyright-infringement-tracker-survey-7th-wave. Accessed 12 Dec 2017.

Vaidhyanathan, S. 2001. *Copyrights and Copywrongs: The Rise of Intellectual Property and How It Threatens Creativity*. New York: New York University Press.

Wlömert, N., and D. Papies. 2016. On-Demand Streaming Services and Music Industry Revenues—Insights from Spotify's Market Entry. *International Journal of Research in Marketing* 33 (2): 314–327.

6

Digital Music Distribution Networks

This chapter analyses the evolution of digital distribution networks since Napster. After a period of transition, iTunes laid the foundation of the digital distribution infrastructure. The direct distribution system between major labels and iTunes allowed major labels to maintain their control. The influx of new demands catered for independent labels accentuated an emergence of new intermediaries. Digital Music Distributors, as these new intermediaries were later dubbed, started as simple digital music aggregators but later, as the digital market continued to grow, came to play a crucial role in shaping digital music convergence. At the other end of the spectrum, a range of services emerged to tap into the affordances of digital networks in order to bring democratic production and musical diversity. Amidst the overall uptick of digital services in general, unexpected problems within the digital music economy arose and new solutions were devised to combat them; the sheer abundance of music choice afforded by new digital services sparked a resurgence of the old model. In the last section, we will broaden the perspective and describe how the music distribution networks have become reconfigured in the digital era.

H. Sun, *Digital Revolution Tamed*, https://doi.org/10.1007/978-3-319-93022-0_6

6.1 Foundation of Digital Music Distribution Infrastructure

6.1.1 Lack of Infrastructure

The predominant discourse surrounding digital revolution prompted by Napster includes implications that technological possibilities are tantamount to the technological implementation. This account, however, fails to take into account the most crucial aspect of technological development. Radical technological innovation rarely follows predicted development trajectories due to the lack of matching innovations, instead is subject to conflicts and struggles amongst a diverse array of players (Sørensen 1996; Williams et al. 2005). Napster, novel though it may have been, was not a thoroughly thought-out technology. It failed to become an enabling technology or "reach adolescence," in Arthur's (2009, p. 148) words, primarily because, at the time, there existed a tremendous amount of technological, social and cognitive constraints to overcome. Because Napster was a radically emerged technology, the surrounding infrastructure spread out slowly, only after years of learning processes by heterogeneous players.

Many interviewees witnessed this radical change in the music industry first-hand. Scott Cohen, co-founder of The Orchard, a digital music distribution company, was one of the pioneers of the digital music business. He started the company in 1995 with his business partner Richard Gottehrer. As their business as a record label did not go well, they began looking for alternative ways to promote the artists on their label. The Internet was a new medium they decided to use. They contacted music fans on the Internet by sending emails to the users of AOL, a popular Internet Service Provider (ISP) in the 1990s that offered everything from chat rooms to bulletin boards and rudimentary search functions. Although the users they contacted represented tiny niches, the rarity of email usage at that time earned them a 100% response rate. They were intrigued by this novel way of delivering music and set up a new digital music company called The Orchard in 1997, the first digital music distributor. They fought bitter battles during the early years and even teetered on the brink of bankruptcy at one point. The hardships that

Cohen experienced provide an insight into the lack of business infrastructure during this phase. He explains that from the Internet connection to storing music files, the infrastructure at that time was far from ready for a commercialisation of the music business.

> The biggest challenge was to even explain digital to people that were not even connected to the Internet. Most people did not have Internet access in the '90s. Broadband didn't exist. The second challenge was how do we even get the things inside the computer. I mean, all these seem so obvious now, but it wasn't obvious back then. Delivery was slow, painful and expensive to encode catalogues of music. Storage was also expensive. The amount of storage that I have on my MacBook compared to what storage was in the '90s would have been tens of thousands of dollars. (Scott Cohen, Interview)

Napster changed this to a certain degree. But the initial reaction of people in the industry to the new digital music business during this period was one of hostility. Scott Cohen continues:

> Not only were they resistant to it, they were actually fairly aggressive with their views that what we were doing was something bad…Then you'd begin to get the business models in early 2000s. But most of those were kind of Web 1.0 models which were just like the old world replicated online. (Scott Cohen, Interview)

A project to commercialise Napster is another episode that demonstrates the lack of infrastructure during the early phase of the digital music era. While major labels were gearing up to pursue litigation to take down the service, independent labels wanted to embrace the new opportunity. One of the examples of this effort was a project initiated by a group of organisations representing independent labels' interests. IMPALA, the Brussels-based Independent Music Companies Association, and Association of Independent Music ("AIM") struck a deal to use Napster's repertoire, enabling consumers to listen to diverse independent music legitimately and compensate the artists at the same time (IMPALA 2001). However, this ambitious project proved to be an incredible challenge due to the unprepared digital music infrastructure.

Helen Smith, the Executive Chair and Secretary General at IMPALA, was in charge of the legal side, and Gordon Rintoul, who currently works for INgroove's Client Services, took on the technical side. Gordon Rintoul says that it required a considerable amount of work and time to turn Napster's P2P platform into a commercial platform:

> There were mechanics that needed to be looked after at that point. Because there were a thousand record labels with all of this content on CDs, and then you had Napster which was a Peer-to-Peer platform, the question became how to make it into an actual commerce-based platform? Even the simplest thing like how to handle the data - there were no spreadsheets like what we use now. We figured out that we could put the data into Excel sheets so we can move them into XML and import them into the database. And out came the core concept of gathering data through Excel sheets, which we use today. At that time, Napster required five fields of data, because they hadn't thought yet of the flipside of how everything's paid for. They only thought about how to get the content onto the platform. We started looking to standardise everything - Excel sheets, data sheets, how publishing would be paid for; we had to look at how a label would be paid, how to deal with individual rights, different territories, all those different things. That took three years of work. Three years of solid work. (Gordon Rintoul, Interview)

This layout has established the foundation for the digital music transaction format and is still largely in use. What this anecdote highlights is the fact that not only was Napster's domestication in the hands of a few recording companies (Spitz and Hunter 2005), there was also a fundamental lack of "matching innovations" (Rogers 2014, p. 11).

6.1.2 Beginning of Legitimate Digital Music Distribution Infrastructure

6.1.2.1 Major Labels' Path

Significantly large financial investment combined with consumers' capricious and unpredictable taste in music made the music business particularly uncertain and risky. Great unpredictability involved in the creative production impelled the record labels to develop a strategy to control consumers' music choices and hence recoup their investment. Above all, the control over distribution was instrumental to influence the decision on consumers' access to final products and thereby curtail the risk (Hirsch 2000). Initially, most labels distributed their albums through their own sales and distribution team, who would contact individual stores. As the volume of records increased, the major labels built their own distribution system in which publishing, record label, manufacture and distribution units were built into the business structure. Known as vertical integration, this system is defined as "the combination of technologically distinct production, distribution, selling, and/or economic processes within the confines of a single firm (Porter 1980, p. 300)." With the massive number of artists and domineering market share, big major labels, in the form of oligopoly, had long controlled the distribution (Negus 1992).

The lowered cost involved in music production and the barrier to distributing music suggested by digital technology was conceived as having the potential to revert this system. Alison Wenham, Chairman and CEO at Association of Independent Music ("AIM"), explains what it means to lose control over the supply for major labels (Fig. 6.1):

> The majors at this point had not grown used to the idea that they were losing control of distribution, control of the supply chain. If you control the supply chain, you control the why, the where, the when and the how much. If you don't control the supply chain, you don't control any of that. And the majors were absolutely terrified of losing that control.
>
> These are companies who have grown up quickly, produced global businesses with very big profits. However, I had some sympathy with their point of view, it was a new environment and huge risks as well as rewards - which were by no means clear. (Alison Wenham, Interview)

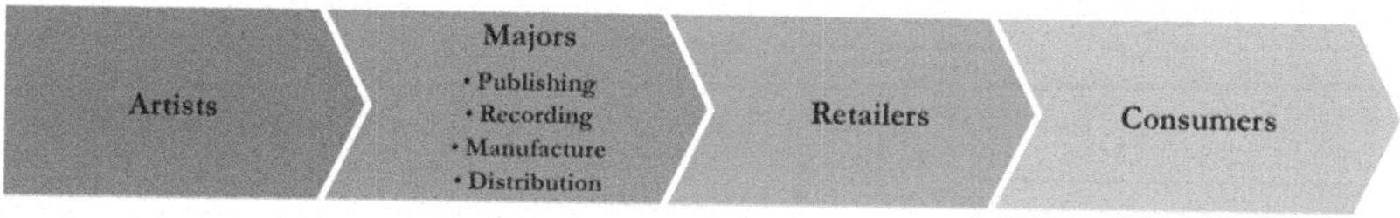

Fig. 6.1 Digital music value chain for major labels

The arrival of iTunes ended the great expectation of disintermediation. To ensure that iTunes had all the catalogues from the major labels, Apple had licensing deals in place. This first successful legal digital music distribution platform became an avenue where major labels could maintain their power by building a direct digital distribution system. The terms and system favourable to major labels have been criticised for allowing major labels to regain their conventional network effects, which stem from a massive budget for marketing and promotion (Arditi 2014). iTunes eventually "len[t] itself to concentrating power in the major record labels. The walls that digital distribution broke down have been replaced by distribution barriers in the form of iTunes" (Arditi 2014, p. 422). This system continued to function for some time. The increased digital music business transaction posed a great challenge to major labels' distribution system and rendered distribution networks considerably reconfigured, through which major labels successfully repositioned themselves and regained market control.[1]

6.1.2.2 Independent Labels' Path

In the conventional system, numerous and diverse distributors and retailers existed in order to cover as many regions as possible. Rich Bengloff, President at The American Association of Independent Music ("A2IM"),[2] recalls this and says:

> Back then, instead of having one distributor of music, you may have some Select-O-Hits, do your distribution in the southeast, Big State your distribution in the Texas, Oklahoma area, CD one stop northeast doing your distribution in the northeast, a variety of different distributors. (Rich Bengloff, Interview)

---

[1]This is discussed further in Chapter 7.

[2]A2IM is a sister organisation of AIM in the USA.

The most efficient way to target fans of independent music is not as same as mainstream music. An industry expert explains that the cost involved in targeting nationwide audiences is not well-suited to independent labels.

> Our strongest suit is urban genres, hip-hop, R&B, also rock, heavy metal, Christian gospel. Some people call them niche or speciality genres. It's not a broad mainstream teen pop feel. The issue with those kinds of genres in the US especially is that to effectively market and promote to that audience, to do it nationally is a huge investment. You have to deal with all the gatekeepers, radio gatekeepers etc. Things get expensive very fast. Since you have to reach the entire population, you spend on reaching people that who are not our audience anymore. (Interview, name unrevealed at his/her request)

Therefore, distributors came into the market to help independent labels distribute their albums to diverse retailers.

When Napster emerged, the independent labels' response was different from that of the major labels. Alison Wenham, Chairman and CEO at AIM, emphasises that in the independent sector, digital technology was regarded as an opportunity, rather than a threat or a challenge.

> When Napster came along, we were in a position to embrace Napster. We felt that it offered a fantastic global platform to music lovers. We felt that the technology had jumped out of the box quickly, was a phenomenon, and the owners were not cynical pirates who created a platform to deliberately rip the music industry off. (Alison Wenham, Interview)

After all, independent labels didn't have much to lose.

> We said, 'We are innovative, agile, with low overheads, we are curious, we are inquisitive and we will try all sorts of things. Go back over the development of new music genres; they all come from independent sector – creating and embracing change is in our DNA. (Alison Wenham, Interview)

iTunes, equally, was an important new avenue for independent labels. Unlike major labels, however, independent labels could not afford to build direct distribution channels with the digital music service providers. This brought about a considerable restructuring of digital music distribution networks.

6.1.2.3 Emergence of Independent Digital Music Distributors

One significant change in the digital music distribution networks is an emergence of a new breed of intermediaries: independent digital music distributors. Consolidated Independent ("CI") was established as a digital music delivery platform during this period. Kieron Faller, General Manager at CI, describes independent labels' lack of knowledge in digital technology as the driving force behind CI's business as a platform:

> They [founders Paul Sanders and Philip Crewdson] saw that there was going to be a need on the independent side of the industry for technical infrastructure. They could see that the majors could afford to have their own systems, because they had the capital to invest in infrastructure and they could kind of manage the technology. Each individual, independent label had no way of doing that, because they didn't have the funds and they didn't have the expertise. (Kieron Faller, Interview)

One of CI's highest profile clients is Beggars Group.[3] The observation that even companies like Beggars Group need technical support for the delivery of digital music drove CI's founders to build an infrastructure for independent labels.

> Even the larger kind of independent labels were very used to physical distribution and they will likely to find it difficult to make the transition across. So the founders saw that a way to approach the issue would be for there to be a centralised infrastructure hub, an infrastructure and service that then dealt with the technical requirements of getting content from one place to another, and effectively spreading the cost of that, across a

[3]Once an underdog at the vanguard of a fledgling post-punk movement, Beggars Group now looms tall as the biggest independent record label in the world, whose roster includes powerhouse acts like Adele and Vampire Weekend. It is comprised of four significant independent labels: 4AD, Matador Records, Rough Trade Records and XL Recordings.

> range of independent clients. So each individual independent label was itself, buying a small fraction of the infrastructure cost. And that's really proved correct. (Kieron Faller, Interview)

A parallel demand, in tandem with the labels' need for assistance, came from digital music service providers. Napster took the unlimited music access genie out of the bottle, and digital music service providers were compelled to cater to consumers who sought niche products. Since many independent labels are specialised to provide niche genres of music and are autonomously owned and operated, the process of acquiring their vast but disconnected catalogues on a case-by-case basis was an immense task. Dominic Jones, Marketing Director at INgrooves, explains how digital music users' demands for independent music catalogues gave rise to the emergence of independent digital music distributors.

> The majors have always had the power because of their ability to do deals directly with the accounts. This lead to the majority of the independent labels getting together and saying, 'We are 25% of the market, don't ignore us.' But because of the fragmentation, because they are made up of 3000 labels, it is much more difficult for the accounts to handle unless those independents go through a recognised distributor, which is how independent distribution was born really. (Dominic Jones, Interview)

Phonofile is a digital music distributor founded in 1995 in Norway. Trond Tones, Marketing Manager at Phonofile, explains that the demand for a middleman who can collect and manage digital music data opened windows of opportunity for companies like his.

> The companies (digital music service providers) wanted to roll out music services. They needed a lot of catalogues. And to get the catalogues, they wanted partners who help them collect these catalogues and send them over in a right format with the right metadata. It would take years and they probably need to hire a huge number of people, and once they attain the catalogues, they won't need all the employees. So they said let's outsource this. That, I think, was a natural thought. And then it became the digital music aggregators. As the digital technology developed, the early aggregators have become digital music distributors. (Trond Tones, Interview)

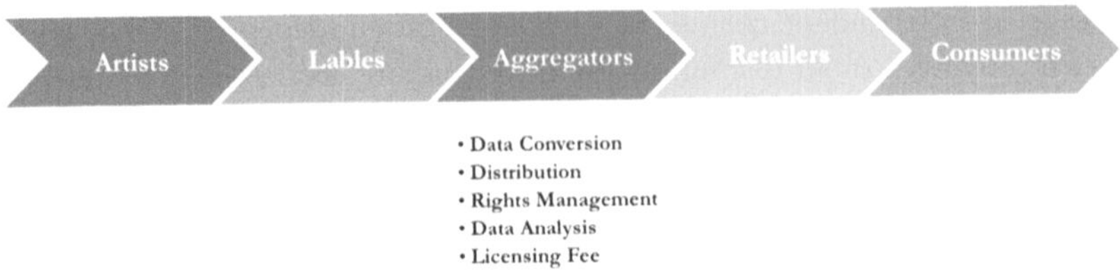

Fig. 6.2 Digital music value chain for independent labels

Digital music distributors also serve a crucial role on a practical level, just as intermediaries for a franchised grocery store would. Scott Cohen captures the nature of independent digital music distributors (Fig. 6.2).

> It's no different than if you go to a grocery store here, Tesco. They don't deal with every farmer. A farmer doesn't come to the store and say, 'I brought some tomatoes and apples.' They can't do that. These companies that distribute all the produce are the ones that deal with all the farmers. They put it all in one big warehouse and then they ship it to all the stores. The people like iTunes, Amazon, Spotify and the hundreds of others…their customers are not their suppliers. They want as few suppliers as possible. They'd want to be able to talk to us once a week. If there are thousands and thousands of suppliers, then they don't know what they should be featuring on their homepage. They just don't know because they can't have individual conversations with their five thousand suppliers. (Scott Cohen, Interview)

While the barrier to pre-filtering their selection has been abolished, digital music service providers still felt the need to manage the quality of their content. This is where digital music distributors fit into the equation. Dominic Jones says:

> We are the conduit to the market for our labels…There's no way that any of those retailers could deal with them all - there's not enough time in the day to hear from 3000 independent labels and three majors. Just couldn't happen. So they need a filter and those filters are distributors or aggregators. (Dominic Jones, Interview)

6.1.2.4 Technical Assistance

Besides the lack of funds and expertise to build an online transaction infrastructure, independent labels were not always equipped with the skills required for digital business. Many tools were developed in the digital age which lowered the hurdles to reproducing, distributing and promoting digital music; these tools, although beneficial in many ways, produced the false idea that digital transactions can be easily managed and maintained by anyone, regardless of background or training. Contrary to this belief, however, most labels quickly came to realise that they needed professional help in this highly technical arena. FatBeats, a hip-hop vinyl distribution company, distributes their digital albums through INgrooves. Tyler McWilliams, Sales and Marketing Director at FatBeats, explains the lack of expertise and the economic consideration were the main reason to choose to rely on aggregators for digital distribution.

> We don't do it ourselves because we simply don't have the staff [who can take care of digital distribution]. Our time and energy is focused on physical distribution, and it's easier to simply use their service at the expense of some margin. To put it simply, the cost of using an aggregator is less than the cost of an additional full time employee. (Tyler McWilliams, Interview)

Gordon Rintoul, who is in charge of the digital distribution client at INgrooves, affirms that technicality is not the labels' main subject of concern.

> First and foremost, labels have never been good at that. Never. You will now have to go back and look all the older albums and look at the spelling mistakes on the back of them when the old like you know when it's the actual vinyl. Look at all the spelling mistakes and errors etc. They've never been good at it. Labels' emphasis is on the creative side – the creation of the music, the ethos and the artists behind it. So there's not very much attention to detail. That's always been the problem. (Gordon Rintoul, Interview)

Digital music distributors' main responsibility was originally converting files from physical formats into digital formats using metadata. Metadata is the information used to identify the unique attributes of an audio file. It is composed of the song title, name of the artist(s), name of the album, music genre, ISRC,[4] publisher and price. For the communication of metadata, the XML format has been widely used.[5] Although it is widely used today, metadata was a novelty to many people in the music industry at the outset of the digital business. Alex Branson, SVP at INgrooves International, shares an anecdote.

> Essentially the problem was there were these record companies…and then technology companies came along, and said to the record companies, 'Okay, this is great. We like your music. Can you send that to me in a particular file format, and can you send me the data in XML?' And guys in the record companies were like 'XM what? Can I send you a word document? Is that the same thing? Can I send you a CD?' There was a long period of time when people were literally doing this. Here's a box of CDs, and if you're lucky you've got a spreadsheet with data typed out. (Alex Branson, Interview)

The problems caused by a labels' deficiency in attention to detail persist in the digital age. Don Gross is a Client Service Manager at INgrooves and is in charge of clearing metadata before sending files to digital music service providers. Gross is often startled to find many labels making simple mistakes on what appears to be crucial information for the labels.

> The biggest problem with it is the labels themselves or the artists dealing with their own data. The number of labels and artists who can't spell their own names is frankly shocking. You just think that some people don't seem to care about their own data. They don't seem to understand that it

[4]The International Standard Recording Code. As an international identification system for sound recordings, it helps manage digital music rights.

[5]It is in transition to Digital Data Exchange ("DDEX").

> has value and this is what people are going to see on the store and read on the websites in all aspects. (Don Gross, Interview)

Digital music service providers' technical standardisation requirements in metadata constitute another layer of technicality that often frustrates labels. While its standardisation effort could prove to be useful in some senses, it sometimes works against artists' creativity. Sharon Matheson, Label Manager at INgrooves, says:

> Metadata has to be so standardised now for iTunes. We know an artist's named DENA and the name is spelled capital D, capital E, capital N and capital A, but in iTunes that comes up capital D, and lower case for 'ena' (Dena). It's very different in all the branding. So metadata standardisation is both a blessing and a curse. (Sharon Matheson, Interview)

In summary, the growth of digital music business sparked by iTunes laid the foundation for digital music distribution infrastructure. Major labels who had sufficient funds and market power built a direct distribution system with digital music service providers. On the other hand, independent labels' lack of capital and technical expertise in the digital music business gave rise to the emergence of independent digital music distributors.

6.2 Digital Music Convergence

Over the years following iTunes' launch, the digital music business slowly began to show signs of an important revenue stream potential. On the one hand, recording companies were making strenuous efforts to maintain their conventional business. On the other, diverse services were springing up supplying a range of tools for artists to tap into the new opportunities suggested by digital technology. However, as the market matured, unexpected issues arose posing barriers to wider adoption.

6.2.1 Direct-to-Fan (D2F) Revolution

A range of tools for Do-It-Yourself (DIY) media production and distribution were perceived as a force for bringing the digital revolution to fruition. It was propagated by the legacy of Napster and the P2P networks, which was "regarded as community empowerment, the reinvigoration of shared passion for music, and a re-signification of intellectual property infringement, especially copyright" (Reia 2014). At the centre of the discussion of DIY's potential to democratise musical production, distribution and consumption is its ability to bypass conventional business frameworks and facilitate subcultures that, for a long time, could only exist in the margins.

The distant history of DIY goes back to the eighteenth century, when, in the wake of new technological developments, a number of musicians began expunging the patronage system—in which aristocratic benefactors bankrolled the creation of artworks—and pursued new careers as self-employed musicians (Scherer 2004). Since 1960s, DIY gained significance for underground music scene as a new cultural form of ensuring self-directed creative practice and subvert the established music industry (Spencer 2005; Reynolds 2006; Lowndes 2016).

A more recent example of DIY initiative in the world of music came in 1977 when the post-punk band Desperate Bicycles released their single "Smokescreen/Handlebars" on their own, without the assistance of any label. Since these experiments, DIY began to carry the connotation of a revolutionary approach—"to fuck the system"—through the empowerment of individuals (Dale 2008, p. 177).

The digital DIY movement can be categorised into three phases. The first was propagated by Radiohead, one of the first bands who tapped into this new opportunity. When their contract with EMI ended in 2007, Radiohead released their seventh album, "*In Rainbows*," on their own by allowing fans to download the songs on their website at a "pay-what-you-want" price—anywhere from zero to £99.99 for handling fees and anything in between. During the first 60 days of the album's release, their website logged over 3 million visits. The net revenue they earned from this album was £2.67 on average, which far exceeded what they would have received from their contract with a major label (Green 2008). This experimentation was succeeded by Trent Reznor of Nine Inch Nails, who, although having enjoyed multi-platinum sales in the 1990s, has outspokenly criticising the music industry for "ripping people off" (*Trent Reznor—Steal This Music* 2007). He encouraged fans to download his songs illegally, condemning the music industry for exploiting consumers' willingness to pay by "forcing" them to purchase physical products (Moses 2007).

Technological advances in DIY, fuelled by social networking tools, permitted artists to expand their DIY activities to include the power of Internet communities. Artists breaking out via so-called Web 2.0 tools can be categorised as the second generation of DIY. These tools of dis-intermediation slowly made inroads for unknown artists who either did not want to sign contracts with labels or simply did not have the ability to do so. MySpace earned Lily Allen, a pop singer, the badge of "the social networker of the decade" (Swash 2009), and Connor Oberst emerged as a breaking new musician through YouTube. A plethora of new digital music avenues also arose to enable musicians to distribute and promote their music for free, legally. Jamendo and Megatune allowed self-releasing artists to distribute their music under Creative Commons License ("CCL") on their platforms.

The lowered barrier to entry and widened adoption of legitimate digital music services spurred a wide range of innovation in DIY tools. Some companies provide tools that help artists connect with their fans directly without having to do deals with labels—also known as Direct-To-Fan ("D2F") services. D2F takes in various forms: (1) crowdfunding services, (2) self-distribution, and (3) artist management.[6]

6.2.1.1 Crowdfunding

Throughout the history of professional musicianship, the success or failure of a career has depended to a large extent on the financial capacity of the artist. The high cost of reproduction and distribution, in

[6]Companies exemplified here are not exclusively categorised as one of the three forms. Often their roles cross over. For example, PledgeMusic does not exclusively provide crowdfunding; it also serves as artist management. The major roles of the companies were used to categorise them in this research.

particular, rendered most artists subordinate to their label. Although the shrinking overheads in music creation alleviated this burden in the digital age, digital tools did not entirely eliminate the importance of financial support in an artist's career. The means to overcome financial constraints, however, changed. Enabling a direct link between artists and fans, crowdfunding services arose as a platform where artists could launch their own project on their own terms without the need for a financial middleman. Fans interested in seeing the works of their favourite artist come to fruition could pledge funds directly. Companies like Kickstarter, PledgeMusic and Indiegogo are the pioneers of this concept. Kickstarter covers a variety of works, whereas PledgeMusic and Indiegogo specialise in music.

Kickstarter's business idea was sparked by the personal inspiration of the original CEO of Kickstarter, Perry Chen, to put on a concert during Jazz Music Festival in 2002. The idea was consolidated when he met Yancey Strickler, the current CEO of Kickstarter, in New York. They became convinced that their idea had merit when they met a group of friends who wanted to pursue their career as artists but could not, due to their own financial limitations. PledgeMusic, meanwhile, emerged to provide an answer for artists struggling to earn a living in the age of declining album sales; it enabled consumers to participate in the creation of a record in exchange for a pre-order (Ingham 2014). By liberating artists from financial dependence on labels, this and other D2F platforms have contributed to catalysing innovative changes.

Participatory Platforms

Principally, these platforms serve as a pipeline of collectivism through which fans become important collaborators in the production of content. On such platforms, users become a crucial part of the design process by participating in the early phase of the project. Fans' further engagement is achieved as a form of barter economy in which users opt to receive something in return. Benji Rogers, CEO of PledgeMusic, said in an interview with Music Week that it is vital for artists to find and cultivate an engagement with hardcore fans who want to engage deeply with the artists they admire.

> Years ago I used to bartend with some of The Hold Steady in the East Village and I just couldn't get them interested in Pledge. But when they eventually tried it and saw the reaction from the fans, they were like, 'Wait, our fans love this, and this is stuff we do for free anyway!' (Ingham (2014), sampled 15 February 2016)

From one viewpoint, this platform is "reminiscent of the Artists and Repertoire (A&R) function traditionally played by the recording industry" (Galuszka 2015). The deep intermingling enables fans to feel responsible for and become very attached to the artists' projects. It can raise or manifest fans' loyalty to artists and willingness to spend money on the project. The generative values created on this platform offer a special embodiment of the project that is "better than free" (Kelly 2008). In the music arena, this is manifested as an answer to the music industry's long-fought battle with piracy. Yancey Strickler observed that direct engagement with artists makes users part of an artist's career by providing financial support.

> Some people think Kickstarter is the most effective anti-piracy tool, because you're asking for upfront fees for all different things, and we exist only if you pay. There's another part of it. You're being a patron of some work that you love. So I illegally downloaded this Radiohead album, but on Kickstarter I'll give 50 bucks, because I want to make up for that. Also, it does feel different now when your money is paid directly for someone versus iTunes where you really don't know what percentage of $9.99 goes to the artist. (Yancey Strickler, Interview)

Artists' Empowerment

Financial independence also means liberation from creative control, which often resides in the hands of labels. These platforms, therefore, empower artists to choose what they think is best for their career while retaining all ownership and rights therein. Amongst the numerous musicians who launched their career through Kickstarter, Amanda Palmer is one of the most well-known cases. As a former member of the Dresden Dolls, she launched her orchestral solo recording project on Kickstarter in 2012 and raised $1.2 million from about 25,000 fans. Her project was hailed as proof that social media could bring about changes in the music business (Clark 2013). For Palmer, this is a platform for "an emerging middle class of artists who don't have to be superstars." In an interview with Forbes, she says:

> Success is no longer getting on MTV or being Madonna or Prince. We're now finding you can have a sustainable life in which you get to make art for people – which actually sounds much better. (Clark (2013) sampled 15 February 2016)

For others, it is a platform for rising to be a major label act. Thanks to their success on PledgeMusic, the Headstones, a Canadian hard rock band, signed a contract with Universal, wearing "PledgeMusic" logo T-shirts (Ingham 2014).

Modern Patronage System

Although platforms like Kickstarter and PledgeMusic might appear to be novel progeny of the digital age, we can in fact trace the roots of their core D2F concept back to the fifteenth century, when the first private patronage relationships emerged. Up until the eighteenth century, most composers earned their living from diverse sources, and securing support from noble and wealthy patrons allowed artists to focus exclusively on creating masterworks instead of facing the humdrum distractions of workaday life. Yancey Strickler thinks that Kickstarter exists in the continuum of the patronage system that potentially transcends, if only in the sense of creative quality, the prevailing industrial complex that caters to the lowest common denominator of mass media:

> We're very much of a legacy of patronage and subscription system, which is how a lot of authors published their books. For the last 70 years, we've been at a war where mainstream culture was primarily subsidised by corporations for reasons of making money. Looking at the history of mankind that is a very small period. I think the development of this ability to extend beyond nobility and royalty of church is obviously a positive

> thing…Some of the dynamics of this system is original, but the notion itself is something that has long been a part of the culture of civilisation. And I think that's part of why it's managed to be accepted in a relatively short amount of time. There is something distantly familiar about it. In a sense, it does make sense. (Yancey Strickler, Interview)

To a large degree, composers supported by nobles faced pressure to create works that catered to their patrons' tastes. In an open-ended participatory platform where anonymous consumers are the sponsors, artists can brave their creativity in whatever form it takes. Yancey Strickler thinks Kickstarter is in line with this principle.

> If there's one place purely preserved for this (creativity), it still will be the big stage. It's not about making judgments on who's worthy of creating art, and who's not. It's just the idea that there are opportunities for people to be creative and make things. I think the world needs a place like that. And that's the ground that we want to create, protect and preserve. (Yancey Strickler, Interview)

Yancey Strickler also suggests that funding from the crowd can have an even more far-reaching influence on culture by liberating the forms of creation, which used to be restricted by commercial interests.

> I think more interesting things that can happen is that the forms that are at stake can change. The album in a form is very interesting. The album is not made of twelve songs, because the artists determined it's optimal to express their set of musical thoughts. Album has twelve songs, because that's something they put on a record, and a record was the way that music could be shared, and a record had to be sold in stores.
>
> So if you change what the initial funding is and change the questions behind it, with time you can change the form itself. If I'm raising money from my fans, rather than from a record label, they don't care if my album is 72 min or if it's three minutes, or if it's an opera that will be performed in a church in Scotland once every 17 years and it will last for two days. And now that people agreed with me that that is a worthy idea, then I can do that, regardless of what the market may feel. That long-term opportunity to change the form to evolve is something exciting to me. (Yancey Strickler, Interview)

6.2.1.2 Self-Distribution

Central to the notion of democratisation in the digital era is the decentralisation, through which the hegemony of large major recording companies could penetrate the market more efficiently and rapidly, by spreading the risk of investments over several artists through the economies of scale (Burke 2011). In the music industry, this market power built a barrier for entry where only a fraction of albums could be recorded, distributed, promoted and finally displayed in the store (Hirsch 1972). Jeff Price co-founded TuneCore in 2006 to provide artists with an avenue for easily distributing their music and generating revenue. Now a former CEO of TuneCore, Jeff Price shared his views on the changes this new means of distribution had brought on Hypebot, a blog on music and technology trends. In this article, he describes the expensive and highly hierarchical structure of physical distribution in the pre-digital era.

> Physical distribution is an expensive, inefficient, costly endeavor of trucks, warehouses, shrink-wrap, inventory systems, finance systems, employees and more. The only way to get distribution was for the artist to do a deal with an entity that had this pre-existing infrastructure – another function of the major labels. In addition, physical retail stores could only stock so many releases before they ran out of room. It was only the majors with their pipelines and money that had access to the shelves of stores like Walmart, the number one music retail outlet in the United States for a period of time. (Price (2012), sampled 15 February 2016)

Digital technology, however, significantly lowered this barrier. Literally anyone, professional or amateur, who had his or her own digital music products, could distribute his or her music on online retail stores. Services such as TuneCore, CD Baby and EmuBands help unsigned artists distribute their music on digital music services. Jeff Price admits that removing the obstacles created by shelf space limitation does not amount per se to an immediate rise to stardom, but companies like TuneCore can reduce the trouble involved in the dissemination (Sisario 2012).

> I'm not going to promise anyone they're going to be a star. I am going to promise that if you pay me a fee for the service, I will distribute your music to the places you want it to go, and I will deal with all the hassles that come along with that. (Sisario (2012) sampled 15 February 2016)

Equal Exposure

Outlets for music have long been considerably limited. This was the case for fledgling artists in particular (Price 2012).

> Most of the twentieth century, exposure in the commercial radio, television and print magazines was virtually impossible if an artist was not supported by a record label. (Price (2012), sampled 15 February 2016)

Although there still exist certain forms of media that are not equally accessible to unknown artists, Jeff Price emphasises that a number of new outlets such as social networking sites offer a cheap and accessible means of exposing works.

> There is now equal access to music discovery outlets – YouTube, blogs, Slacker, Pandora, Spotify, digital music stores' discovery features, Twitter, Facebook and other social networking applications are open to everyone, not just the elite few artists signed to labels. The only media outlet not open to everyone is commercial radio, but with that going the way of the 8-Track over the next few years, the last stranglehold of the traditional music industry will be gone. (Price (2012), sampled 15 February 2016)

Transparency

Traditionally, the high risk and the uncertainty in the success of a recording have produced an imbalance in the relationship between record labels and artists. Burkart (2010) summarised:

> To make many small financial commitments to artists and bands as a way to search for the big hits, which will be more heavily financed, and tightly controlled by contract. The economies of scope and scale required

> to sustain this business model required bureaucratic hierarchies with gatekeepers at every level. Therefore, new artists' access to channels for financing, music production, distribution, and marketing is highly restricted. (Burkart 2010, p. 22)

This power imbalance, skewed towards the labels and often caused by the complicated nature of contractual terms, has largely been the root of the conflict between artists and labels. Transparent and straightforward accounting, therefore, is especially appealing to artists. In his book "How Music Works," David Byrne, lead singer of the American band Talking Heads, says the great advantage of direct distribution is transparency in sales records:

> I prefer to get accounted to monthly by TuneCore (as opposed to quarterly by Redeye), and for a onetime flat fee of twenty-five dollars rather than paying 10 percent monthly fees. The big advantage for anyone supplying the digital service providers [download stores like Amazon and iTunes] direct or via Tunecore, is you get paid monthly. Over the last twelve months we've averaged over $3000 per month in income from iTunes sales on that record. (Byrne 2012, p. 241)

Significantly, for some artists, it proved to be lucrative.

> Within three weeks of the digital files being available online on our own websites, we sold enough to cover our recording costs, which added up to $49,000, and included travel, the mixing engineer, graphic design, flights, and extra musicians. Based on my own experience, that seemed amazing to me. With a standard record deal, it would normally have taken six months to a year to recoup those costs. And then there would have been other miscellaneous costs to recoup - the music video (there wasn't one), that open bar after the concert, the car service to the airport. (Byrne 2012, p. 242)

6.2.1.3 Artists' Management

Although it is a tremendous achievement for anyone to make their albums available online, being a professional musician entails a lot more than putting out albums. Artists' careers and their potential success are intimately bound up with the creation of fandom. The concept of fandom emerged in the early nineteenth century, with remarkable virtuosi such as Paganini and Liszt whose ineffable charisma, on top of their talents, captivated audiences (Théberge 2006). Geographical obstacles, however, afforded fans only limited means to express their admiration (Galuszka 2015). The Internet changed this. The unprecedented degree of access enabled both fans and artists to engage with each other in an ongoing and reciprocal way (Théberge 2006).

Companies such as TopSpin, ReverbNation and Music Glue provide tools for artists to harness the benefits that digital technology has brought. Founded in 2006 by Shamal Ranasinghe and Peter Gotcher, a co-creator of Pro Tools,[7] TopSpin provides tools for artists to manage their career and connect with fans directly without having to sign contracts with labels. Stephen O'Reilly, Marketing Manager at TopSpin, explains the background of TopSpin as a continuation of Pro Tools.

> Pro Tools was a company about how to create music. And then almost the next step was how do you distribute your music to your fans, and how do you grow your audience, and turn those audiences into customers for artists to make a living. That was the vision of the company. (Stephen O'Reilly, Interview)

Fan Building

For emerging artists, these tools are used to create their fan base. Stephen O'Reilly emphasises the significance of creating a fan base in the early phase of an artist's career.

> When bands are starting out, they're not in the business of selling music, they're in the fan acquisition business trying to acquire fans, acquire people who'd be interested in your brand, and then be passionate about you. We always recommend that you have two thousands of email addresses

---

[7]Pro Tools is a digital audio workstation enabling people to record their music. By displacing the need to record albums at a professional studio, Pro Tools is regarded to have precipitated the digital revolution in music production.

> before you worry about selling some music. Because when you got that audience, then you can turn on the top in the commerce. (Stephen O'Reilly, Interview)

Fan Engagement

Ian Rogers, who was CEO for TopSpin until he moved to Beats Music in 2014, thinks the company's contribution is to cultivate an environment where all strata of artists can actively engage with their fans.

> I think another difference between the proverbial yesterday and today is that we're moving from a mass market to mass niches, so you have to know what the first niche is that you're targeting and then go after it. You don't put the music out there and see who adopts you; you have to know when and how and where you fit. (Owsinkski 2011, p. 243)

Digital technology has made it possible to glean more accurate data on almost every aspect of an artist's career; managing their career requires a different set of skills. The tools artists can use include collecting fans' email addresses, building their websites, selling merchandise products and ticketing their gigs or concerts.

Autonomy

Music Glue, a D2F platform provider headquartered in London, proved to be a crucial platform for career development for artists such as Mumford and Sons, Enter Shikari and Ben Howard. Joe Porn, Squadron Leader at Music Glue, observed the great potential this platform could bring.

> The ability to sell directly to the customers has the potential to change everything because you are generating direct income yourself. You are setting your own prices. You are, hopefully, creating an ecosystem and the environment. Your customer comes to you and purchases from you – they like your music or your brand as you are. So, depending on doing

certain things, you could seek great success. You make yourself heard in various ways and good life, one is writing good music, or building a fan base. There are lots of things you can do.

It's maybe not as romantic as signing to a record label and flying around the world and doing all that stuff. It's quite most bands' life. Actually, if you love playing, you love listening to music, if you can make a living from it, fantastic. I like doing what I'm doing and I make a living from it. (Joe Porn, Interview)

In summary, D2F tools ranging from crowdfunding to artist management and self-distribution tools have enabled opportunities unprecedented previously. Though the revolutionary potential this novelty has brought is unquestionable, it is more of an option than a "fully fledged alternative" to the conventional creative production (Tschmuck 2016, p. 18). Some argues that the utopian portrayal surrounding D2F is overstated, calling it "fan exploitation" in which "fanancing" is capitalised by the industry (Scott 2014), while others view it both as an exploitation and an empowerment (Galuszka and Brzozowska 2017). There is also a growing awareness that the impact of this platform remains only in cultivating subculture, and that it has not been adopted by the mainstream (Galuszka 2012; Rogers 2013; Reia 2014). In the next section, I will discuss the underlining dynamics lurking in the digital music industry that posed challenges to this potential being realised in the market.

6.2.2 Attention Economy

6.2.2.1 The Promise of Celestial Jukebox and the Reality

For a long time, consumers' choice of music depended largely on the availability in the market. Napster undermined this system. As far as legitimate music consumption is concerned, however, the recording industry has held its grip for a period of time. iTunes provided a wide variety of music at a reasonably lowered price. However, it was still a world where legitimate sale of choice was limited. Until recently, the number of catalogues on digital music services was crucial to attracting more customers. Attaining catalogues from labels, especially major labels, was a major challenge for many digital music service providers, and it was not uncommon to see companies close their businesses due to lack of catalogues. Kieron Faller, General Manager at Consolidated Independence ("CI"), an independent music distributor, recalls this time:

> There was a period I think, until a few years ago, where people like iTunes and Spotify and Deezer, particularly, if these services were launching, they would say –we've got 50 million tracks. We've got 20 million tracks. We've got 25 million tracks. Whatever. And it was kind of – the bigger the number, the better at that point. (Kieron Faller, Interview)

While some other services, such as YouTube or Grooveshark, could be credited for presenting an immense number of catalogues, the debates on the legality of these services fell short of achieving unbounded music choices. Spotify's arrival changed the game entirely. The subscription-and-advertising model that afforded unlimited access achieved remarkable success and enabled almost everything to be available online with less friction of legality. With this legal and unlimited access to music, Spotify was acclaimed as "exactly what music fans had been waiting for, fulfilling the long-sought dream of a 'Celestial Jukebox' – a service that makes every song always available, freely and legally" (Pollack 2011).

6.2.2.2 Tyranny of Choice

With the rise of streaming business, the idealised vision of the Celestial Jukebox faced an unexpected challenge: abundance of choice. In the face of limitless world catalogues of music, the majority of digital music users were more perplexed, than thrilled, at not knowing what to listen to. Music industry analyst Mark Mulligan (2014) stated that "30 million tracks (and counting) is a meaningless quantity of music. It would take three lifetimes to listen to every track once. There is so much choice that there is effectively no choice at all" defined it as "Tyranny of Choice." The abundance of choice, indeed, has not only become meaningless, it has also created music choice fatigue. Kieron Faller says:

> People haven't worked out the usability problems. If you are on Spotify and you search for Frank Sinatra, that's 500 albums. No one actually wants to see that list of 500 albums. (Kieron Faller, Interview)

Kieron Faller thinks the frustration of pre-Spotify consumers with the difficulty of access to music has now been replaced by the annoyance of finding the right track.

> I think that's one of the key challenges for streaming services particularly. And they are starting to address, but how do you clean out that annoyance? It's just confusing, and the same with sound-alike stuff, for example, like karaoke. And you just want one good version of each track on the platform. But in terms of rights, it's actually quite difficult and complicated to decide. Why should you prefer one record label's "Best of …" to another? How do you make that choice? Are you allowed to make that choice? (Kieron Faller, Interviwe)

6.2.2.3 The Long Tail and the Attention Economy

An argument that is closely pertinent to the discussion of the Celestial Jukebox is the Long Tail economy, a notion advocated by Wired Magazine editor, Chris Anderson (2006). Forecasting a fundamental shift in the cultural economy, he propagated the idea that reduced cost involved in creative production will bring a shift away from the economy suited for brick and mortar, and hence "away from a focus on a relatively small number of hits (mainstream products and markets) at the head of the demand curve and toward a huge number of niches in the tail" (Anderson 2006, p. 52). In other words, through the lowered barrier of entry, products catering for minority tastes become available and consumers are given more diverse choices. The collective sum of consumption of these diversified niche products would make up enough market share to surpass mainstream music consumption. This unprecedented opportunity of individual expression would pose a threat to the conventional business model, Anderson (2006) suggests, and would be ultimately conducive to cultivating creativity and cultural diversity. Many interviewees agreed that some of these opportunities had materialised. Rich Bengloff, President at A2IM, agrees that the traditional barrier to entry has been eliminated.

> Traditionally the only way to monetise was to get into the physical retail and that's how it worked. You had to buy a cooperative advertisement to get into retail. Whether it's promotion or monetisation, we had no access. Things moved forward and the good news is now everybody has an access, especially direct access to fans which we never had before. (Rich Bengloff, Interview)

However, the current status quo is quite distinct from this prediction. Underling the departure is the unexpected challenges. The lifted barrier of access, in fact, came with the problem of fiercer competition. Rich Bengloff continues: "The bad news is everybody has access, so how do you get noticed?" (Rich Bengloff, Interview)

Departed from the prediction of the shift from hits to niche, the majority of artists still suffer from obscurity, with hit-driven business remaining paramount to the digital music economy. Behind it lies the fact that the shelf barrier removed in the digital era has been replaced with a new barrier. Dominic Jones, Marketing Director at INgrooves, stresses that the barrier to entry approximates to the barrier to getting on people's radar in the digital era.

> In the physical world we have CDs and vinyl. The biggest hurdle to overcome is getting record shops to want to stock them in the first place because you actually have to sell them physical things and you have to ship them from our warehouse to their warehouse and to their shop and convince them that people are going to be walking through the door to buy them. In the digital world I think it is very different because you are shipping them a master file and, with a few exceptions, most of the large retailers will take everything that you want to deliver to them.

> The hurdle with digital is getting the most profile for your release, making sure it is on the homepage or genre page or on a newsletter. If you look at iTunes, you only have so much space. But then they have scrolling sections. Well…you could scroll forever if you wanted to or if they wanted to scroll everything to accommodate all the new releases and bestsellers. Having one of the banners on iTunes gives you all the advantages over those that don't have them. (Dominic Jones, Interview)

The quintessence of the issue is how to grab audiences' attention. In contrast to what is commonly believed, the digital music sphere does have competition for a limited space. The difference is that the limitation that was closely related to physical space in the conventional setting is replaced by the limitation of virtual space—attention. This is what economist Herbert Simon (1971) predicted at the dawn of the electronic age.[8]

> When we speak of an information-rich world, we may expect, analogically, that the wealth of information means a dearth of something else – a scarcity of whatever it is that information consumes. What information consumes is rather obvious: it consumes the attention of its recipients. Hence a wealth of information creates a poverty of attention, and a need to allocate that attention efficiently among the overabundance of information sources that might consume it. (Simon 1971, pp. 40–41)

Scott Cohen, co-founder of The Orchard, explains why the contemporary music business model based on subscription/streaming belongs to this category.

> If you look at services like Spotify, they're not in the streaming business, a delivery mechanism, they're not in the ad business or subscribing business, they're in the attention business. It's really about how much time we spent on a given artist inside the service! And if you can get somebody to spend five minutes a week, an hour a week on your stuff, the implicit

[8]A similar concept was advanced by Benkler (2006) who defined it as "Babel objection" that the curatorial power will continue to remain significant in the vast sea of digital contents.

message is that they can't spend their time on somebody else's. You can't listen to two songs simultaneously. In the attention economy, the game is can we get people to pay attention to your stuff, instead of somebody else's. (Scott Cohen, Interview)

So far we looked at the unprecedented opportunities that digital technology has brought, as well as the new challenges for this potential being to be realised in the market. The next section expands this view and examines how digital convergence is changing the dynamic of the digital recording business.

6.3 Digital Music Value Networks Reconfigured

Digitisation suggested an opportunity to disintermediate the value chain. By allowing artists to bypass intermediaries and reach out to their fans directly, disintermediation could render intermediaries unnecessary or obsolete. This shortened value chain was expected to repair the long-sustained problems in the music industry, including: (1) the power imbalance skewed towards major labels that is closely related to a lack of compensation for artists, and (2) the majors' control over the distribution system, which often was criticised for a lack of cultural diversity and inflated price of consumer products. As many observed, digitised distribution did not lead to a diminished chain or function or made conventional intermediaries redundant. Rather, the recording industry is experiencing "the changing patterns of intermediation" (Kretschmer et al. 2001, p. 433), or what Leyshon (2001) described as "reintermediation." Not only is the contemporary music industry replete with "fundamental strands of continuity" (Rogers 2013, p. 34), it is also witnessing new patterns enabled by digital technology. In order to analyse the gap between the technological expectation and the materialised technology, this section expands the view that encompasses the entire value networks and provides a comprehensive understanding of the changes value networks of the recording industry.

6.3.1 Changing Value Networks

Value chain analysis postulates the value-creating logic in an industry. Porter's (1980) value chain framework signalled the commencement of understanding how firms achieve competitive advantage by differentiating their product or service in value-adding processes. To understand the contingent nature of industrial development, Stabell and Fjeldstad (1998) developed a value network analysis. It is widely used to capture the complex constellations of value creation networking context. Many studies have drawn attention to apprehending the value chain and value networks in the music industry. Leyshon's (2001) value networks, above all, provide a useful framework for understanding how the four major networks in the music industry were configured in the pre-digital era and the first infancy of the digital era. The allocation of the different functions of the industry in the four musical networks is particularly valuable in depicting the complex relationship amongst heterogeneous forces and the blurred interaction amongst the four networks. Drawing upon this framework, this section demonstrates how these networks are undergoing changes in the digital era.[9]

6.3.1.1 D2F Networks

The most pronounced changes can be found in D2F networks, which were extremely limited before digital tools became available.[10] The diverse platforms enabled by D2F technologies greatly improved artists' autonomy by affording the capacity to create, promote and distribute music on their own. This alternative means of digital tools are undergoing experimentation in all four networks, enabling a direct relationship between artists and fans throughout the entire process of music production, distribution, promotion and consumption. Some artists choose to brave the vicissitude of DIY throughout the whole process, but D2F tools are not exclusively used by DIY artists. Some labels harness these

---

[9]The conventional value networks are discussed in Chapter 3, Sect. 3.2.

[10]The changes enabled by D2F have been discussed in depth at this chapter, Sect. 6.2.

tools for artists who are signed to them. More discussion on how DIY practices are adopted will be discussed in the following section.

6.3.1.2 Networks of Creativity

Networks of creativity are composed of players involved in music composition, production and recording. Traditionally, recording companies played a vital role in providing artists with access to specialised labour and facilities. In exchange for a contract, labels offered the wherewithal to work with professional record producers, sound engineers and session musicians, and to use the recording studios for both rehearsals and actual recordings. Signing contracts was essential for labels to ensure they would recoup their investment in highly risky projects, of which less than 10% would actually make a profit (Cummings 2010).

The most distinct change in networks of creativity has been the possibility for aspiring artists to record music and bypass conventional intermediaries. This lowered barrier to entry, including cheaper and more powerful tools for music production and dissemination, has generated a wide range of options for artists to choose how to manage their career, leading to the emergence of what Prior (2010) has called a breed of "new amateurs." For example, access to professional help with music production is not a prerequisite for some artists, who have the capacity to produce their music on their own. Alison Wenham thinks the new changes in the digital era have fostered creativity in the recording industry.

> This is a golden period for creativity, because you have so many choices on how you want to run the business side. Creativity is a given, that is sort of K in the equation, that won't change. (Alison Wenham, Interview)

However, its impact still remains in the margin of subculture (Galuszka 2012; Rogers 2013; Reia 2014). Distinct from the prediction that DIY will subvert the business structure, major labels who own large catalogues successfully repositioned themselves in a business structure driven by licensing (Rogers and Preston 2016). As Kretschmer et al. (2001) pointed out, DIY practice can be useful only with concrete fan bases and adequate financial capacity for marketing and promotion.

The attention economy arose in the digital era rendered the lifted barrier of entry ensnared with fiercer competition. D2F tools such as crowdfunding therefore are more appropriately apprehended as a tool for fan building than a displacement of intermediaries (Tschmuck 2016). In addition, the wide range of DIY tools did not crowd out the professional skills in recording and production. Rather, the sheer abundance of contents also made highly skilled engineers and highly qualified studio technicians remain significant in producing high quality recordings (Spilker 2012). A notion of "artepreneuership," artists empowered with entrepreneurship, has drawn significant attention as a solution to achieve disintermediation (Tschmuck 2016). Increased awareness of an artist's autonomy, as well as the entrepreneurship-fused artisanship, will no doubt bring great benefit to the digital music economy. Considering the reintermediation is very much an issue of structural, however, artepreneurship alone is not likely to suffice to disintermediate the industry, at least in the foreseeable future (Fig. 6.3).

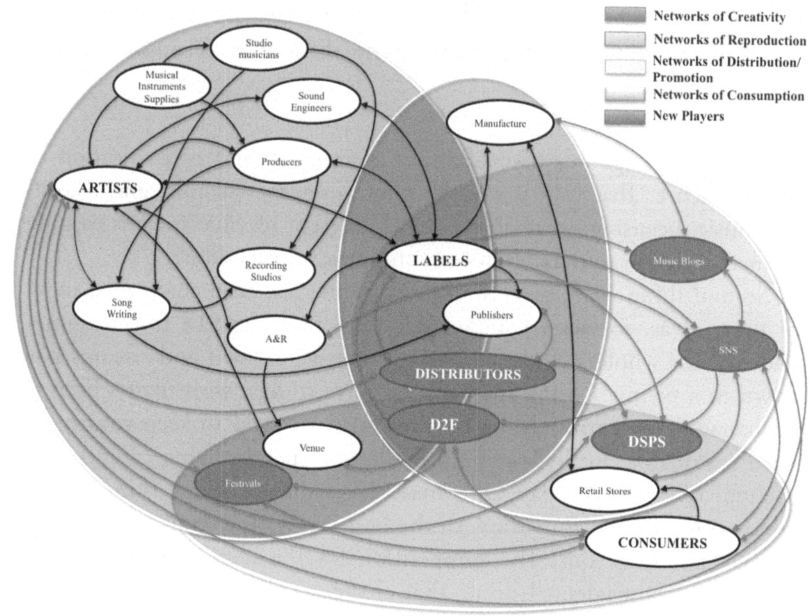

Fig. 6.3 Digital music value networks (*Source* Modified from Leyshon (2001)'s networks of music economy)

6.3.2 Networks of Reproduction

Networks of reproduction used to be a highly capital-intensive area of the music business through which large-scale production and logistics supported the brick-and-mortar infrastructure. As the demand for physical products has significantly reduced, these networks have undergone a tremendous reconfiguration. Most major labels closed down their own reproduction units. Sony DADC used to handle reproduction for UMG, Sony and EMI until February 2012, when Anderson Merchandisers acquired US distribution rights for CD from Sony DADC. This means that 82% of global CD distribution is handled by one company. Only Warner's reproduction is handled by Cinram (CNW 2010).

Many independent labels' reproduction units have also been closed down or downsized. (Wikström 2013) indicated that the record industry has seen a 25% reduction in its workforce since 2000. Besides laying off employees, labels strove to generate revenue from other sectors. Victor Zara, CFO at Razor and Tie, an independent label in Brooklyn, shares his experience of overcoming the difficulties brought about by declining sales.

> One of the things was diversification of revenue, and diversification of musical genre. That way, if we're in publishing, merchandise and recording music, licensing, we're able to have different revenue streams coming from all different sources. That's one thing we've been doing.
>
> Second thing we've been doing is, revenue has been challenged in all of these areas, so when you can sell Celo Disc for $18 for consumer and $12 for wholesale, physical wholesales were down and streams pay down to a penny. I think the way you have to deal with that is by way of managing cost strongly. So by all means you have to keep your overhead reasonable. Really watching marketing spends, being careful with the type of events you pay. Of course, the challenge of that is there's still competition to you to work with the best talent, and so ultimately may or may not work out. The competition for the best people, competition for the best talent, I think, that creates a dilemma. (Victor Zaraya, Interview)

One interesting change is the growth in vinyl consumption, which has given rise to a renewed increase of vinyl reproduction. This is striking, especially considering the continued decline of CD sales. Vinyl's growth has been on the rise for ten consecutive years, achieving the highest growth in 2017 since 1999 (BPI 2018). Although it takes only very marginal sales of the global recording revenue, vinyl is likely to stay treasured by music aficionados. More details will be discussed in the Section 5.5 of this chapter on the networks of consumption.

6.3.3 Networks of Distribution/Promotion

6.3.3.1 Networks of Distribution

As discussed in Chapter 3, Sect. 3.2, major labels built direct distribution systems with digital music service providers, while independent digital music distributors emerged to help independent labels' digital music transactions. As the digital music business grew, a considerable restructuring took place in the networks of distribution.

Major Labels' Struggles

Through a vertically integrated system, majors have long kept a tight grip on the distribution of music products in the market. Faced with digital disruption, major labels were "terrified" by the idea of losing this control.[11] To maintain it, they took all measures believed necessary. The efforts to maintain their tight hold on the legal and regulatory frameworks are well-known. What is less well-known is the way their grip was loosened on technological frameworks.

The direct distribution system that major labels built with iTunes lasted for a period of time. However, when the amount of digital music transactions increased, major labels realised that their outmoded system

[11]Major labels' path is discussed in more detail at Sect. 6.2.1 in this chapter. A detailed analysis can be found at Chapter 7.

was failing to address their needs efficiently. Sony and Warner had to outsource their distribution to Sony DADC (Christman 2012). The problem was especially acute with Universal, the largest label in the world. Universal's outsourced system from Oracle was imposing a tremendous burden; as a result, they conducted market research and decided to use INgrooves' distribution system.

Windows of Opportunity for Independent Music Distributors

This struggle lends itself particularly well to the argument over how the independent sector's nimble approach could champion the major labels' monolithic fashion in the digital context. The partnership underpins the often-overlooked side of digital music business history—the majors' struggle to maintain their supply chains, which served as a crucial means of control in distribution. On the flip side, the struggle that majors faced has opened up opportunities for independent players. As far as technical possibilities are concerned, this is the first in the history of the modern music business; the industry is now seeing a level playing field where independent labels use the same distribution platform as the major labels. Later, this asymmetric partnership between major labels and independent players led to a restructuring of the industry, ultimately contributing to a resurgence of the market control by major labels.[12]

6.3.3.2 Networks of Promotion

In conventional networks of promotion, the key was to overcome the risk caused by the hefty cost involved in producing and distributing physical music products, as well as consumers' fickle taste. To minimise the risk, filtering process was formulated to ensure selected music was widely reached to intended audiences. Henceforth, consumer's access to

[12]For more discussion on the resurgence of market control, read Chapter 7.

music was considerably limited to the items that have previously been filtered as a result of power negotiations. The lifted barrier of entry into digital music networks changed this hierarchical filtering process and significantly diversified the music discovery channel. Recent changes in the networks of promotion will be discussed in the following section.

Diversified Promotion Channels

The diversified promotion channels in the early Internet era are exemplified by some successful cases such as Radiohead's "pay-what-you-want" experiment for their IN Rainbows album (Byrne and Yorke 2007) and Nine Inch Nail's case of giving up their *Ghosts I-IV* album for free on file-sharing networks (Rose 2007). The remarkable change in this field was accelerated with the so-called Web 2.0 technologies, which tightly bridged the connection between artists and consumers. Web 2.0 social networking sites meant expanded horizon of artists and fan relationships as expanded friendship and hence signalled a tremendous reconfiguration in music taste (Beer 2008). MySpace arose as the first legitimate digital music promotion avenue where artists voluntarily uploaded their music for free; musicians such as Lily Allen and the Arctic Monkeys successfully used this platform to create buzz on their pages. YouTube facilitated user participation to contribute to improved exposure of diverse music.

More recently, new services have enhanced connectivity even further. For instance, the Berlin-based music-sharing platform SoundCloud has become an increasingly important music discovery outlet by facilitating diverse engagement such as reposting, favouriting and commenting. Shazam, a British music service, helps people discover music on the go. Using fingerprint technology, Shazam matches an identified song to a database and enables users to find the searched-for music on their favourite digital music services. Originally developed to help people detect songs, Shazam is proving to be more useful as a hit predicator. Its interactive map allows users to search the most Shazam'd songs in a designated area. It has suggested that the more Shazam'd a song is, the more likely the song is going to be the next big thing. Its near precise indication of which songs are catching on has positioned it as the must-have app for music agents to find new talent (Thompson 2014). As Wikström (2013) states, "The connectivity of the network is radically improved. The barriers that previously stopped everyone, except for a few resource-rich players, from distributing information to members of the network have almost completely disappeared" (Wikström 2013, p. 92) As a result, the distinction between distribution and promotion and the link between exposure and sales have become unclear, resulting more marketing budget with more obscure returns on investment (Wikström 2013). The unprecedented opportunities for artists who are willing to experiment with a new mode of music promotion are also criticised to be better suited for artists who already built sold fan base than aspiring artists (Rutter 2011, p. 172). New tools emerged in the digital era are more appropriately perceived as alternative than a means to displace the existing intermediaries (Young and Collins 2010).

Digital Music Discovery

In the conventional networks, consumers' musical choices were considerably restricted by the filtering process that was subject to negotiations of conflicting interests and power relations. With the rise of streaming services, legal and unlimited access to music known as "Celestial Jukebox" has become a common place. The main discussion expressed in the discussion of the Celestial Jukebox was that the access to the vast music choices would serve to help people discover and appreciate music otherwise was not available, and therefore would cultivate cultural creativity and diversity. Underpinning the presumption is that people are predisposed to enjoy the wide scope of musical choices when available, and that peer recommendation and sharing on the Internet would be a better predicator for people's music taste than the existing tastemakers. As the streaming services are increasing their user bases, however, it is becoming clear that the majority of users are not primed to discover lesser-known or unknown music, but, as Rogers (2013) argued, are "uncritical" consumers and "occasional" purchasers of popular hits:

> This consumer band is largely uncritical and by virtue of the fact that the people within it only purchase music on very rare occasions, it is the easiest market for record executives to satisfy. While it is not essential to sell to this mass market in order to achieve commercial success, it is this segment of the consumer base that generates the biggest hits, essential to sustaining the major labels. (p. 174)

As a result, the digital music discovery networks were estranged from the prediction that intermediaries will become redundant. Instead, digital music discovery shows a strong strand of continuity and discontinuity where the existing music discovery structures still remain paramount and new promotion outlets are adding their weight to digital music choices. This change is illustrated in Fig. 6.4, a framework modified from Hirsch (1969)'s organisation structure of popular music.

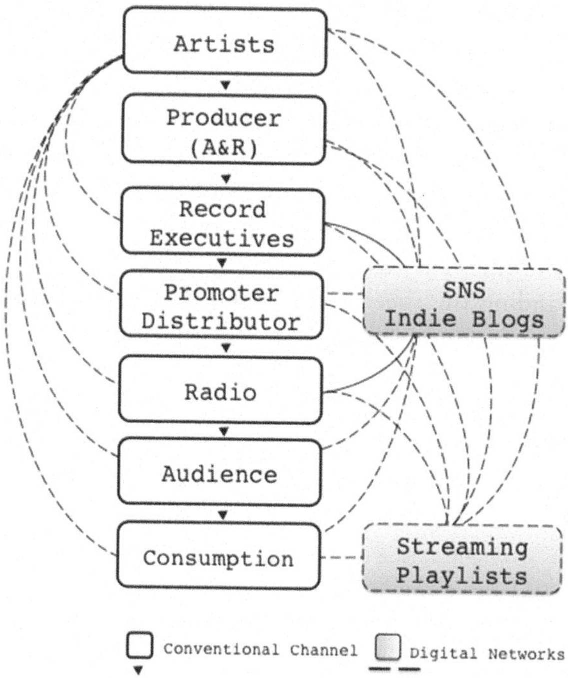

Fig. 6.4 Digital music discovery networks (*Source* Modified from Hirsch (1969)'s the Organization of Pop Music Industry)

This process emphasises that "each object must be 'discovered', sponsored, and brought to public attention by entrepreneurial organisations or non-profit agencies before the originating artist or writer can be linked successfully to the intended audience" (Hirsch 1972, p. 640). While this structure continues to exist, new discovery channels, such as social network sites ("SNS"), independent music blogs and streaming playlist, are creating new digital music discovery dynamics. Major new changes will be further explored in the following section.

Radio

Before the advent of radio, the major way to discover music was to go to a music venue, be that a street, church or a concert hall. As radio became a basic home appliance used in almost every household, it brought "a feeling of connectedness" through everyone listening to the same tune on the radio (Taylor et al. 2012, p. 4). The popularity of radio soon became deeply interlinked to the recording business, for which radio airplay played a central role in disseminating new records (Hirsch 1969; Peterson 1990). The significance of this role is manifested in the recording business practice called "payola," through which recording companies bribe DJs on commercial radio station to guarantee radio play of their records.

Notwithstanding the sheer number and diversity of music discovery outlets, airplay on commercial radio still remains essential for music discovery. In a recent research by Nielsen Music, radio was reported as the most relied-upon medium for new music discovery, (Nielsen Music 2017). An industry expert in radio broadcasting affirms the significance of the radio that still persists in the digital age with two main reasons, the ripple effect and the massive number of listeners.

> Radios are still the number one sort of discovery mechanism for new music and have been for some time and I think more than ever. At the moment, stations like Radio 1, for example in the UK, are really, really important because it has a ripple effect throughout the rest of the industry and that could help with life, it can help with TV, it can help with

> press, it can help with all sorts of other areas of the business. So, it's really important. Also, the reach of radio is huge. Radio listening actually went up in the last couple of years. We reached the vast majority of the UK population through radio. So, it's a really, really important part of the overall. (Interview, name unrevealed at his/her request)

The majority of consumers want to have what music they should listen to be dictated to them, and unlimited access to music has not changed that trait. Even the most engaged music aficionados need this direction.

> Sometimes you don't know whether you like that music until you are told maybe why you should like it, and having someone explain to you why something is important or why they think it's good or has a certain degree of passion or some sort of selling mechanism could make a difference between someone liking the song or not liking it really, or of seeing it or hearing it in a very different way. I think, as long as radio is the best in doing that, it will be the best style. (Interview, name unrevealed at his/her request)

Radio's role in the success of the music business was significant enough to be called the "lifeline" of a record company (Hirsch 1969, p. 32). Although streaming is increasingly poised to replace radio's role (Miller 2017), its prime importance is likely to stay at least for sometime. Whereas radio airplay followed a Top 40 pre-selection filtering structure in conventional recording business settings, the diffused networks of digital music discovery and the subsequent changes on the way people discover music have brought changes on how songs receive airplay. Radio stations are now taking diverse factors into account, including macro-industry forces, their network of circles, charting information, heuristic approaches to using social media and personal intuition (Schreiber 2016). What this suggests is a way to redirect the plugger's attention. However, the plugger's role still remains crucial.

> The plugger's reputation is obviously important too because if you come in with a record and you say, I think this is really good, this is going to be really big. If you are someone that they've trusted in the past and

> someone who has been right in the past… that's really the integrity and you need to be able to formulate arguments in a way that is true to your eyes but also works and convinces and persuades the gatekeepers of the radio to play it. (Interview, name unrevealed at his/her request)

Emergence of Independent Music Blogs

The sheer abundance of music contents on the digital music discovery networks came with the dilemma of what a music analyst Mark Mulligan called the "Tyranny of Choice." The challenges of the choice overload brought a renewed need for tastemakers who could curate, guide and direct the music choices (Barna 2017). While tastemakers in the conventional structure were somewhat limited to established media and curators, diverse players, ranging from individual music enthusiasts to professional tastemakers, have come into play to hold a curatorial role in the digital networks. Amongst them, independent music blogs, such as Pitchfork, Brooklyn Vegan and Stereogum (in the USA) and Drowned in Sound and Line of the Best Fit (in the UK), are increasingly poised to exert a significant influence on songs' popularity. Many of them existed since Napster, but the plenitude of music contents on streaming platforms magnified their roles. Rich Bengloff, President of A2IM, thinks these diversified media outlets are especially helpful for promoting independent music.

> For publicity things were goods, now they are much better because of Brooklyn Vegan, Dali and Pitchfork, and all the online. There's hundreds of online blogs. Before you only need to get only one selection, especially with mobile fourth generation phones out there, and the search engines are much better. (Rich Bengloff, Interview)

Pitchfork is currently the most prominent player in the indie rock music critic websites. The site began in 1995, when Ryan Schreiber, a nineteen-year-old high school graduate, began posting reviews of indie music and interviews with bands he persuaded to contribute on a website (Lindvall 2010). As Napster and its progeny enabled an untrammelled garden of music choices, the website began to grow (Lindvall 2010). Pitchfork's success owes much to the efficiency of online media, timely publication and low-cost production and discovering marginalised artists, resulting in "reputation as the flagship of online music discussion, and the ultimate example of the potential for fan-built e-zines to completely re-shape previous systems of taste, reviewing and recommendation (Waugh 2015, p. 104)." Pitchfork has become an undeniable force of music review arbiter when its chief role was recognised in discovering breakout artists such as Clap your Hands Say Yeah, Arcade Fire and Sufjan Stevens (Lindvall 2010). Many interviewees acknowledged that their importance is ever heightened by the increasing growth of streaming business, especially because of the abundance of content.

> Pitchfork media, it's just a great website/blog that if they give you an amazing review - probably the most important medium for indie rock. The question is can [you] get them to even listen? Yes. Can you get them the answers? No. There's too much shit out there. (Scott Cohen, Interview)

The Line of Best Fit is an independent music blog in the UK. Paul Bridgewater, an editor at The Line of Best Fit, thinks the role of independent music blogs is equivalent to the test bed of new talents, which is the traditional role of A&R. In this way, independent music blogs are an essential part of the entire system of promotion. Paul Bridgewater says:

> Outside we're known as a natural vehicle for publicising content and bands. We have to try and test a formula for three or four bands for the last few years that have gone through really good things. So it was low risk for them. It is like we are almost like partners in the process of the artist development. In other words, indie blogging is becoming an essential part of the promotion system. It's like a whole kind of network, an organic network that has been developing outside of the rim of labels. Where blogs and sites feed into these things and labels kind of see what rises at the top. (Paul Bridgewater, Interview)

However, as the significance of blogs has increased, concerns have been raised as to the authenticity of finding real gems. Contrary to the strong appeal of an alternative voice for the music on the margin, the expanded coverage of music that includes mainstream music, combined with the ever-increasing influence over songs' popularity, is criticised to mirror the roles once taken up by established media (Carter and Rogers 2014; Waugh 2015).

Streaming Playlists[13]

With streaming services' pervasive adoption by the market, they are playing an increasingly influential role in promotion. Spotify as the market leader has led this change in which curated playlists are increasingly positioned as a vital source for new music discovery. Curated playlists arose in response to users' changing demands and market conditions. The digital music discovery features, from basic keyword search to algorithm-based discovery, Curated Playlist, Discover Weekly, Daily Mix, Release Radar and recent Autoplay, have evolved to help people discover new music. Clearly, streaming playlists are instrumental in increasing number of new music is being discovered on this new music listening platform.[14] Just as radio's airplay was essential for songs' discovery and popularity, streaming playlist is increasingly situated to create momentum for songs' popularity. For example, Meghan Trainor's 2015 song "All About That Bass" garnered a critical momentum for popularity when it was added to a Spotify-curated playlist (Page and Ning 2014).

As the prominence streaming playlist has over songs' popularity increased, however, playlists have come under criticism that "[S]treaming playlists will become like radio playlists: reachable only by labels and artists with the resources to afford robust promotion" (Peoples 2015), and hence bringing the resurgence of the market control.

---

[13]More details on the development and the implications of streaming playlist are discussed in Chapter 4, Section 4.3.

[14]The cross-border discovery has been reported to be the most distinct change (Mulligan 2016; WIN 2017).

6.3.4 Networks of Consumption

CD sales have been in decline since Napster's appearance on the market. Most large retail stores have closed down. After many years of struggle, iTunes remained the number one digital store for some time. This began to change with the striking growth of streaming/subscription-based services. The music choices which used to be subject to market availability have been opened up, rendering almost all music available in the market. The increased uptake of streaming services is bringing increased number of population to legal services for music consumption platform. The overall consumption has increased dramatically, with only 15% of users aged over 12 years still consume music illegally (music constitutes 7%) in the UK (UK IPO 2017). The year 2017 marked the third consecutive year growth and the "fastest growth this Millennium" in the UK music, with 9.5% increase from 2016 and more than half of the music consumption (50.4%) is coming from streaming (BPI 2018). The dramatic rise of streaming music business is driving an overall growth of the music consumption, with other areas such as music festivals and vinyl generating revived growth. In the following section, the growth of digital music consumption is discussed further in these three major aspects: Streaming, Festival and Vinyl.

6.3.4.1 Growth of Streaming Music Consumption

According to IFPI Digital Music Report 2017, 112 million users have subscribed to paid streaming services, being "the key driver of growth" (IFPI 2017, p. 7). In the UK, streaming is responsible for more than half of music consumption, with 1.5 billion tracks streamed weekly (BPI 2018). The growth is evident in the independent music sphere as well, reporting $2.1 billion revenue, an astounding 80.4% increase in 2016 from the pervious year (WIN 2017).

Although streaming is an undeniable force of growth in digital music consumption, this is a view from the industry which does not necessarily represent other various stakeholders in the digital music valuation networks. As an example, Mulligan (2015) probed the fragmentation of music consumers in the digital music era and demonstrates the shifting patterns in music consumption: music aficionados, who make up 17% of music consumers, used to constitute 61% of music spending.[15] In other words, the lowered barrier to music consumption has turned some of the majority of passive listeners into paying customers, but it also reduced the massive amount that music aficionados used to spend. Streaming is still in its infancy and hence a forecast of the future should encompass the far-reaching implication of this novelty (Sun 2018).

6.3.4.2 Increase of Vinyl Consumption

Amidst streaming services' increasing growth, the music industry is witnessing the comeback of vinyl, a medium presumed long dead. CDs still account for a much larger piece of music sales than vinyl, with vinyl taking up only 3% compared to CD's 30% (BPI 2018). However, vinyl's growth is meaningful in a few aspects. Vinyl's growth has been on the rise for ten consecutive years, achieving the highest growth in 2017 since 1999 (BPI 2018), whereas the CD continues to decline.

The revival of vinyl is interesting especially when one considers the ease of access to all kinds of music, what Kasabian called "ubiquitous listening" (Kassabian 2001, 2013). What drives people engrossed over this past medium known as "retromania" (Reynolds 2011)? Ironically, the revived popularity of vinyl is, at least partly, attributed to the very essence that brought us to digital music: ease, convenience, ready accessibility. In times of information overload, digitised music not only compressed the file size but also significantly eliminated the intimate experience of music listening. Vinyl, as a supplementary medium to digital music, therefore, serves to supplant that experience which you do not get in the digitised musical experience. The physicality, warmth and even smell, as Osborne (2016) argues, are the unique attributes of vinyl that digital music cannot quite come close. Tyler McWilliams is a Sales and Marketing Director for FatBeats, a hip-hop vinyl distribution company, and has seen the ebb and flow of vinyl. He agrees to this view and

[15] For music user fragmentation, read Severin (2014).

says the revival of vinyl's popularity is a response to a missed experience in a digital era where music has become disposable whereas vinyl often can bring an immersive experience.

> Once upon a time, listening to music was more like watching a film. You put on the record, you took special care to take this item out of its sleeve, take care not to put your finger prints on it, you put it on the platter, pick up the needle, put it down. And you adjust your stereo system to make sure the volume levels are right. You sit down, and listen to your album beginning to end. So it was more of a commitment to the music. In the age of digital downloads and streaming, there is an experience that is lost in the process. Music is disposable, and consumed in small little bites. You listen to a song, switch the song before it's even over, skipping around. So, music listening is no longer such an immersive experience. (Tyler McWilliams, Interview)

Despite the astonishing growth in vinyl, however, the glory of vinyl as a populist medium thrived on 1970s is not a likely outcome at least in the foreseeable future. The intrinsic qualities that developed interest for this past medium are fundamentally connoseuirs. McWilliams calls this the "bourgeoisie product" suited for consumers who want to distinguish themselves from the mass consumers by "consciously" spending more. He says:

> It's now a collector's medium. It is what I would call an upper-class kind of product, almost a bourgeoisie product, a niche product, because there are cheaper alternatives. Digital downloads are much less expensive than vinyl. CDs are much less expensive than vinyl. And you can still buy CDs. So today's vinyl consumers are consciously choosing to spend more, because they want higher quality and a more attractive product. Like buying vintage wine vs. the bargain bin variety, or eating at a restaurant vs. cooking your own food, or buying Versace vs. Old Navy. It's a choice for quality. So the average vinyl consumer now is someone who has fine taste. (Tyler McWilliams, Interview)

When it comes to the future of the vinyl, the phenomenon of "retromania" will also likely to change. A significant number of vinyl consumers are from digital generations who have no previous vinyl account to resort to.

The vinyl consumption is therefore no longer merely nostalgic "retro" but also reflects "fluctuations" arising in the streaming era, absorbing a new generation who have not been exposed to the vinyl experience previously (Waugh 2015).

6.3.4.3 Increase in Festivals

The developments in music technologies have long been associated with the eclipse of live music. Primarily, the growth of live music owes to decreased revenue from recorded music. Live music is increasingly perceived as a "a means of survival" (Larkin 2006), and artists have been advised to perform more live concerts to generate revenue. Krueger (2005) calls this the Bowie Theory, coined for British singer-songwriter David Bowie's caveat to musicians that "[m]usic itself is going to become like running water or electricity…You'd better be prepared for doing a lot of touring because that's really the only unique situation that's going to be left" (quoted in Pareles 2002). Frith (2007) ignited renewed interest in live music as being more than just a means of survival. He reversed the prevailing idea that live technology has reduced the boundaries but in fact helped live music flourish. He opposed the notion that "[c]inema organists were made redundant by talking pictures; pit orchestras were replaced by pre-recorded tapes, pub singers by jukeboxes, dance halls with dance bands by discos with DJs (p2)," and argued that live music "has expanded the boundaries via technologies of amplification and festival events with large audiences (p2)."

This change is indicated in the explosive growth of live music particularly festival (McKay 2015; Robinson 2016). The growth is especially notable in the UK, with more than half of the UK population, 30.9 million, attending live music and 3.9 million festival attendance in 2017 (UK Music 2017). Some niche or boutique festivals are expanding their horizons to attract different segments of demographics who tend to be averse to blatantly commercialised forms of festivals managed by corporate sponsorship (Robinson 2016, p. 69). The diversity of the cultural forms delivered in the forms of festival moved the festivals beyond the sporadic experience, and to be increasingly positioned as an essential popular culture consuming avenue. Its far-reaching influence infiltrated into musical experience that brings the collegiate experience of music prompted (Taylor et al. 2016) to term "festivalization of culture."

New fan engagement tools, as well as the immediate access to music on streaming services, are increasingly integrated for festival experiences. For example, new services such as Songkick, Concertsin and Bandsintown keep music fans posted about future events happening near their location. Streaming services are particularly becoming an important destination for festivals and are actively used pre- and post-festival by those who prepare for upcoming festivals and reinforce their music experience after the festival (Kjus and Danielsen 2014; Maasø 2016). Others also noted that technology offered the greater sense of intimacy, the diversified means of interaction and fan building (Danielsen and Yngvar 2017) and the possibility as an important economic driver for musicians, along with associated products such as merchandising and recordings have thus increased musicians' revenues (Holt 2010).

However, record companies have adopted a new strategy, called 360 deals, to generate revenue from live music (Marshall 2013). Over time, stadium filling superstars have tended towards individual concerts. Festivals remain geared to less known artists who cannot afford the heavy cost involved in touring, in addition to a few known artists who can guarantee good ticket sales. The saturated market of festivals also raises concerns over the multinational firms' market dominance (McNulty 2017).

6.4 Concluding Remarks

Through the evolution of digital music distribution infrastructure and value networks, this chapter detailed a process of reintermediation, in which a new breed of intermediaries has emerged to solve unexpected problems that have arisen in large-scale digital music transactions. The chapter then advanced the way the convergence of novelties and continuity have produced new conditions in the digital recording industry. D2F tools have suggested new opportunities to allow artists to develop their career without conventional gatekeepers. However, the sheer abundance of content enabled by the removed entry barrier has given rise to the new digital music ecology of "attention economy." Underpinning this change are digital music users who, in the face of unlimited access to music, want their choices dictated to them. In the expanded view of entire networks in the digital recording industry, we observed how this convergence is bringing changing dynamics to the four major networks of creativity, reproduction, distribution/promotion and consumption.

References

Anderson, C. 2006. *The Long Tail: Why the Future of Business Is Selling Less of More*. New York: Hyperion.

Arditi, D. 2014. iTunes: Breaking Barriers and Building Walls. *Popular Music and Society* 37 (4): 408–424.

Arthur, W.B. 2009. *The Nature of Technology: What It Is and How It Evolves*. London and New York: Allen Lane.

Barna, E. 2017. The Perfect Guide in a Crowded Musical Landscape: Online Music Platforms and Curatorship. *First Monday* 22 (4). Available from https://doi.org/10.5210/fm.v22i4.6914

Beer, D. 2008. Making Friends with Jarvis Cocker: Music Culture in the Context of Web 2.0. *Cultural Sociology* 2 (2): 222–241.

Benkler, Y. 2006. *The Wealth of Networks: How Social Production Transforms Markets and Freedom*. New Haven, CT: Yale University Press.

BPI. 2018. Rising UK Music Consumption Enjoys Fastest Growth This Millennium [online]. *BPI*. Available from https://www.bpi.co.uk/news-analysis/rising-uk-music-consumption-enjoys-fastest-growth-this-millennium/. Accessed 29 Jan 2018.

Burkart, P. 2010. *Music and Cyberliberties*. Middletown, CT: Wesleyan University Press.

Burke, A.E. 2011. Music Business. In *A Handbook of Cultural Economics*, 2nd ed, ed. R. Towse. Cheltenham: Edward Elgar.

Byrne, D. 2012. *How Music Works*. San Francisco, CA: McSweeneys.

Byrne, D., and T. Yorke. 2007. David Byrne and Thom Yorke on the Real Value of Music [online]. *Wired*. Available from https://www.wired.com/2007/12/ff-yorke/?currentPage=all. Accessed 10 July 2017.

Carter, D., and I. Rogers. 2014. Fifteen Years of 'Utopia': Napster and Pitchfork as Technologies of Democratization. *First Monday* 19 (10). http://firstmonday.org/ojs/index.php/fm/article/view/5543/4122 or http://dx.doi.org/10.5210/fm.v19i10.5543.

Christman, E. 2012. Warner Music's Digital Distribution Going to Sony DADC: Sources [online]. *Billboard*. Available from https://www.billboard.com/biz/articles/news/1098895/warner-musics-digital-distribution-going-to-sony-dadc-sources. Accessed 31 Jan 2018.

Clark, D. 2013. Amanda Palmer: Proof That Social Media Is the Future of Business. *Forbes*.

CNW. 2010. Cinram Signs New Agreements with Warner Music Group [online]. Available from http://www.prnewswire.com/news-releases/cinram-signs-new-agreements-with-warner-music-group-108702959.html. Accessed 24 Feb 2016.

Cummings, A.S. 2010. From Monopoly to Intellectual Property: Music Piracy and the Remaking of American Copyright, 1909–1971. *The Journal of American History* 97 (3): 659–681.

Dale, P. 2008. It Was Easy, It Was Cheap, so What?: Reconsidering the DIY Principle of Punk and Indie Music. *Popular Music History* 3 (2): 171–193.

Danielsen, Anne D., and Yngvar K. Kjus. 2017. The Mediated Festival: Live Music as Trigger of Music Streaming and Social Media Engagement. *Convergence: The International Journal of Research into New Media Technologies*. Online First, 1–21.

Frith, S. 2007. Live Music Matters. *Scottish Music Review* 1 (1): 1–17.

Galuszka, P. 2012. Netlabels and Democratization of the Recording Industry. *First Monday* 17 (7). Available from https://journals.uic.edu/ojs/index.php/fm/article/view/3770/3278 or https://doi.org/10.5210/fm.v17i7.3770.

Galuszka, P. 2015. New Economy of Fandom. *Popular Music & Society* 38 (1): 25–43.

Galuszka, P., and B. Brzozowska. 2017. Crowdfunding: Towards a Redefinition of the Artist's Role—The Case of MegaTotal. *International Journal of Cultural Studies* 20 (1): 83–99.

Green, C. 2008. Radiohead Sales Show Fans' Loyalty to Illegal Sites. *The Independent*, August 4.

Hirsch, P. 1969. *The Structure of the Popular Music Industry: An Examination of the Filtering Process by Which Records are Preselected for Public Consumption*. Ann Arbor, Mich.: Institute for Social Research, The University of Michigan.

Hirsch, P.M. 1972. Processing Fads and Fashions: An Organization-Set Analysis of Cultural Industry Systems. *American Journal of Sociology* 77 (4): 639–659.

Hirsch, P.M. 2000. Cultural Industries Revisited. *Organization Science* 11 (3): 356–361.
Holt, F. 2010. The Economy of Live Music in the Digital Age. *European Journal of Cultural Studies* 13 (2): 243–261.
IFPI. 2017. IFPI Global Music Report 2017: Annual State of the Industry. Available from http://www.ifpi.org/news/IFPI-GLOBAL-MUSIC-REPORT-2017.
IMPALA. 2001. Independent Record Labels Strike Historical Deal with Napster [online]. *IMPALA*. Available from http://www.impalamusic.org/docum/04-press/press_0106_1.html. Accessed 21 Jan 2015.
Ingham, T. 2014. Living on the Pledge. *Music Week.*
Kassabian, A. 2001. *Hearing Film: Tracking Identifications in Contemporary Hollywood Film Music*. New York: Routledge.
Kassabian, A. 2013. *Ubiquitous Listening: Affect, Attention, and Distributed Subjectivity*. Berkeley: University of California Press.
Kelly, K. 2008. The Technium: Better Than Free [online]. *The Technium*. Available from http://kk.org/thetechnium/better-than-fre/. Accessed 28 Feb 2016.
Kjus, Y. and A. Danielsen. 2014. Live Island in the Seas of Recordings: The Music Experience of Visitors at the Oya Festival. *Popular Music and Society* 37 (5): 660–679.
Kretschmer, M., G.M. Klimis, and R. Wallis. 2001. Music in Electronic Markets—An Empirical Study. *New Media & Society* 3 (4): 417–441.
Krueger, A.B. 2005. The Economics of Real Superstars: The Market for Rock Concerts in the Material World. *Journal of Labor Economics* 23 (1): 1–30.
Larkin, J. 2006. Live Boom Raises Data Question. *Music Week* 10: 10–11.
Leyshon, A. 2001. Time-Space (and Digital) Compression: Software Formats, Musical Networks, and the Reorganisation of the Music Industry. *Environment & Planning A* 33 (1): 49.
Lindvall, H. 2010. Behind the Music: An Interview with Pitchfork Founder Ryan Schreiber. *The Guardian*, October 21.
Lowndes, S. 2016. *The DIY Movement in Art, Music and Publishing: Subjugated Knowledges*. New York: Routledge.
Maasø, A. 2016. Music Streaming, Festivals, and the Eventization of Music. *Popular Music and Society*, 1–23. https://doi.org/10.1080/03007766.2016.1231001.
Marshall, L. 2013. The 360 Deal and the 'New' Music Industry. *European Journal of Cultural Studies* 16 (1): 77–99.
McKay, G. (ed.). 2015. *The Pop Festival: History, Music, Media, Culture*. New York: Bloomsbury.

McNulty, B. 2017. Has the UK's Festival Scene Reached Saturation Point? [online]. *Financial Times*. Available from https://www.ft.com/content/622d56e2-157f-11e7-b0c1-37e417ee6c76. Accessed 27 Feb 2018.
Miller, L.S. 2017. Paradigm Shift: Why Radio Must Adapt to the Rise of Digital. *Entertainment and Sports Lawyer* 28 (16).
Moses, A. 2007. Nails Frontman Urges Fans to Steal Music—Web—Technology—smh.com.au. *The Sydney Morning Herald*, September 18.
Mulligan, M. 2014. Tyranny of Choice. *Music Industry Blog*.
Mulligan, M. 2015. Why the Music Aficionado Was to Blame for Declining Music Sales in 2014. *Music Industry Blog*. Available from https://musicindustryblog.wordpress.com/2015/02/05/why-the-music-aficionado-was-to-blame-for-declining-music-sales-in-2014/.
Mulligan, M. 2016. Cross Border Listening: Borderless Hits and Curated Playlists. *MIDiA Research*.
Negus, K. 1992. *Producing Pop: Culture and Conflict in the Popular Music Industry*. London: Edward Arnold.
Nielsen Music. 2017. Nielsen Music 360 Report 2017. Nielsen.
Osborne, R. 2016. *Vinyl: A History of the Analogue Record*. London: Routledge.
Owsinkski, B. 2011. *Music 3.0: A Survival Guide for Making Music in the Internet Age*. 2nd ed. Milwaukee, WI: Hal Leonard Books.
Page, W., and K. Ning. 2014. Anatomy of a Hit: How Meghan Trainor Made the UK Chart Without Selling Downloads. *Spotify Insights*.
Pareles, J. 2002. David Bowie, 21st-Century Entrepreneur. *The New York Times*, June 9.
Peoples, G. 2015. 'Playola' Infiltrates Streaming Services: Pay for Play 'Definitely Happening' [online]. *Billboard*. Available from http://www.billboard.com/articles/business/6670475/playola-promotion-streaming-services. Accessed 28 Jan 2016.
Peterson, R.A. 1990. Why 1955? Explaining the Advent of Rock Music. *Popular Music* 9 (1): 97–116.
Pollack, N., 2011. Spotify's Celestial Jukebox [online]. *Wired UK*. Available from http://www.wired.co.uk/magazine/archive/2011/02/start/spotify-celestial-jukebox. Accessed 28 Feb 2016.
Porter, M.E. 1980. *Competitive Strategy: Techniques for Analyzing Industries and Competitors*. New York: Free Press.
Price, J. 2012. How Technology Destroyed The Traditional Music Industry. *Hypebot*.
Prior, N. 2010. The Rise of the New Amateurs: Popular Music, Digital Technology and the Fate of Cultural Production. In *Handbook of Cultural Sociology*, ed. J.R. Hall, L. Grindstaff and M. Lo, 398–407. Routledge.

Reia, J. 2014. Napster and Beyond: How Online Music Can Transform the Dynamics of Musical Production and Consumption in DIY Subcultures. *First Monday* 19 (10). http://firstmonday.org/ojs/index.php/fm/article/view/5552/4131 or http://dx.doi.org/10.5210/fm.v19i10.5552. Accessed 6 Oct 2014.

Reynolds, S. 2006. *Rip It Up and Start Again: Postpunk 1978–1984*. New York: Penguin Books.

Reynolds, S. 2011. *Retromania: Pop Culture's Addiction to Its Own Past*. London: Faber and Faber.

Robinson, R. 2016. *Music Festivals and the Politics of Participation*. London: Routledge.

Rogers, J. 2013. *The Death and Life of the Music Industry in the Digital Age*. London: Bloomsbury.

Rogers, J. 2014. Canary Down the Mine: Music and Copyright at the Digital Coalface. *Socialism and Democracy* 28 (1): 34–50.

Rogers, J., and P. Preston. 2016. Crisis and Creative Destruction: New Modes of Appropriation in the Twenty-First Century Music Industry. In *Business Innovation and Disruption in the Music Industry*, ed. P. Wikström and R. DeFillippi, 53–72. Cheltenham, UK: Edward Elgar.

Rose, F. 2007. Secret Websites, Coded Messages: The New World of Immersive Games. *Wired Magazine* 20: 01–16.

Rutter, P. 2011. *The Music Industry Handbook*. London: Routledge.

Scherer, F.M. 2004. *Quarter Notes and Bank Notes: The Economics of Music Composition in the Eighteenth and Nineteenth Centuries*. Princeton: Princeton University Press.

Schreiber, D. 2016. The Influence of Disruptive Technologies on Radio Promotion Strategies in the Music Industry: A Case Study of One Micro-Firm's Decision-Making Practice. In *Business Innovation and Disruption in the Music Industry*, ed. P. Wikström and R. DeFillippi, 13–32. Cheltenham, UK: Edward Elgar.

Scott, S. 2014. The Moral Economy of Crowdfunding and the Transformative Capacity of Fan-ancing. *New Media & Society*. https://doi.org/10.1177/1461444814558908.

Severin, K. 2014. Music Consumer Segmentation: From Lagging Indicators to Leading Indicators. *MIDiA Research*.

Simon, H.A. 1971. Designing Organizations for an Information-Rich World. *Computers, Communications, and the Public Interest*, 37–72.

Sisario, B. 2012. TuneCore Chief Shakes Up Music with His Own Words. *The New York Times*, May 6.

Sørensen, K.H. 1996. *Learning Technology, Constructing Culture: Socio-Technical Change as Social Learning*. Trondheim: University of Trondheim, Centre for Technology and Society, No. 18/96.

Spencer, A. 2005. *DIY: The Rise of Lo-fi Culture*. London: Marion Boyars.

Spilker, H.S. 2012. The Network Studio Revisited: Becoming an Artist in the Age of 'Piracy Cultures'. *International Journal of Communication* 6: 773–794.

Spitz, D., and S. Hunter. 2005. Contested Codes: The Social Construction of Napster. *Information Society* 21 (3): 169–180.

Stabell, C.B., and Ø.D. Fjeldstad. 1998. Configuring Value for Competitive Advantage: On Chains, Shops, and Networks. *Strategic Management Journal* 19 (5): 413.

Sun, H. 2018. The Times They Are a-Changin': Digital Music Value in Transition from Piracy to Streaming. In *Digital Piracy: A Global, Multidisciplinary Account*, ed. S.C. Brown and T.J. Holt. Arbington, Oxon and New York.

Swash, R. 2009. Lily Allen: Social Networker of the Decade. *The Guardian*, November 29.

Taylor, J., A. Bennett, and I. Woodward (eds.). 2016. *The Festivalization of Culture*. London: Routledge.

Taylor, T.D., M. Katz, and T. Grajeda. 2012. *Music, Sound, and Technology in America: A Documentary History of Early Phonograph, Cinema, and Radio*. Durham, NC: Duke University Press.

Théberge, P. 2006. Everyday Fandom: Fan Clubs, Blogging, and the Quotidian Rhythms of the Internet. *Canadian Journal of Communication* 30 (4): 485–502.

Thompson, D. 2014. The Shazam Effect. *The Atlantic*.

Trent Reznor—Steal This Music. 2007. Available from https://www.youtube.com/watch?v=IFXivarypE4.

Tschmuck, P. 2016. From Record Selling to Cultural Entrepreneruship: The Music Economy in the Digital Paradigm Shift. In *Business Innovation and Disruption in the Music Industry*, ed. P. Wikström and R. DeFillippi, 13–32. Cheltenham, UK: Edward Elgar.

UK Intellectual Property Office. 2017. Online Copyright Infringement Tracker Survey (7th Wave)—GOV.UK [online]. Available from https://www.gov.uk/government/publications/online-copyright-infringement-tracker-survey-7th-wave. Accessed 12 Dec 2017.

UK Music. 2017. *Music Tourism: Wish You Were Here—The Contribution of Live Music to the UK Economy*. London: UK Music. Available from https://www.ukmusic.org/assets/general/Report_WYWH_17.pdf.

Waugh, M. 2015. 'Music That Actually Matters'? Post-Internet Musicians, Retromania and Authenticity in Online Popular Musical Milieux. Ph.D. Dissertation, Anglia Ruskin University.

Wikström, P. 2013. *The Music Industry: Music in the Cloud*, 2nd ed. Cambridge, England: Polity.

Williams, R., J. Stewart, and R. Slack. 2005. *Social Learning in Technological Innovation: Experimenting with Information and Communication Technologies*. Cheltenham: Edward Elgar.

WIN. 2017. WINTEL 2017—Worldwide Independent Market Report.

Young, S., and S. Collins. 2010. A View from the Trenches of Music 2.0. *Popular Music & Society* 33 (3): 339–355.

7
Case Study—INgrooves

This chapter provides an in-depth empirical investigation on INgrooves and addresses the reintermediation process took place on the digital music distribution networks. It details INgrooves' innovation process that parallels the process; digital music distribution networks have become reintermediated. INgrooves' beginning of the business demonstrates how iTunes' arrival gave rise to the emergence of new intermediaries as middlemen between digital music service providers and independent music labels. The partnership between INgrooves and Universal Music Group illustrates major labels' struggle to build an infrastructure suited for digital music transaction, the way they successfully repositioned themselves in the digital music business environment, as well as the changing dynamics where we witness a resurgence of the market control.

H. Sun, *Digital Revolution Tamed*, https://doi.org/10.1007/978-3-319-93022-0_7

7.1 Beginning

Robb McDaniels,[1] an American by birth, was brought up in London during the early years of his childhood. At the age of fourteen, living in the USA, he visited London to see one of his best friends and was smitten by the music culture deeply ingrained in Londoners' life: everyone he met had a set of turntables in their bedroom and was DJing almost as a daily habit. The most unforgettable of all was the Notting Hill Carnival. There, the DJs who played music on the rooftops were worshipped as rock stars (*This Week in Music—Interview with Robb McDaniels* 2012). It prompted him to become a professional DJ later, but he soon discovered that it was not necessarily the best career path being based in the USA. Putting his passion for music aside, he deviated to the finance world, working as an investment banker at Marsh & McLennan Securities. Despite rapid career advancement, he felt misplaced in the finance world (Greenburg 2012). McDaniels says:

> I would go into the bathroom before meetings and just be like, 'What am I doing? This just doesn't feel right.' (Greenburg (2012), sampled 15 February 2016)

He finally made up his mind to pursue his passion. He drew insights from his previous working experiences such as the time at a vinyl record shop on Newbury Street in Boston. He also received inspiration from Mob, an American singer-songwriter and a DJ who had licences for major commercials. He began drawing up a business plan in the attic of his house in 2001.

Unlike many other music companies, which evolved from the physical businesses, INgrooves was a digital music company from the outset. It originated from Robb McDaniels' fascination with the unprecedented opportunity of the digital music experience that Napster had presented.

[1]Robb McDaniels resigned CEO in December 2014 and remains on the company's board of directors. The position was replaced by Bob Roback, former Head of Music at Yahoo, in August 2015.

> I've been a big fan of the original Napster. It was amazing that you could find all this music from all over the world and get it to your fingertips. It's one of the reasons why I really wanted to bring dance & electronic music to the United States and help commercialise it. (Robb McDaniels, Interview)

The business took off in 2002, led by McDaniels, with many dance labels as partners. During the early phase, the focus of the business was to license dance & electronic music in Europe for TV commercials or video games in the USA.

> We didn't start initially with the downloading as a big component of our business model. The initial vision was to represent music, mostly dance & electronic music from UK and Europe, and represent it for licensing for TV commercials and video games here in the United States. (Robb McDaniels, Interview)

They began acquiring rights as "synchronisation" for popular catalogues and helped rights owners to exploit their contents.

7.2 iTunes and the Emergence of Digital Music Aggregators

The infancy of the digital music business, following Napster's shutdown, witnessed the consequence of the briefly attempted digital revolution, a huge chasm between consumers' expectation and what the industry could offer. It also saw an influx of new trials, as well as errors. Often depicted as delayed innovation, this phase is dominantly discussed in two contested arguments: one is the argument raised by the recording industry that piracy kills the industry, and the other is the criticism levelled at the industry that its resistance to the change delayed the innovation. The dichotomy of the discussion, however, overlooks an important factor—the lack of accompanying infrastructure. Neither Internet access infrastructure nor legitimate digital music transaction was ready for digital music business, let alone people's perception towards this novelty.

By the time iTunes became popular, things were rapidly changing. Dial-up Internet access had been replaced by high speed broadband. iTunes had facilitated the uptake of mobile digital music listening devices. As an increasingly popular avenue, it also allowed lines of businesses to set up digital music transactions. Before the business officially launched, iTunes had already built direct lines of business with major labels. It was almost impossible for the service to handle thousands of independent labels in the market. Neither could iTunes just have ignored indie labels; they needed to cater for digital music users who had already been exposed to the unlimited access to music enabled by Napster. A new breed of intermediaries was born to fill the gap between digital music service providers and independent labels. It marked the beginning of the reintermediation of the digital music business, and a turning point for INgrooves. Robb McDaniels was excited by this unexpected opportunity. All the information on the catalogues INgrooves held for other types of digital transaction became an essential asset in extending the service to digital music downloads.

> When iTunes launched, a lot of these clients asked, 'Hey, can you help us get our content on to iTunes and the other digital music services?' INgrooves was representing this music for exploitation and TV films and video games here in the United States. But very quickly, we recognised that once we had all this information on the catalogues, once we had these rights, it was very easy to extend it for digital download. So we immediately began to expand our services to include downloading and did deals with iTunes, Rhapsody and the legal form of Napster and so forth. (Robb McDaniels, Interview)

The ever-increasing access to digital technology sweeping across the nation and generation gave rise to the idea that digital transaction was within anyone's reach. However, quite contrary to this belief, commercial transaction of digital content entails professional skills. Everything involved in digital distribution, from converting information contained on physical products into digital, digital rights management to the methods of settling payment was a novelty, and thereby required special expertise. Few independent labels, let alone artists, were prepared to carry out even the simplest tasks of business in digital terms.

iTunes' success sparked a sudden demand for digital music distribution, and INgrooves needed to scale the platform. McDaniels says:

> That was in 2003. That was when we also realised that in order to effectively become a digital distributor, we needed to have a platform to manage the delivery of these assets. (Robb McDaniels, Interview)

He had a basic idea about how to build the system, but his knowledge of technology was nothing compared to his affinity for music. This gap was bridged very fortuitously. His life insurance salesman happened to be a former HR Director at Napster, and put him in touch with David Kent, a former Director of New Technology at Napster, who later became CTO at INgrooves.

> The guy who came to sell me life insurance, this is to show how things happen, had been HR Director at Napster. He started asking me what I was doing as I was going on my life insurance policy, telling him I promise I never smoked weed, I don't go skydiving…all that good stuff. So I tell him what I'm doing, and he said 'Look, I gotta go, and you gotta meet someone.' It was David Kent. He's been the primary architect of our enterprise software application which is today what really empowers INgrooves and even Universal Music Group. (Greenburg (2012), sampled 15 February 2016)

In the beginning, INgrooves' business was focused on carrying out this basic task of converting CD to digital formats and sending the information to digital music service providers. Deals with good artists also helped the business. Alex Branson, SVP at INgrooves International, explains:

> The business began in literally converting. It was just about getting them ready to suddenly go to Rhapsody, iTunes or Amazon. So pretty much for the first six years of the company, 2002 till 2008, it very much grew organically. They tried to bring some big artists. One of the main labels is called BSL. They did very well. And that's probably one of the things that kept the company going financially during those years. (Alex Branson, Interview)

During the dawn of the legitimate digital music business period, many music companies appeared and vanished. Despite the ebbs and flows, INgrooves' business continued to grow. Robb McDaniels thinks the secret of this growth is a combination of capital, forbearance and strength, as well as luck.

> It's tough to survive. We've gotten ourselves into this generational shift in consumption patterns from physical but this is the digital. This isn't a flash in the pan overnight type of opportunity. It certainly takes access to capital to help you survive the ups and downs. It takes patience and fortitude, but there's a little bit of luck sprinkled in there as well. (Greenburg (2012), sampled 15 February 2016)

In 2005, INgrooves had two of these ingredients—capital and luck. It raised $2 million of investment from a venture capital firm, which led to a considerable sales increase of $1.6 million in 2006 and $4.7 million in 2007 (Greenburg 2012). The stroke of luck was McDaniel's acquaintance with Al Teller, a music industry veteran who had held numerous top executive roles including Head of Columbia Records and Head of MCA Records (which later became part of Universal Music Group). INgrooves' technology impressed Al Teller enough to convince him and his contacts to make a financial investment as well as build human credentials. He introduced INgrooves to Universal, which ignited INgrooves' advancement soon afterwards (Greenburg 2012).

7.3 Beyond Distribution

7.3.1 Marketing/Promotion

Over the years, digital music sales grew, so did the number of digital music distributors. INgrooves felt the need to distinguish itself from the competitors. The pursuit of establishing a unique advantage as a digital music distributor soon resulted in an advancement in its position as a middleman between labels and retailers. Alex Branson explains:

> We came as a distribution company…but over time that stopped being enough. There were a lot of other companies came into this place. We thought about market force as a marketing company. We spent time calling retail accounts – 'We've got this new record, really good. Here's some information about it. What opportunities do you have this week, or the week it was released?' We participated – 'Is there a feature that we can have on homepage, or a genre page, or a special price-drop promotion, maybe we could create a special label sample that you can feature?' We can have that link to back to the catalogue. There are lots of different deals that retailers can do. (Alex Branson, Interview)

Behind this change lay an unexpected problem that the digital music industry had begun to face. Contrary to the prediction that an abolition of the barrier of entry would lead to democratisation of access, it generated problems both for artists and consumers: it became even more difficult for artists to have their music heard, and consumers faced a "Tyranny of Choice" (Mulligan 2014). Underpinning this dilemma was the arrival of attention economy that economist Herbert Simon had predicted in 1971.

> (I)n an information-rich world, the wealth of information means a dearth of something else: a scarcity of whatever it is that information consumes…Hence a wealth of information creates a poverty of attention and a need to allocate that attention efficiently among the overabundance of information sources that might consume it. (Simon 1971, pp. 40–41)

In the face of unlimited access to music, it turned out that most consumers do not want to search for music amongst 300 million tracks. The majority of users want to be told the music to which they should listen. The sheer abundance of choice enabled by streaming services had led to complicated control over ways of creating hits. This dilemma brought back the industry's long-established practice: filtering. Dominic Jones, International Sales and Marketing Director at INgrooves, thinks that this largely is similar to the traditional music business where select few albums were displayed in retail stores, only shelf space competition has been replaced by attention competition.

> In the physical world we have CDs and vinyl. The biggest hurdle to overcome is getting record shops to want to stock them in the first place because you actually have to sell them physical things and you have to ship them from our warehouse to their warehouse and to their shop and convince them that people are going to be walking through the door to buy them. (Dominic Jones, Interview)

However, there are differences in the digital era. What is distinct from the past is that the removed entry barrier has itself been replaced by a new barrier, in this case the problem of maximising exposure in the diversified channels of music discovery.

> In the digital world I think it is very different because you are shipping them a master file and, with a few exceptions, most of the large retailers will take everything that you want to deliver to them. The hurdle with digital is getting the most profile for your release, making sure it is on the homepage or genre page or on a newsletter. If you look at iTunes, you only have so much space. But then they have scrolling sections. Well…you could scroll forever if you wanted to or if they wanted to scroll everything to accommodate all the new releases and bestsellers. Having one of the banners on iTunes gives you all the advantages over those that don't have them…We have to convince those retailers that our releases should be higher profile and bigger priorities than those of all our competitors. (Dominic Jones, Interview)

The arrival of attention economy in the music industry came as a belated connection between what consumers wanted and what the industry had to offer. In the conventional system, where the recording industry had considerable control over the music to which people listen, recording companies' main concern was maximising the odds of exposure. Although the way music becomes popular already entails a certain degree of uncertainty, the changing dynamics prompted by digital technology have made it even more complicated. As the streaming services expand into mainstream adoption, what songs get featured or playlisted on streaming services has become one of the most, if not the most, significant elements for music marketing and promotion.

Consumers' unchanged demand to be told the music to which they should listen, combined with labels' strong appetite to wield their control over people's listening, has left leeway for retailers to manipulate what they highlight. Retailers have always worked directly with major labels. However, the enormity of the independent catalogues available resulted in a need for help from digital music distributors like INgrooves, who had already built a relationship with independent labels and retailers and were thus well-positioned to move into digital music marketing and promotion. INgrooves' marketing team came into prominence. The major role of INgrooves' marketing team is to choose the top 10 albums from 6000 new releases per week.[2]

Considering the significance of grabbing the attention, it is important to know on what criteria do these companies rely to choose these 10 out of 6000. The quality of the album has always been thought to be of the utmost importance. However, as Frith (2002) pointed out, the reason why we like certain music or why certain music is popular is not an objective means of determining objective aesthetics of music, but a socially determined preference. The "popularity" of a song, therefore, is less an outcome of an absolute aesthetic definition than a socially determined collective consumption. It leaves the criteria of prioritising albums cannot be not solely based on the quality of albums or sales. As a middleman between labels and digital music service providers, INgrooves need to take both parties into consideration. The criteria that INgrooves take into account for the labels are the important albums that labels emphasise and their relationship with these labels. Dominic Jones says:

> It's partly those labels that shout the loudest and say 'this is really important to us'. Part of it will be the relationships that we need to maintain with key labels and priority labels. That might be to do with who signed them, in which part of the company. It might be to do with future relationships we want to maintain, it might be down to historical

[2] This figure is based on the interview conducted in 2013.

> relationships or it might be just down to perceiving that a great label that have a good roster of artists are more important than sales. (Dominic Jones, Interview)

Equally important is providing the information that digital music service providers want. For digital music service providers, what sells well often is deemed to be significant and this is closely interlinked to the wide publicity of the songs. Dominic Jones continues:

> We have to provide the ammunition for the labels to let the accounts know that the band's fans will be coming to their sites or people will be coming into their shops to buy these releases and here are the things that will drive them towards you. Those things are generally promotion at radio, press, TV or increasingly good use of social media. Primarily what I think we should be trying to indicate on those priority sheets are the 10 most important things that we have got this week which are led by the basics of press, radio, TV and touring. Most retailers want to know that public has heard about it, read about it or seen it. I used to say to labels, if a retailer hasn't heard about you, read about or seen your act, why would they want to stock it? (Dominic Jones, Interview)

There are exceptions where artists rise to the top without relying on conventional promotion channels. Although this exceptional stardom syndrome is nothing new, what are new are the diversified routes that digital technology has enabled. D2F tools particularly suggested an unprecedented opportunity through which unsigned artists can rocket to stardom. In reality, most musicians still suffer from obscurity. Underlying the problem is that whereas the competition of jockeying for entry has disappeared, the barrier of getting noticed still exists. As Dominic Jones says,

> You can't just approach The Times and say, 'hello, I have got this new album'. It has to go through [the process]. I mean in some cases, if you are [a] recognised artist that might work, but still they would rather be approached by somebody who is bringing them the cream of what is out there. (Dominic Jones, Interview)

As affirmed by other scholars (Rogers 2013), the long-sustained market practice structured by commercial interests is still firmly rooted in the popular music-making process. Furthermore, new intermediaries that have emerged from digital music business are becoming part of the entire process.

> They want to know what's going on at press, radio and TV. Radio wants to know what's going on in retail and press and TV. TV wants to know what's going on at radio, press and retail. So everybody needs to know how the promotion is building. We [INgrooves] are collating the information of the best promo to then present to the retailers…[and] giving them the reasons why they should be giving it profile. (Dominic Jones, Interview)

7.3.2 INresidence (Artist Services Division)

Having acquired considerable market knowledge and technical ingenuity, INgrooves was prepared to bring their prowess to bear upon the way artists could stand out from the noise. In 2013, the company, which already had tools for cultivating artists' careers through digital and physical distribution on a global level, marketing/promotion and rights managements all in-house, found a niche market they could enter. Under the name of INresidence, INgrooves provides a suite of "marketing and promotions services to established artists and labels looking for a better, and more fair, all-encompassing distribution solution" (Pham 2013). This new set of business crystalises INgrooves' three unique advantages: a global distributor, a technology company and an expert in the independent sector.

7.3.2.1 Global Distribution

Quite distinct from the widely perceived prediction that the recording industry would experience a radical change through disintermediation, the digital music industry is more reintermediated than ever before. One of the reasons that brought about this reintermediation is that not all artists are endowed with business skills. Alex Branson comments:

> The problem with the disintermediation is that they're still gonna organise themselves. The recording artist isn't going to be the world's best businessman, because they're talented musicians or singer-songwriter[s] or whatever. Not everybody has all the skills they need to do it. So they need a little bit of help. (Alex Branson, Interview)

Building a fan base and making noise amongst the crowd still remains the biggest hurdle for most artists. Alex Branson continues:

> How do you build your fan base? Those (D2F tools) are probably great if you're super-talented at all the social networking services etc. The challenge is how we can get hold of the noise? It's very difficult. It's very easy for a record company to consume the marketplace. And I think what has been lost a little bit is that professionalism, sometimes, what used to be confined to record companies, what they need to do in order to make their music more popular than the other ones. How do you convince them yours is the better one? (Alex Branson, Interview)

Toby Peacock, International Labels Director at INgrooves, believes the niche was created through the narrowed margin in this area.

> I don't think the record labels can afford to get away with the kind of business they used to in the '80s. I don't think the margins are that big anymore. (Toby Peacock, Interview)

As a global digital music distributor, INgrooves can distribute and do marketing and promotion on a worldwide scale. Toby Peacock says:

> I think as everything becomes more global especially digitally, distribution through a company like INgrooves makes more sense, compared with signing different deals with several record companies for various territories. Now it's much more of a global thing. We have to offer a worldwide deal and a worldwide solution, not just North America. (Toby Peacock, Interview)

In addition to the digital side, physical distribution equips INgrooves to reach out to worldwide fans effectively.

> We can affect an efficient global physical release, because we're running direct marketing relationships with each of those partners. They act like a local office for us, helping us navigate the ever-changing marketplace. (Alex Branson, Interview)

7.3.2.2 Technology Company

While digital technologies are perceived to have opened up great opportunities for artists by providing diverse options, it is not the preferred method of all artists. To artists who are not familiar with these changes, digital technology is, in fact, an obstacle to entry. This is especially true for established artists that have been away from the field for a while. This is how INresidence picked up Mazzy Star, an American alternative rock band that was acclaimed in the mid-1990s. The band already had a solid fan base, but had not released an album in 17 years. For bands like Mazzy Star, there are many things on which they need catch up in the digital music business environment. Toby Peacock says:

> Although they [Mazzy Star] are very aware of how the music industry works, they're probably not quite so informed about how it works today [compared to the way] it was 17 years ago. So, when you're talking about digital and social media, there's a lot of education that has to happen with the band and management. If it's talking about a free track giveaway or promotion with a digital blog or retailer, it's kind of 'how does it work?' You have to explain why we're doing it, why it might be a good thing and what the payback might be etc. etc. If it's an album exclusive being streamed upfront for a week; 'what does that actually mean? Does it mean people can download it or not?' There is that education. (Toby Peacock, Interview)

As a technology company, INgrooves can also be better positioned in using digital data. In choosing which artists to work with, the quality of sound comes first, which in many cases means the marketability. An interesting change that has arisen in the digital music business is that the way of measuring marketability has become more data-based. Toby Peacock explains:

> I think it always has to come back down to the music. Is the music good? The next question then becomes: Is there a market for the artist and where are their fans? With artists nowadays engaging with social platforms to promote themselves they can gauge very quickly, from the data coming back from these platforms, not only reactions to the music but also where their fans are located. It has helped open up the market, not only as these platforms are available to any artist but also as they cross borders. (Toby Peacock, Interview)

Rather than relying on an intuitive ear alone by going to gigs to find raw talent, intermediaries in the digital age can use other indicators to reduce the risk of investment by looking into the data, such as followers on social media. Toby Peacock continues:

> There still needs to be some curators that make decisions on what is 'good' and then champion the artist. But sometimes you might not understand the project or its popularity and why they have got all these digital followers? Then the questions become more business-like and less emotional: There is a fan base to reach, how can we monetise it? It's no longer just about going out to see bands live and saying, 'Okay, I get this. This is good, I can see how this might work' but also supporting that instinct with data available. (Toby Peacock, Interview)

Toby Peacock believes that, as a technology company, INgrooves is in a great position to produce a better output using the data available to them.

> Working at a music company like INgrooves that is also tech savvy and on projects globally means that we can better understand what is happening where and when and react accordingly. (Toby Peacock, Interview)

Robb McDaniels agrees with this.

> We are actually paying an artist more accurately. Rather than one artist benefitting from selling a CD which only has two songs on it that the fan wants, the fan will now only pay for the two songs that they want and then have money to pay for [an]other bunch of artists for music that

> they want to have access to. So it's potentially a more fair and equitable distribution solution. (Robb McDaniels, Interview)

7.3.2.3 Independents' Expertise

INgrooves' strong foothold in the independent music field is a unique asset for artists who want to label themselves as independent and need leverage to develop their career. Toby Peacock explains:

> From an independent artists' point of view, there is still resistance to entering into a major label scenario. For me, the days of the career artist on major labels are a lot harder to see. There seems to be more bands that have successful debuts but by second or the third album [has] and diminishing return[s] for the label; that will be the end. In some ways though this is where label services can really help an artist with a fan base to still release records successfully without having to give up rights to the major labels who are no longer prepared to support. (Toby Peacock, Interview)

INresidence has one of the attractive qualities of independent labels—providing more control over the way artists pursue their careers. Because artists have online access through the INresidence system, they have a better idea of the way to move things forward and do not have to give up the lion's share of their income as was the case in the pre-digital era. This also forces INgrooves to ensure they are much more bespoke in terms of artist management. Toby Peacock continues:

> The artists that have been around the block with the major labels can take more control of their expenditure with a label services deal and are often surprised by some of the costs that can be involved with a campaign. When artists are involved directly you start to have conversations such as 'Actually, this is my money. No, I don't think we should be staying at this particular hotel or need to be flying over there.' Artists have more say in what is best for them and where their money is better spent. We try to be more bespoke and use our insights to spend wisely. It's a lot more having conversations with the artist. (Toby Peacock, Interview)

The best vantage point of INresidence comes from its close relationship with retailers. Armed with its well-established connections, INgrooves can exercise influence over the acts to which music retailers pay more attention. Alex Branson explains:

> One of the things that we did this week is 'Someday'. It went over to Spotify. As you log on Spotify, splashing pages come up. And it's advertising the catalogue from the record company called Om Records. That special promotion we do with Spotify is very very effective. Explore or discover the new music. That's sort of the thing we do. (Alex Branson, Interview)

7.4 Partnership with Universal

INgrooves had a significant momentum for growth in 2008 when Universal Music Group ("Universal"), the world's largest music label, made a strategic investment. The partnership underpins the often-overlooked side of the digital music business history—majors' struggle to maintain their supply chains, which served as a crucial means for control in distribution. On the flip side, this same struggle opened up opportunities for independent players, which eventually led to a restructuring of the industry.

7.4.1 Universal's Struggle

Through a vertically integrated system, majors have long maintained tight control over distribution of music products in the market. In order to maintain its control, they built their own distribution system in the beginning. Universal realised that their outmoded system was failing to address their needs efficiently. As is widely known, digital technology's disruption of this control was largely tackled through legal means: a plethora of regulatory measures were adopted to strengthen copyright protection and numerous legal allegations were made not only against the companies, but also their consumers. While the majors convinced legislators of their views to a large degree, the difficulty of maintaining control was partly coming from their own internal system.

> They built their own platform. It managed their business for about a decade. So they did well enough. But it began to break down a little bit. (Robb McDaniels, Interview)

An industry entrepreneur encapsulates this:

> If we think about the troubles majors experienced in building distribution system [it] makes it daunting [that] this once-used-to-be-a-very-small-company could. While we believe big companies would be able to afford the world's best engineers and the best system available, this is not the case with digital music distribution. (Interview, name unrevealed at his/her request)

An industry expert gives an insight into why major labels' formal and monolithic approach could not survive in digital music networks.

> There is an approach to building software that is very, very much an ISO 9000 approach, which takes you two years to produce anything. But it is kind of so formalised and documented that it has left a paper trail of exactly what's running. By the time we get there what might be running is obsolete but it's highly formalised. (Interview, name unrevealed at his/her request)

Gordon Rintoul, who works at Client Services at INgrooves, shares a more detailed description of what happened. He explains that Universal nearly went bankrupt for the increasing amount of fees they had to pay to Oracle for outsourcing the licence.

> I don't talk too much about it but I know how much some of the major[s] spent on it. And they very very nearly bankrupt themselves. They spent money that they thought is necessary to build up [the] platform. If you're technical, you're not going to do it with Oracle, because [of] the cost of the Oracle license. There's also [the] individual cost of

> every time someone connects to that database. So [the] end of scenario that can run completely out of thing if you got thousand people accessing that database [with] no middleware, then all of these licenses is going to cost [a] fortune. Not just that. You have to hire Oracle engineers etc., etc. (Gordon Rintoul, Interview)

In essence, the new methods of music production and distribution in the digital age exhibited fundamental changes that diverge considerably from the conventional approach. This novelty thereby required a significantly different method of building a system. This is how Gordon Rintoul built a digital music distribution system early on for Rightsrouter as a former co-founder.

> So, for example, my system that [was] built back in 2003 was [a] very clunky type of system, but what? We built it for a couple thousand pounds and the system I built when the company took over the cost. And then it did what the other one that couldn't do as much does it, and would eventually [have] been much better if we kept on playing money into it. But how much money are you going to spend on those situation[s] here with just becomes completely up in front? You're never going to get your returns. (Gordon Rintoul, Interview)

Gordon Rintoul thinks that it is more about the mindset than technicality per se.

> So this was the mentality of the major labels at that time: 'Is this Oracle going to be like shiny if we're going to go with this, we're going to go with that and what about these apps'. And sooner or later when someone's pull[ed] the plug on it, because they got into maybe spending 30, 40, 50 100 million like on the system developments and they have to stop it. A major broadcaster is a classic example, that they had the system where the ones to go through digitising the program and probably all their catalogue and they put a plug on it after spending 100 million on it. (Gordon Rintoul, Interview)

In building INgrooves' distribution system, One Digital took the opposite approach to the conventional method. Based on "dynamic integral approach," INgrooves achieved a more efficient, adaptable and fast distribution system. An employee at INgrooves explains:

> The entirely opposite approach [to the conventional system] is a dynamic integral approach to building software and it's designed in its organisation, in its implementation. We don't have an outlying approach but we got here, we leapfrogged everybody else because of sort of the opposite approach to building software. I'm not saying it was an undisciplined approach but it was very, very different in many of its aspects. I think that that is the strength of the platform. I think it makes more adaptable. I think it makes it faster in production turnaround. (Interview, name unrevealed at his/her request)

Central to the partnership through which major labels loosened their control over distribution was the majors' organisational structure, which was fundamentally out of sync with the fast-changing nature of digital technology. Many interviewees at INgrooves think the partnership is owed to major labels' status as behemoths. For example, Sharon Matheson, Label Manager at INgrooves, emphasises how independent labels can perform better in the fast-changing digital business environment whereas major labels' horizontal structure can be a hindrance to adapting to new changes.

> The indies are always first to move. The indies are small but flexible. That's one thing great about INgrooves: despite being a multinational company, we can change so quickly, whereas Universal isn't really able to do that. They are more of a linear company rather than horizontal. So there are so many decisions to be made all along. There's not just one guy in the top that is going to do that and then filtering all the way down. There are so many different departments, different teams, all across the world. They can't move very fast. (Sharon Matheson, Interview)

7.4.2 Partnership

Universal undertook market research to look for a potential partner, with two strategic aims in mind: a company that had a cost-efficient and scalable digital delivery system, as well as a strong foothold in the independent sector. Robb McDaniels explains:

> They (Universal) had been researching the marketplace around the world. They wanted two things. They wanted a company that had a technical platform that was 'next generation', that was cost-efficient and more scalable than their internal systems. They wanted to use a new platform to handle their digital supply chain. And then they were also looking for a company that had a presence in the independent music industry because they realised that the independent music industry was expanding and they wanted better representation with the independents. (Robb McDaniels, Interview)

Impressed by INgrooves' "unmatched technology and the value-added services" (Universal Music Group 2008) and perhaps the existing relationship built through Al Teller, the head of MCA Records, as an additional incentive, Universal chose to use INgrooves as their new distribution provider.

In 2008, Universal made a strategic investment in INgrooves, making Universal the major stakeholder in Isolation Networks Inc., the parent company of INgrooves. Through this alliance, Universal used INgrooves' distribution platform, One Digital, to deliver all of Universal's North American digital content to the major music services. This partnership took INgrooves' system to another level. It furnished INgrooves with the capital to invest in developing "the finest and the most comprehensive digital distribution platform" (Universal Music Group 2008). As the largest global recording label, Universal required a sophisticated system, as its needs were much more complicated than most other record labels. Alex Branson explains:

> That enabled us to bring in a lot more resources, we were able to develop the platform specifically for Universal, which meant that there was a lot of learning. Because Universal, being who they are, has very special types of deals that they do with retailers and lots of different types of ones. And they're often very different commercially to independent record company deals. It's more intricate: it has more price tiers, different ways

> of expressing territories or streaming, audio and video, lots of different things. For us from a technology point of view, it presented a challenge, because it was new. But they've been very happy. We delivered all on time on budget. It's by far the best platform in the world of all time. (Alex Branson, Interview)

7.4.2.1 Technical Level Playing Field

The partnership with Universal produced a tremendous synergy impact through knowledge transfer from Universal. Robb McDaniels says:

> There's been a lot of knowledge transfer from Universal. They have a lot of smart people there. Being able to work on a platform that gets them ready for [the] digital world as it obviously helps us as we get the rest of our content partners ready for the digital world. So yeah, there has been a lot of good synergies with that relationship. (Robb McDaniels, Interview)

One crucial impact of this partnership is the market validation, through which INgrooves attained the majors' authentication. Alex Branson explains:

> All of a sudden, the largest record company in the world is using our platform to deliver all their music to all their stores. That's quite a statement, quite an achievement. (Alex Branson, Interview)

Robb McDaniels thinks this change even has the potential to level the playing field. The fact that major labels and independent labels can have access to the same distribution platform is something that would not be possible in conventional settings.

> It has been a very important part of our business for the last five years. Obviously, it provided us with the validation of the marketplace to go and really sell our services to independents and to management companies. They get access to the similar platform, technologies and expertise that Universal uses. So it puts the indies on a level playing field with the majors. (Robb McDaniels, Interview)

7.4.2.2 Opens Up Niche Market for Independent Distributors

The union of the world's biggest label and an independent digital music distributor epitomises the way high street fashion can win over haute couture. An employee at INgrooves thinks this is possible due to the niche created by major labels' neglect of the ecology of the digital music environment.

> They (Universal) neglected a simple aspect of multiplication and almost ruined their business as a result – and we are all about multiplication. There are so many retailers multiplied by so many types of assets with so many intellectual property restrictions. We are absolutely scrupulous. Our business is built on being 101% compliant with intellectual property law from the get-go, and there are so many labels and artists and suppliers of content that when you multiply all the dimensions it's inherently unmanageable. That's what we do. We manage the unmanageable. (Interview, name unrevealed at his/her request)

In other words, Universal's resistance to embrace the digital novelty opened up an opportunity for INgrooves. Robb McDaniels explains that this is better understood as a process of finding a league of its own.

> Historically, they [major labels] could certainly be blamed for a variety of errors. But I'm also in a position where our company has benefited from those errors. Some major labels were resistant to embracing technology and its impact on business was one of the reasons why Universal outsourced its business to us. We benefited from that. So, labels are focused on marketing, developing artists, and promotions and less about the nuts and bolts of distribution. So I think it's one of the things that they're getting better at. But we benefited from the past, so I'm not going to speak too negative about that. (Robb McDaniels, Interview)

7.4.3 Acquisition of Fontana Distribution

In 2012, INgrooves took another step to further strengthen its partnership with Universal. It purchased Fontana Distribution, which was Universal's North American independent physical digital distribution solution.

The acquisition came when INgrooves' growth was accelerating upward. Robb McDaniels explains that INgrooves was looking for extra help to accelerate the growth.

> Our INgrooves team had really knocked the cover off the ball in 2011. And they grew by ninety per cent that year. We just needed some additional people to help manage that growth. (Greenburg (2012), sampled 15 February 2016)

This growth was partly sparked by Shamrock's investment in 2010, which required INgrooves to build a new media for e-books, and to scale it so as to incorporate physical distribution. For INgrooves, it was essential to provide a single point of centralisation for both the physical and digital distribution service, so as to enhance the relationship with the partners. Robb McDaniels affirms this position.

> It was important for us since a lot of our labels had a single point of centralisation for their digital and physical distribution, instead of digital through us, and physical through another partner. We became big and important enough that a lot of our clients wanted to be in that central place. So the best thing for us to provide the best possible service to our most important labels was to have physical distribution and marketing within the same group as digital distribution and marketing. (Robb McDaniels, Interview)

This time, INgrooves went out to market to find the best partner, and Fontana was the partner it chose. Robb McDaniels explains that it was a strategic decision that benefited both INgrooves and Universal in terms of attracting more labels.

> We purchased them from Universal. Fontana was Universal's North American independent physical and digital distribution solution. Of course, the digital distribution ran through our overall deal with Universal so it came to our platform. It was important for us as digital crossed the 50% of revenue threshold in North America. We had a very straightforward deal with Universal. For many strategic reasons, it was good for them as it was good for us. It helped us grow in the business and attract some pretty labels. (Robb McDaniels, Interview)

This begs the question, however, of what was good for Universal. The timing is a crucial clue. The acquisition coincided with a time when Universal was trying to purchase EMI. EMI had experienced a dramatic decline of business in the digital age. After a few changes of ownership, EMI put its music publishing business, including Abbey Road Studios, up for sale in 2010 in an effort to reduce its debt (Bates 2010). Universal intended to acquire EMI, but had to divest its music assets in order to get approval from the regulators including the European Commission and US Federal Trade Commission. The sell-out of the Fontana division was supposed to reduce 2% of the market share and alleviate the concerns raised by Impala and A2IM, organisations representing independent labels' interests (Christman 2012). Robb McDaniels does not deny the role that this played in the acquisition.

> I think that might have been part of it. It's also not a core of business for them and was viewed as not very strategic. (Robb McDaniels, Interview)

7.4.4 Implications

This partnership, however, has been a double-edged sword for INgrooves. All interviewees at INgrooves were unequivocal in stating that Universal maintains a very small share of the ownership at INgrooves. Robb McDaniels asserts that INgrooves' business is not influenced by Universal.

> We just had to make sure that the independent music industry knows that we're not owned or controlled by Universal. The work we do for them is very separate from what we do for everybody else. (Robb McDaniels, Interview)

INgrooves' share was reduced by Shamrock's investment, making Universal's share less than it first invested. However, this partnership could have far-reaching ramifications if it succumbs to the pitfall of letting majors regain their control over the supply chain. This is a special concern because INgrooves is not the only digital distribution aggregator in which majors have a stake in the ownership. Established in 1997, The Orchard is another major player in digital music distribution. It owns eight million independent music tracks, constituting the largest number of catalogues. In 2012, Sony Music Entertainment made a strategic investment in The Orchard and has 51% of its ownership.[3] Scott Cohen explains that the partnership with Sony was the result of a business strategy to purchase Independent Online Distribution Association ("IODA"), which was then another main digital distribution company. He also emphasises that this partnership will not affect the business of The Orchard.

> Sony had a large equity stake in IODA and when we were going to buy IODA, what we ended up doing was creating a new venture; so taking IODA which was controlled by Sony and The Orchard. Setting up a new company, this new company is called The Orchard. Now try to think how many equity stakes a company like Sony has in different companies whether they're software companies, hardware companies, movie companies, music companies, it's what Sony does. They have a piece of lots of things. And if you ask people at Sony about it, most people would not even know they exist. (Scott Cohen, Interview)

An expanded horizon of the distribution of independent music illustrated in Fig. 7.1 provides a striking feature of contemporary digital music distribution. All three main independent music distributors, INgrooves, The Orchard and Alternative Distribution Association ("ADA"), have partnered with major labels, and all three major labels, Universal, Sony and Warner, distribute their own indie labels' catalogues through their indie label distribution partners.

Kieron Faller, General Manager at CI, sharply criticises the approach other digital music distributors have taken, for he thinks it questions the very legitimacy of independent music sector.

---

[3]In 2017, Sony further merged its independent distribution unit RED into the Orchard (Christman 2017).

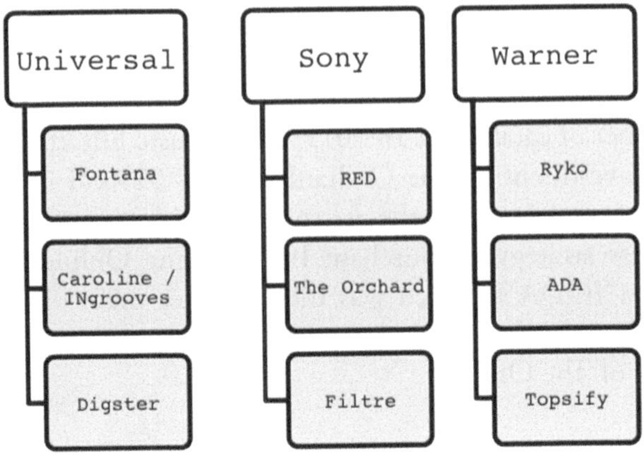

Fig. 7.1 Digital music distribution networks by ownership

> ADA, which is part of Warner Music Group, is particularly strong in the States in physical, and that's called Alternative Distribution Alliance. Alternative to what? IODA (Independent Online Distribution Alliance) did start independent, but once it was owned 51% by Sony…independent of what? (Kieron Faller, Interview)

He then warns that majors' ownership in the independent sector could have a detrimental impact on the industry by allowing majors to regain market dominance through consolidation.

> You might not think that it matters that much who manages The Orchard and to an extent, if you are an Orchard customer, maybe it doesn't matter that much to you in a direct, on a day to day way…You are helping Sony that has a greater dominance in the market…the fact that The Orchard has collected together with the small labels and then Sony came in and bought The Orchard is quite a straightforward kind of sum for that. (Kieron Faller, Interview)

Kieron Faller's remark obliges us to explore much more closely whether majors' ownership of independent labels indeed bears any relation to their market dominance. A debate on majors' ownership provides a particular lens through which we can find the links. According to the statistics released on Billboard, there is a discrepancy between the ways of calculating the market share (Christman 2013). One is to calculate it by ownership, and the other is by distribution. When the market share is counted by ownership, all large independent distribution shares by Alternative Distribution Alliance, Caroline, RED and INgrooves are absorbed into major labels' market share, marginalising independent labels' share at 12.3%. On the other hand, distribution-wise calculation shows independent labels' market share as almost tripled to 34.5%.[4] Organisations representing independent labels' interests have been outspoken about the increasingly high market share of independent labels.

> Our market share is actually higher than the major labels...32% on Spotify and close to 40% on Pandora. The RIAA claims they represent 99% of the industry, but they don't. Our members own their businesses. Sometimes they use the majors as their distributor. But actually they don't use major labels as their distributor for their digital. So that's really a lie. They don't parse it when they claim 99%. iTunes is about 40% of the business in the US. They do the direct deals with half of our members. So that's sort of distorting, isn't it? To claim that market share. (Rich Bengloff, Interview)

Why do they fight so hard for this market share? Simon Wheeler says this is interlinked with major labels' strategy of exaggerating their market share in order to maximise their album exposure on streaming music platforms.

> There are many different components in the deal which can be beneficial to the company. For getting that amount of shop window space... Universal said I have got 40% market share so I am 40% of your front pages for their artists. And Sony would say the same and Warner would say the same, and when you add up their market shares you will probably get to 150%. Because everybody exaggerates their market shares, it means

[4]According to a recent report by Worldwide Independent Network (WIN), independent market share arose to 40% but the issue of "distorted" market share driven by distribution-based calculation still continues (WIN 2017).

> that there are no space left for other people. And they're surely quite aware of those top mechanics. It could be quite tricky, and some people are very pleasantly aware and transparent and very honest and some people aren't. (Simon Wheeler, Interview)

According to a report released by an independent music organisation WIN (2017), 52% of independent labels which do not have an infrastructure for a global distribution use major labels for distribution, resulting in increased market share for major labels and hence more bargaining power to leverage. Maintaining stakes in other parts of the industry has widely been used as a way to read market trends and prepare for potential risks or changes. For major labels, it was direct vertical integration that they used to manage their control over the market. With recent changing dynamics, direct vertical integration has become difficult; thereby market control has become very complicated. Major labels are escalating their efforts to maximise their control. Besides the conventional methods—extensive spending and legal allegations—they are trying to maximise the exposure of their catalogues on digital platforms. Market share is thus crucial to increasing their odds of creating hits. A closer look at the implications of this will serve to correct the imbalanced market power, as well as cultural creativity and diversity.

7.5 Concluding Remarks

INgrooves' emergence as a digital music distributor underpins a few significant changes lurking in the music industry. First, it signifies the reintermediation of the music industry. Despite the hyperbolic account of the disintermediation enabled by digital technology, it has been proven that the prediction did not materialise for the following reasons: first, not all artists are equipped with business skills, and secondly, the abolished barrier to entry resulted in increased competition and therefore increased the need for artists to have their music heard.

The growth of INgrooves also reveals the unknown history of the digital music industry. While the majors strove hard to maintain control of the supply chain through every means possible, the grip was loosened from the inside. Universal built its own distribution system in an effort to continue its control, only to admit its failure at the brink of bankruptcy. This opened up an opportunity for INgrooves and unveiled the fact that independents' nimble approach could champion majors' monolithic take on the novelty. It represented a great leap forward for INgrooves. The irony here is that by allowing majors to extend their market power by letting them overstate the market share, independent digital music distributors could indirectly enable major labels to regain control.

References

Bates, S. 2010. Beatles for Sale: EMI Puts Abbey Road Studios on the Market [online]. *The Guardian*. Available from http://www.theguardian.com/business/2010/feb/16/abbey-road-studios-sale-emi. Accessed 16 Nov 2013.

Christman, E. 2012. INgrooves to Purchase Fontana. *Billboard*, March 2.

Christman, E. 2013. Fourth Quarter Market Share Report: Indies & Market Share [online]. *Billboard*. Available from http://www.billboard.com/biz/articles/news/5763065/fourth-quarter-market-share-report-indies-market-share. Accessed 28 Nov 2013.

Christman, E. 2017. Sony Merges RED Into The Orchard: What the Music Giant's Latest Consolidation Means for Indie Labels [online]. *Billboard*. Available from https://www.billboard.com/articles/business/7817640/sony-music-orchard-red-indie-distributors-merged. Accessed 27 Feb 2018.

Frith, S. 2002. Music and Everyday Life. *Critical Quarterly* 44 (1): 35–48.

Greenburg, Z.O. 2012. INgrooves: Proof You Can Make Money on Music, Even If You're Not Apple. *Forbes*.

Mulligan, M. 2014. Tyranny of Choice. *Music Industry Blog*.

Pham, A. 2013. Questions Answered: Robb McDaniels, Founder/CEO of INgrooves/Isolation Network [online]. *Billboard*. Available from http://www.billboard.com/biz/articles/news/1560617/questions-answered-robb-mcdaniels-founderceo-of-ingroovesisolation-network. Accessed 9 Oct 2014.

Rogers, J. 2013. *The Death and Life of the Music Industry in the Digital Age*. London: Bloomsbury.

Simon, H.A. 1971. Designing Organizations for an Information-Rich World. *Computers, Communications, and the Public Interest*, 37–72.

This Week in Music—Interview with Robb McDaniels. 2012. Interview. Music Biz 2012.
Universal Music Group. 2008. Universal Music Group Distribution (UMGD) Expands Digital Services with INgrooves Strategic Alliance [online]. Available from http://www.universalmusic.com/corporate/detail/544. Accessed 8 Oct 2014.
WIN. 2017. WINTEL 2017—Worldwide Independent Market Report.

8

Digital Revolution Tamed in the Recording Industry

This final chapter summarises the central theme and arguments of this book. It offers a discussion on the ways this book recontextualised the understanding of digital disruption in the recording industry and overcame the previous linear and simplistic accounts. In the following section, I readdress the complicated process of digital music valorisation where the protracted nature of the digital music business innovation highlights the reason why digital revolution has been tamed. Lastly, the chapter reviews major points this book explored to explode the myth surrounding digital revolution in the digital recording industry.

8.1 Recontextualising Digital Disruption in the Recording Industry

The prelude to this study was the widespread perception that digitisation and the dematerialisation of cultural content that undermined existing methods of trading music embedded in physical artefacts and opened up the possibility of distributing content over the Internet. The arrival of Napster, the first popular digital music service based on P2P

H. Sun, *Digital Revolution Tamed*, https://doi.org/10.1007/978-3-319-93022-0_8

file-sharing technology, stimulated widely circulated predictions of a seismic shift in the digital recording industry. Though there was consensus that the industry was embarking upon far-reaching changes, there was little agreement about the nature and implications of these changes; the various conflicting interests involved in music networks articulated competing visions of technology-induced change. On the one hand, many media accounts and academics produced a utopian vision of the industry. John Perry Barlow (1994, 1996) argued that the mechanism of Intellectual Property Law would no longer exist in the digital world. Nicholas Negroponte (1996) proclaimed that copyright law as a Gutenberg artefact would dissolve in the new mode of cultural production and therefore level the mass media playing field. It was believed digital technologies would serve to bring about the demise of the conventional recording industry and the end of the copyright regime (Kelly 1998; Shirky 2001; Alderman 2002; Ku 2002; Knopper 2009). For example, Alderman (2002) described the digital recording industry as "struggling to maintain control and remain relevant" and said:

> The big-record-label-dominated music business that developed in the last century is now under assault by successive waves of young techies such as Napster's Shawn Fanning and Gnutella creator Justin Frankel and their tsunami of followers. These arbiters of innovation share several traits, namely technical ingenuity and priorities that fall polar opposite to traditional business…Technology brings power, and the level of technology now in the hands of individuals will present challenges to everyone with a vested interests in the status quo. (Alderman 2002, pp. 1–2)

Their argument was that the decreased costs involved in music recording, combined with the ability to create a perfect duplication of music files at zero cost, would shorten the value chain in the recording industry by diminishing the roles of intermediaries or rendering them redundant. The dematerialisation of cultural artefacts has been heralded as the end of copyright: the possibility that artists can retain copyright over the sound recordings with higher returns and greater control over their works would undermine the control that is in the hands of a few major recording companies. New opportunities such as lowered barriers to entry, including cheaper and more powerful tools of music production and dissemination, would level the playing field (Théberge 2001; Bakker 2005). Peer production would reverse the long-lasting trend of the pre-Internet era typified by capital-intensive production and centralisation of information (Benkler 2006). Non-proprietary production would offer the opportunity to shift the conventional methods of production, distribution, and consumption of cultural products. The opportunity to gain unlimited access to music known as "Celestial Jukebox" would serve to help people discover and appreciate music otherwise was not available, and therefore would cultivate cultural creativity and diversity.

On the other hand, the notion of a terminal crisis was formulated largely by the recording industry. The technological possibility of the ease of duplication, in conjunction with large-scale distribution of free music through P2P file-sharing networks, was perceived as a great challenge to the conventional recording music business which grants exclusive rights to copy. Decrying the possible change and innovation as a threat, the recording industry created the rhetoric of "digital crisis" to describe the economic downturn of the recording industry. The primary evidence supporting this argument was a decline in physical sales, with P2P file-sharing often cited as the main cause of the decline in sales. Denouncing all kinds of P2P file-sharing as "digital piracy" or "copyright theft," the recording industry mobilised a campaign to promote the idea that "piracy kills the industry." They contended that piracy damages the fiscal soundness of the industry, making record companies unable to continue investing in the creation of music for the public. The decline of record sales, therefore, was frequently equated with harm to artists and to the detriment of the musical experience and cultural creativity. For example, the Recording Industry Association of America ("RIAA") asserted,

> While downloading one song may not feel that serious of a crime, the accumulative impact of millions of songs downloaded illegally – and without any compensation to all the people who helped to create that song and bring it to fans – is devastating. (RIAA 2007)

Both views, however, offer an essentially techno-centric vision, which focuses almost exclusively on P2P distribution and its consequences when explaining how music was traded/valorised and infers from this a radical transformation of the industry. This book presented some steps towards mapping out the actual process of change. It explored the recent history of digital music business and examined changes in real time as they unfolded. This proximity has allowed detailed insights, though recognising that this may be at the cost of analytical distance. I sought to overcome this potential shortcoming by addressing developments from a number of viewpoints in the sector, through which a set of heuristics in different settings allowed me to explore the technological developments over multiple locations (Pollock 2009; Hyysalo 2010; Williams and Pollock 2012).

The early history of the digital recording industry reveals the complex responses of the key established players: major labels. On the one hand, they reacted defensively, resisting new forms of distribution and seeking to reassert prior forms of copyright. On the other hand, they also sought to ensure that they were not displaced by new forms of digital distribution. In an effort to maintain their long-established business structure, major labels employed diverse strategies including lobbying for stronger copyright enforcement and development of DRM technologies (Burkart and McCourt 2006; Hesmondhalgh 2006; Cummings 2010; Carter and Rogers 2014). Alongside these attempts to stigmatise and criminalise P2P, the major labels also sought to develop their own digital music services. However, the subscription business model attempted delivered a limited number of streams, incomplete catalogues and restricted usage. This left a large gulf between market affordances and digital music users' demands for new digital music consumption.

However, not all players resisted the digital changes. Independent labels, which had less to lose, embraced the new opportunities. Some independent labels tried to commercialise Napster. A group of organisations representing independent labels' interests, such as IMPALA and AIM, struck a deal to use Napster's repertoire, enabling consumers to listen to diverse independent music legitimately and compensate artists at the same time. However, this project did not materialise. This was due to Napster's domestication being in the hands of a few recording companies (Spitz and Hunter 2005) and because there was a fundamental lack of supporting assemblies. Large-scale infrastructure for digital music transactions was not ready, and Internet connection and bandwidth were still an issue in many countries.

When the change happened, as often seems to have been the case in the history of the recording industry, the key breakthrough was made by a technology firm. In this case, it was Apple. As a computer manufacturing company, Apple wanted a music service to promote their portable media player, the iPod. Apple developed a media management application called iTunes and created a gateway to consume music on a legal platform. Its innovative approaches, such as a-la-carte download options and seamless integration with music playing devices at a lowered price, proved to be an alternative model for a commercially successful music business. It allowed labels to generate revenue from digital music, enabled users to consume music legitimately at a lowered price and gave more opportunities for independent musicians to distribute their music online. However, this was not the final stage in the process: whilst it addressed the recording companies' concerns, a large proportion of digital users who had been exposed to the free option remained unwilling to pay for music.

iTunes' model proved to be insufficient in undercutting piracy and left a space for experimentation with new digital business models, most of which were geared towards providing a free service. This book covered two such popular digital music services: Last.fm and YouTube. Both services offered free access to a large number of catalogues based on an advertising model, and both faced challenges of negotiating copyright licensing deals with major labels. The way they dealt with the challenges changed the fate of their development path. Last.fm closed down some of its popular features to avoid paying hefty licensing fees to the labels and its popularity began to wane. YouTube took a more compliant approach by adopting measures to enhance the legitimacy of the service, such as Content ID and reaching an agreement with major labels. YouTube continues to be a popular digital music service.

In a situation where major labels' power in maintaining control over legitimate digital music services persisted, the friction between the market response and digital music users continued. The entrenched market created around physical sales also remained unresolved. Two possibilities could have resolved this issue. One was the network effect enabled by P2P file-sharing which, in principle, could create sufficient additional value for artists so they could pursue their professional careers without having to rely on intermediaries.[1] The network effects of P2P file-sharing or the sharing economy, however, are increasingly perceived as one of the options available to artists rather than as a new channel to replace the pre-existing system (Galuszka 2012; Rogers 2013; Reia 2014). Another way is to build the commercial viability of a new technology that could achieve a critical mass (Graham et al. 1996). No business model has been able to achieve this, largely due to a lack of understanding of how to match new technical capabilities to digital music users. In the digital recording industry, it was compounded by the conflicts between major labels, who wanted to extend their market control, and consumers, who withheld their willingness to pay for music.

Spotify's solution to this market entrenchment was to offer large-scale access at low cost, which appeased both labels and consumers. By configuring changing users' requirements and realigning multiple visions and interests, Spotify's resolution is making unwavering inroads to the industry's dilemma of how to make people pay for music (IFPI 2017). The company, however, also posed a few paradoxes to make this business sustainable. Spotify's licensing deals were traded with the company's equity at a meagre amount from the labels (Jerräng 2009). Labels' ownership in Spotify raised a serious concern that this signified majors' usurpation of control in the digital music business (Teague 2012; Barr 2013). Its lack of consideration for artists' commercial gains also left Spotify embroiled in debates on inadequate remuneration for artists. Its new role as an essential route for stardom, spurred by the increasing significance of playlist in tandem with the encroachment of the commercial interest, is raising concerns of "playola" in which "[S]treaming playlists will become like radio playlists: reachable only by labels and artists with the resources to afford robust promotion" (Peoples 2015).

---

[1]Gayer and Shy (2006), Oberholzer-Gee and Strumpf (2007), Zentner (2006) discussed the way that the network effects of P2P file-sharing as a promotion and discovery tool can create sufficient additional value in the market.

A significant reconfiguration was also observed in digital music distribution networks. The arrival of iTunes spawned a new breed of intermediaries, digital music aggregators, to solve unexpected problems arising in the digital era: large-scale digital music transactions required middlemen between digital music services and independent labels. Digital music services dealt with major labels directly, but could not reach out to thousands of independent labels by themselves. Likewise, independent labels had neither sufficient funds nor knowledge to build a digital music distribution infrastructure. iTunes' platform, which allows traditional bargaining power stemming from marketing and promotion, has been criticised for having created the entry barrier needed for major labels and rebuilt the walls broken down by digital technology (Arditi 2014). As the digital transaction volume increased, major labels' distribution systems began to break down. This unexpected problem opened windows of opportunity for digital music distributors. Independent distributors' nimble approach proved to work better in the digital environment than majors' monolithic approach.

Overcoming the Dichotomy

The debates over the disintermediation of digital technology in the recording industry so far have fallen within the ambit of the dichotomy between utopian and dystopian understandings of the industry. By focusing on either the challenges or the opportunities imposed by technologies, such views often ignore the diversity and heterogeneity of the actors involved in the innovation process and the way their enrolments play out in the development of technology. In order to bridge this gap, this book centred upon moving beyond technological determinism by unpicking the social processes involved in innovation. The result is a multifaceted intertwining of choices involved in designing and developing technologies in heterogeneous networks. This book also presented the gradual improvements in technological changes that arise over time, as well as the reflexive efforts of factors involved in the development of technologies. From this, we observed that technological developments were not immediately apparent, but must be discovered in the course of making technologies work in the market.

Of central importance to overcoming the dichotomy was the users' appropriation or domestication of technologies through the process of tinkering and finding meanings of technologies. Radical technological change would both allow very different ways of meeting user needs and lead to the creation of new markets. The gulf between people's everyday use of digital technology and the supply creates uncertainties about which product will be attractive to consumers and thus be commercially viable. In this book, I showed that innovation continues in the process of an artefact being appropriated and domesticated (Fleck 1988). It highlights that the ultimate power remains with users in making choices and finally ensuring that a technology is adopted in the market. Therefore, a technology has to be encultured in a particular circumstance during the process of consumers making sense of it (Silverstone and Hirsch 1992; Lie and Sørensen 1996). The proliferation of trial and error and the struggles that digital music companies experienced in the course of matching and discovering digital music users' constantly changing demands highlight the crucial role that users play in the technological innovation of the digital recording industry. The uneven trajectory of technological development in the industry sheds light on the choices, complexities and contingencies involved in the innovation process through which technologies are appropriated, domesticated and embedded in the market.

By extending the focus on the mutual shaping of technological and societal change, combined with the contested choices, this book produced a picture that moves beyond the prevailing account of the digital recording industry, which places a single point of focus on the point of sales. By exploring the multiplicity of actors and sites of innovation, this book demonstrated that different players struggle in a constantly changing environment to develop their own commercial space amongst a constellation of players and to stabilise their space in that configuration. In contrast to the widely adopted notion that music is just a point of distribution, the empirical analysis of this study revealed the complexity of the processes involved in the development of digital technology. Although conventional mechanisms for valorising music by selling material products were obliterated by the dematerialisation of music, digitisation did not lead to a simple, e.g. technologically driven, transformation of the industry. In the process of developing digital music distribution, a whole chain of players had to be realigned in the networks of digital recording industry—licensing, distribution and valorisation. This reconfiguration of digital technology was achieved through a significant realignment of interests amongst heterogeneous players who tried to situate themselves in the legitimate digital music business practice so as to fit their needs in technological and socio-legal infrastructure. The interactions and negotiations of conflicting interests and differing commitments produced a reworking of relationships and guided diverging choices in the market where market conditions and consumers' requirements were constantly evolving. The detailed innovation processes in which digital technology was implemented and domesticated disclosed a complex and constantly evolving landscape in which the development of digital technology was far removed from the smooth uptake as envisaged by the technology deterministic visions, and was instead imbued with tension and contradictions.

8.2 Messy Process of Digital Music Valorisation

The technical availability of trading cultural contents without conventional middlemen cultivated the widespread idea that the conventional business models revolving around the distribution and sale of physical artefacts would be overthrown (Kelly 1998; Shirky 2001; Alderman 2002; Ku 2002; Knopper 2009). The complexity of goals and interests and the various exigencies involved in the process of innovation, however, render the trajectory of technological developments uneven. In examining digital disruption in the recording industry, this book observed that a significant technological innovation was manifested in the process of building a commercially viable business model. Through empirical analysis of the evolution of digital music business models, this book suggests a new framework to understand the business model.

Strategic conceptions of business model design arising from the Business School presume that it is possible to develop business models for new services through a one-off rational calculative act. Presupposing that other players' behaviours can be anticipated adequately and that it is straightforward to bring the other players into alignment with the plans, this approach conceptualises the way business models emerge through a calculative process. Their chief concern has been to identify archetypal characteristics that constitute a template of the way a firm operates and creates value for the parties involved (Zott and Amit 2010). Other attempts ensued to conceptualise business model "ideal types" that can be formulated as a typology (Baden-Fuller and Morgan 2010; Baden-Fuller and Haefliger 2013), subsequently making successful models institutionalised (Mikhalkina and Cabantous 2015).

At the heart of the discrepancy between the promise of digital revolution and the actual process of how its potential has become tamed in the recording industry, there was a messy account of digital music valorisation process in which business models were shaped over time by aligning multiple forms of interests and visions through trial and error. The empirical analysis observed the difficulty of technological change, in which companies reconfigure their business model through the learning process informed by feedback from the consumers who slowly find meanings in technologies. Over the course of this iterative process of "learning by interacting" (Sørensen 1996), where the linkages between users and suppliers are achieved, business models mutated into something different from the initial design. From this observation, this book illustrated the multiplicity of actors and sites of innovation in order to depict the constellation of players involved in the innovation process. In doing so, I placed business models within a broader context and observed the actual process of innovation across all of the networks of business: production, distribution, valorisation and consumption. The dispersed and highly complicated networks of the music business across a wide range of players, sites and phases highlight a configurational process of business model shaping that is not conducted by a single player, but instead emerges through an interaction amongst heterogeneous players with different interests and diverging motivations and negotiation power. The evolutionary view of business models has therefore produced a more effective understanding of the digital recording industry than deterministic accounts of the technology-driven view of industrial restructuring or instrumental visions of strategically planned technological change. Based on this empirical analysis, this book proposes the concept of an emergent process of business model shaping in which business strategies emerge en route in the process of technologies being appropriated and domesticated in the market.[2]

The two successful business innovation case studies have exemplified how the emergent process of business model shaping operated in the digital recording industry. Quite contrary to the claim that business models calculated in advance can lead to successful innovation, the detailed empirical analysis of in-depth case studies demonstrate that business models are rarely fully formed from the outset, instead being configured over time in relation to complex heterogeneous networks and evolving user requirements. The proliferation of trial and error carried out in the digital recording market, in particular, underpins the unpredictability of outcomes and the complexity of interactions around the development and use of the technology. INgrooves' case demonstrated the significance of the intermediate use of technologies in order to make the business model relevant and meaningful to an array of players involved in the business. Spotify's case encapsulated the crucial role that users play in deciding which business models can succeed in the market. No matter how well a business model is designed, and the final decision about its success remains with users, who have the ultimate veto power. However, information about potential users can hardly be complete. It is particularly challenging to gauge actual users in the case of radical technologies, which do not have previous data to rely upon. The significance of measuring users' needs has become heightened as digital technology has endowed users with the power to withhold their willingness to pay. The illustration of the evolution of music discovery features on Spotify—from simple search to digital music curation—signified the choices users can bring to bear in the process of refining

[2]This is first suggested and guided by Prof. Robin Williams. This concept is further developed in understanding Chinese digital music market (CREATe 2017).

business strategies. The intertwining innofusion and domestication process in the implementation and use of the business captured the iterative nature of business model shaping in the process of understanding users' appropriation of new technologies (Fleck 1988; Williams et al. 2005).[3]

8.2.1 Case Summary 1—Spotify

Since the advent of Napster, a diverse array of trials and experimentation has taken place in the market to valorise music on the digital music networks. A period of uncertainty ensued with no clear way forwards. A series of moves took place such as iTunes, Last.fm and YouTube, leaving the piracy issue unresolved. Spotify arose in 2006 in the midst of piracy's golden era. The business began with a vision to provide a solution better than P2P file-sharing. The key attraction of P2P file-sharing lay in its ease of use and free and unlimited access to music, with the major weakness of illegality. Spotify's solution was an easier-to-use service with a lowered fixed price to legal access to a worldwide catalogue. This freemium-based streaming music business model, what Halmenschlager and Waelbroeck (2014) called "fighting free with free," targeting a different segment of users who had more willingness to pay, proved to be sufficiently attractive to consumers to be commercially viable. However, the key success factor lay less with the solution per se than with the process of making this model work in a constantly changing environment. Far from straightforward, the process of business development was imbued with contingency, uncertainty and challenges.

The major challenge for Spotify's model was attaining licensing deals with major labels. For major labels, Spotify's model, with a freemium-based lowered monthly fee for large-scale access, was a bitter pill to swallow. For a new innovation opportunity to arise in a harsh

[3]The study did not conduct a direct observation of users in understanding their contribution to the technological development in the digital recording industry. Instead, the role and importance of users were observed indirectly through a detailed fieldwork with key intermediaries in the digital music valorisation process, which involved an extraordinary attention to users.

market conditions, niche, or a protected space, can serve as "incubation rooms" for a radical novelty to break through (Kemp 1994; Kemp et al. 1998; Geels 2002). The protected space for Spotify is not found in the usual suspects. Sweden's failed copyright enforcement policy brought the country the notoriety of being a haven for piracy and home to two major pirate organisations: the Pirate Bay and the Pirate Party. Hence, it was felt that there was nothing to lose in offering new experimentation. The music business spiralled downward and Per Sundin, Chairman and CEO of Universal Music in Sweden, laid off 200 employees. Sundin's mother who was watching an election debate for endorsing piracy in 2006 phoned him to tell him to get a new job (Lynskey 2013). Spotify's technical superiority and the willingness to license, which was a rare combination back then, persuaded Sundin to convince his bosses to support the service. All major labels, along with Merlin, an independent music licensing agency, had 18% of shares in Spotify when it was incorporated (Jerräng 2009). After trying Spotify's demo, Per Sundin said to his team,

> This is Jesus coming to town! If this fucks up, we're going to be dead. So let's go all in. (Lynskey (2013), sampled 15 February 2016)

One significant ingredient to Spotify's successful innovation is its efforts to make this technology relevant and attractive to digital music users. Sung-Kyu Choi, Global Head of Content Operation at Spotify, explains Spotify's efforts to find and match what the users wanted.

> We filled the gap for the consumers. They've been shouting about it. In Sweden, for instance, everyone said I download it illegally, but I want it to be legal, but I don't have any good alternative. (Sung-Kyu Choi, Interview)

Spotify also continuously refined technology by learning consumers' requirements. The latency, a delay in playback, was the largest bottleneck to attaining popularity for streaming services before Spotify. Daniel Ek's previous experience of running μTorrent, one of the largest Torrent trackers for BitTorrent, served a crucial role in solving this problem. Knowing that the P2P network is very efficient for fast and seamless searching and downloading, Spotify integrated a P2P network in pre-fetching data and thus resolved this issue. In order to make Spotify's freemium service work in the market, Spotify had to convert people to premium. The premium service features evolved based on information from Spotify users, who slowly figured out what worked best for them. Spotify's premium service began as an advertising-free service. Later, attuning to the increasing uptake of smartphones, Spotify developed its "offline mode" feature, which allowed users to listen to their saved playlist without Internet connection. It dramatically reduced the friction in downloading and transferring files to mobile devices. Realising that "offline mode" was the most important vantage point for converting people to its premium service, Spotify made this feature available exclusively to premium service users. A Spotify employee explains the background:

> We have a very good free offering that is fantastic which is also now works on mobile. Users find out that they love music and they love Spotify and they decided that they want to be able to listen on demand anywhere, they want offline music and they want to get rid of the ads. And that effectively converts them to be paid users instead of being free users. So we have a tremendous belief in our model, how it works. (Interview, name unrevealed at his/her request)

Contrary to the widely believed idea that digital music has to be free, although important, free music was not all that mattered to digital music users. The offline feature gained Spotify a 20% conversion rate in 2008, making the service the first successful freemium-based digital music business model. By proving that the model would work in the market, Spotify began to expand and established a business model of access replacing the previous ownership. Through an iterative process of "learning by interacting" (Sørensen 1996), Spotify now offers 30 days' free premium service in an effort to attain more premium service subscribers.

The changing strategies involved in digital music discovery underpin the emergent process of refining a business model in the light of constantly evolving market conditions and user requirements. As the number of subscribers increased, Spotify learned that their user requirements diverged from the initial prediction about users. Spotify's beta version was modelled after a P2P file-sharing website. Presuming that digital music users would know what they wanted, Spotify provided a basic keyword search on its service. Soon after Spotify's official launch, its user base grew meteorically. This expanded user base and exponential growth in its music library prompted Spotify to pursue technological advances in music discovery. It offered algorithm-based personalised recommendations based on the previous tracks to which a consumer had listened and what other people with similar tastes had been streaming. As the streaming market crossed further into mainstream adoption, Spotify realised that the majority of users, in fact, wanted their music choices to be presented to them.[4] The company therefore began providing its own curated playlist. A Spotify employee explains this change:

> When Spotify started out, what it had was really a search box where you could input your search query and you could find any music in the whole world…That became a huge success especially in Sweden where people were very used to Pirate Bay, where people were used to having music in the computer and searching for it…As the market is growing and more mainstream users, if that's what you call [them] are coming into streaming, into Spotify and they don't have the same drive to search music. They want it to be presented to them, with less friction and at least that's one hypothesis that we have. So then we felt that we needed to create, we have to reduce friction while still increasing the quality of music recommendations that you get. (Interview, name unrevealed at his/her request)

Spotify's playlist is increasingly becoming an important destination for digital music discovery. An unexpected outcome of this is Spotify's new role as a tastemaker. Empowered with massive user base and top-notch data analytics, Spotify is also veering towards a hitmaker. Lorde, a 16-year-old New Zealand singer-songwriter, is one of those who rose to

[4]In fact, "Hit-heavy, skinny-tail" distribution has also been observed on P2P file-sharing networks (Page and Garland 2009).

stardom overnight through Spotify. Will Page, Director of Economics at Spotify, explains how Sean Parker's[5] playlist on Spotify brought her this instant stardom.

> Here's the streams from Spotify from 19th of March to 16th of April... What happens on the 2nd of April? So this is not a radio plugger or PDs, promotion department, this is just drinking a coffee, like that song, put it on my playlist and he [Sean Parker] has 850,000 followers to that playlist. Pretty mad, huh? So much so that by the second week, she got to number two in the US viral chart. Crazy, for a 16-year-old-girl in New Zealand. (Will Page, Interview)

As Spotify is increasingly positioned to exercise influence over consumers' choices and become an essential route to stardom, concerns have been fuelled that it is bringing back the industry's old practice of market manipulation and contributing to the resurgence of the market control of the majors (Sun, forthcoming; Peoples 2015).

8.2.2 Case Summary 2—INgrooves

INgrooves is a digital music distributor providing custom services for artists and independent record labels. The company was set up by Robb McDaniel with a vision of commercialising European dance electronic music for TV commercials and video games in the USA. The company began acquiring rights as "synchronisation" for popular catalogues and helped rights owners to exploit their contents.

With the arrival of iTunes, the business moved in a different direction. iTunes sparked large-scale legitimate digital music business transactions, and independent labels needed help with getting their content onto this new digital music consumption avenue. All the information on the catalogues INgrooves held for other types of digital transaction became essential assets in extending the business into digital music

[5] Co-founder of Napster. He negotiated licensing deals with Warner and Universal on behalf of Spotify for its launch in the USA and now serves as a board member for Spotify.

downloads. This change in business reveals the way that unexpected issues arose in the digital era. As the control of distribution has always been essential for controlling the market, major labels built a direct distribution system with iTunes. Unlike major labels, however, independent labels could not afford to build direct distribution channels with digital music service providers. Although many tools were developed in the digital age, which lowered the hurdles to reproducing, distributing and promoting digital music, converting files from physical formats into digital formats was still a considerable obstacle to overcome for most independent labels. Alex Branson, SVP at INgrooves International, shares an anecdote:

> Essentially the problem was there were these record companies. And then technology companies came along, and said to the record companies, 'Okay, this is great. We like your music. Can you send that to me in a particular file format, and can you send me the data in XML?' And guys in the record companies were like 'XM what? Can I send you a Word document? Is that the same thing? Can I send you a CD?' There was a long period of time when people were literally doing this. Here's a box of CDs, and if you're lucky you've got a spreadsheet with data typed out. (Alex Branson, Interview)

This brought about the emergence of digital music aggregators. The demands for this new breed of intermediaries are fourfold: (1) whereas major labels had the capital to build the digital music distribution infrastructure, independent labels did not have either the funds or the negotiation power to build a direct distribution channel with digital music service providers; (2) quite contrary to the belief that digital transaction is easily carried out, commercial transaction of digital contents entails professional skills and tasks involved in digital distribution, such as converting the information contained in physical products into digital, digital rights management and settling payment was a novelty and thereby required special expertise; (3) it was almost impossible for digital music service providers to handle thousands of independent labels in the market, and they could not just ignore the independent labels in order to cater to the digital music users already exposed to the unlimited access to music enabled by Napster; and (4) the abundance of content brought about by the abolished barrier to entry required music service providers to control the quality of their contents to ensure better consumer experiences.

In terms of the growth of the company, Robb McDaniel's entrepreneurship played a crucial role. As the demand for digital conversion increased, INgrooves sought to scale the platform. The problem was solved fortuitously. An insurance agent for Robb McDaniel happened to be a former HR Director at Napster. He put him in touch with David Kent, a former director of new technology at Napster. David Kent, now CTO at INgrooves, was the primary architect of the enterprise software application, which was essential for INgrooves' growth. Robb McDaniel raised venture capital to expand the business. His contact with Al Teller, head of MCA Records (which later became part of Universal), played an important role in taking the company to the next level.

As the digital music business grew, the main business shifted from a simple aggregator to a distributor whose business line included features such as marketing and promotion. The change in this direction underlines an important change that emerged in digital music consumption. As streaming services enabled unlimited access to music on a legal platform, the abundance yielded a "Tyranny of Choice" (Mulligan 2014a) in which the majority of consumers could not decide between the 300 million tracks available in the world. This is what Herbert Simon (1971) called an "attention economy."

> When we speak of an information-rich world, we may expect, analogically, that the wealth of information means a dearth of something else – a scarcity of whatever it is that information consumes. What information consumes is rather obvious: it consumes the attention of its recipients. Hence a wealth of information creates a poverty of attention, and a need to allocate that attention efficiently among the overabundance of information sources that might consume it. (Simon 1971, pp. 40–41)

Such changes presented a new role for INgrooves as a middleman between independent labels and digital music service providers.

Out of 600 new albums released weekly, INgrooves' marketing team chooses 10 albums to highlight for digital music service providers, bringing back the industry's old strategy of filtering. Dominic Jones, International Sales and Marketing Director at INgrooves, explains:

> In the physical world we have CDs and vinyl. The biggest hurdle to overcome is getting record shops to want to stock them in the first place… because you actually have to sell them physical things and you have to ship them from our warehouse to their warehouse and to their shop and convince them that people are going to be walking through the door to buy them.
>
> In the digital world I think it is very different because you are shipping them a master file and, with a few exceptions, most of the large retailers will take everything that you want to deliver to them. The hurdle with digital is getting the most profile for your release, making sure it is on the homepage or genre page or on a newsletter. If you look at iTunes, you only have so much space. But then they have scrolling sections. Well…you could scroll forever if you wanted to or if they wanted to scroll everything to accommodate all the new releases and bestsellers. Having one of the banners on iTunes gives you all the advantages over those that don't have them…We have to convince those retailers that our releases should be higher profile and bigger priorities than those of all our competitors. (Dominic Jones, Interview)

Another unexpected problem took INgrooves' business to a new level. Through a vertically integrated system, major labels have long maintained tight control over distribution of music products in the market. Universal built their own distribution system for digital transactions, which they could afford to do in the beginning. As digital music transactions increased, Universal realised their outmoded system was failing to address their needs efficiently. Despite the common belief that large companies would be able to afford the world's best engineers and the best systems available, this was not the case with digital music distribution. This is attributed to the fact that the organisational structure became fundamentally out of sync with the fast-changing nature of digital technology. An industry entrepreneur encapsulates this:

> If we think about the troubles majors experienced in building distribution system [it] makes it daunting [that] this once-used-to-be-a-very-small-company could. While we believe big companies would be able to afford the world's best engineers and the best system available, this is not the case with digital music distribution. (Interview, name unrevealed at his/her request)

Universal built a partnership with INgrooves to use INgrooves' distribution system. The fact that the largest record label chose to use INgrooves' system acted as a market validation. Although independent labels and major labels were on a level playing field in technical terms, subsequent business development raises a question about this. By acquiring Fontana, Universal's North American independent physical digital distribution division, INgrooves helped Universal to finalise its ambition of purchasing EMI. By reducing the Big Four (major labels) to a Big Three, this acquisition led to market consolidation. The "attention economy" intensified the competition for exposure. By allowing major labels to overstate their market share (Christman 2013) and therefore increase the exposure of major catalogues on digital music services, the partnership between independent digital music distributors and major labels is leading to an unexpected consequence of indirectly contributing to the resurgence of market control.

8.3 Demystifying the Hype of Digital Revolution in the Recording Industry

Technological innovation in the recording industry entails a complex interplay amongst a diverse array of factors such as digital technology, copyright regulation and the more or less conflicting interests between heterogeneous players such as major labels, other intermediaries, music consumers and artists. Radical technological innovation is subject to conflicts and struggles, and therefore typically deviates from the envisioned technological trajectory.

Only through an analysis of the whole network can we fully understand the intricate interplay between innovation actors and their interaction in the economic, cultural, legal and institutional context (Russell 1986). SST and SLTI provide a generic account of the processes by which technologies are shaped in particular historically structured contexts and configurations of actors. To emphasise the heterogeneity and loose coupling of players involved in the development of digital technologies, SLTI employs the term "socio-technical constellations" (Williams et al. 2005). This metaphor describes not only the closely organised array of players but also the loosely connected linkages amongst players, especially with some groups who remain on the fringe. However, it does not provide specific accounts of the changing landscape of the digital music economy. Here I turned to the substantive literature in this domain and in particular Leyshon's (2001) networks of music economy. Developed upon Attali's (1985) political and economic music value framework, Leyshon's (2001) value networks explore the allocation of the different functions of the industry in four musical networks. His networks of musical economy depict the constellations of four major networks in the music industry. This framework is particularly valuable for capturing the complex relationship amongst heterogeneous forces and the blurred interaction amongst the four networks—creativity, distribution, distribution/promotion and consumption.

In demystifying the hype of the digital revolution in the recording industry, this book demonstrated a vital role played by intermediaries, particularly in developing the whole system of viable commercialisation of music. Multimedia developments typically call for collaboration amongst heterogeneous constellations of players with diverging power, interests and commitments, and therefore often carry uncertainties and difficulties in development, implementation and use of technologies (Williams 2000). The most pronounced uncertainties relate to future users whose needs constantly change in emerging contexts; therefore, active intermediation is often involved in order to mitigate the gap between supplier and use. There has been a deep uncertainty about how to build a commercially viable service that will be attractive to digital music users and how much or even whether they will be willing to pay. In the digital recording industry, this process involves a negotiation amongst a diverse array of players in a legal and socio-technical context. Spotify's crucial role as an intermediary in this aspect is what Nicoll (2000) described as the ability to build an internal socio-technical constituency by mobilising the necessary resources and configuring users' demands in a naturalistic environment. In bringing the streaming service to mainstream adoption, Spotify played a key role in domestication by making the technology relevant and attractive to digital music consumers, and bringing P2P users onto the legal music consuming platform.

The increasing complexity of technology requires combining many different kinds of knowledge, specialities and multi-level sets of skills. The production of this combination is highly dependent on the infrastructure of knowledge, skills and proficiency or meso-level characteristics (Sørensen and Levold 1992). In building inter-organisational systems, theoretical knowledge alone is not enough. Practical, often tacit, knowledge embodied in living persons is vital to innovation. INgrooves, as a system-building intermediary, played a crucial role in building the inter-organisational system and making digital music transaction work. The INgrooves case also illustrated that the nature of the tacit knowledge circulates better in a certain hierarchical setting: despite the majors' capital and resources, the independents' approach fits better with the digital distribution system and could not be transferred to the major labels.

In assessing the digital revolution in the recording industry, most existing studies focus on a single locus, drawing attention to major labels' influence on either innovation or innovative approaches by independent labels or artists. Its linear approach has fallen short of providing a comprehensive account of the technological change. To overcome this shortcoming, this book looked at multiple loci—record labels, aggregators, service providers, artists and users, and presented their respective roles and contributions to technological development and innovation practices. By attending the interaction and intermingling of the diverse actors across the entire networks of the digital recording industry, this book identified the chains of interplay amongst these diverse players, and hence produced an interweaving dynamics in the heterogeneous digital music networks, and hence moved beyond a simplistic and linear understanding of the digital recording industry.

The account drawn from the socio-technical constellations of the digital recording industry proved to be far removed from the prediction of an imminent and radical transformation of the industry and highlights flaws of focus on dematerialisation of commodity. A comprehensive analysis of the interaction and intermingling of the diverse actors across the entire network of the digital recording industry produced a new landscape, which moves beyond the simplistic and linear understanding of the industry. The complexity of choices, uncertainties and contingencies involved in the innovation highlights the complex and often contested processes in which technologies are actually adopted, employed and embedded in society.

8.4 Discussion

This book was instigated by the interesting shift the recording industry was beginning to witness. Prompted by Spotify's streaming music service, it had begun to recover from the economic downturn persisting since Napster. The research set out to provide a better understanding of the changes at this critical time in the contemporary digital recording industry in which digital music users were becoming more attracted to legal and paid services than to free, often illegal options. While the increasing revenue generated from a digital platform could potentially signal the economic recovery of the recording industry, it was clear to me what was unfolding in the digital music industry was estranged from the radical transformation of the digital recording industry initially predicted.

In understanding the changes in the digital recording industry, much current scholarship has pursued a narrow focus, in part through disciplinary framings either upon the law or technology's impact on the market. This has often produced a simplified account of change that does not do justice to the complexity and multidimensionality of these developments. To move beyond these linear accounts of technological change, this book widened the perspectives that include the diversity and complexities of socio-technical factors influencing technological innovation (Williams and Edge 1996). An analysis of the whole network is required to fully understand the intricate interplay between innovation actors and their interaction in the economic, cultural, legal and institutional context (Russell 1986). To that end, I developed a framework of the socio-technical constellation of the digital recording industry, which allowed us to examine the circuit of the innovation process in which heterogeneous players struggled to stabilise their location in relation to a changing environment. In understanding the constellation of the digital recording industry, the study identified four major factors: digital technology, copyright law, users and business models. In this framework, law and users were not directly addressed in this research, except insofar as they were addressed by the interview respondents. Here I summarise the respective role of these factors.

8.4.1 Digital Technology

This book offers a more complicated view of digital technology, which did not follow the deterministic view that the dematerialisation of cultural contents would lead to radical transformation of the industry. The complexity of goals and interests and the various exigencies involved in the process of innovation rendered the trajectory of technological developments uneven. Multiple forms of interests and visions were aligned through trial and error along the way in order to find ways to valorise digitalised music. The iterative process of "learning by doing" (Arrow 1962) underpins the linkage between users and suppliers that had to be discovered in the course of making technologies work in the market.

8.4.2 Copyright

Quite contrary to the prediction that the disintermediated market will allow artists to retain their legal rights for their own sound recordings and overturn the control in the hands of major labels built through access to copyright law, copyright law continued to exert strong influence in the shaping of digital recording industry. In the form of copyright licensing deals, copyright enabled major labels to retain their market control by mobilising the negotiating power. This is not to say that copyright was a single factor which steered the market. It was reflexive of the heterogeneous factors, including the market conditions and users' constantly changing demands. To demonstrate the multifaceted role of copyright law that is subject to negotiation amongst players with divergent motivations, interests and power, the study drew upon Sørensen's (1996) concept of "learning by regulating."

8.4.3 Users

Although the elusive nature of the audiences' fickle taste has always meant that some level of control continues to reside with users in the music business, the business structure built around physical artefacts has given a considerable power to recording companies to control the price and music choices. Digital technology lifted this control and empowered digital music users to be able to enjoy music for free and to wield great influence in the shaping of digital music services. Digital music users did not merely follow the technological functionalities or legal enforcements. In the process of adoption, consumption and use of technology, users' responses were a direct influence on the shaping of digital music services. The protracted process of bridging the gulf between users' requirements and supply highlighted the instrumental role of users attached to valorisation dimension of the digital music services. Distinct from the widely circulated assertion that "nothing can compete 'free'", free, albeit important, was not all that mattered. Though the research design only allowed me to observe users indirectly through the various intermediaries who have a direct access to consumers, the study observed that digital music users' requirements are more complex and constantly changing, manifested in changing strategies of the innovation.

8.4.4 Business Model

The development of new business models in the digital music sector was far removed from current conceptions within Strategic Management writings in Business Schools, which presume that a one-off calculative act suffices to develop and replicate a successful business model. Instead, this book identified a protracted process of trials and errors learning within and between a number of new digital music start-ups. Over the course of the iterative process of finding ways to valorise music on the digital music networks, business models were reconfigured in response to diverse factors such as users' selective decisions to purchase and appropriate technology, and licensing deals with major labels. Through two detailed case studies of players who had managed to develop and sustain successful business models, the study presented how business models emerge in a dispersed and complicated network and that process technologies are encultured in the market (Silverstone and Hirsch 1992; Lie and Sørensen 1996).

In summary, the multiplicity of actors and innovation sites and the intricate interaction amongst the constellation of players in heterogeneous networks provide a much more complicated picture of the industry than the simplistic understanding induced by technology-driven visions. In the broadened framework, which considers a wider range of innovation processes and a wider array of players, this book depicted the comprehensive innovation process subject to power struggles unfolding in the legal, societal, technological and organisational settings. This complicated account of the industry helped me overcome the bias I myself had when embarking on the research. Reading this book has hopefully contributed to developing a more sophisticated and nuanced understanding of technological change.

References

Alderman, J. 2002. *Sonic Boom: Napster, MP3, and the New Pioneers of Music*. London: Four Estate.

Arditi, D. 2014. iTunes: Breaking Barriers and Building Walls. *Popular Music and Society* 37 (4): 408–424.

Arrow, K.J. 1962. The Economic Implications of Learning by Doing. *The Review of Economic Studies* 29 (3): 155–173.

Attali, J. 1985. *Noise: The Political Economy of Music*. Manchester: Manchester University Press.

Baden-Fuller, C., and S. Haefliger. 2013. Business Models and Technological Innovation. *Long Range Planning* 46 (6): 419–426.
Baden-Fuller, C., and M.S. Morgan. 2010. Business Models as Models. *Long Range Planning* 43 (2–3): 156–171.
Bakker, P. 2005. File-Sharing—Fight, Ignore or Compete: Paid Download Services vs. P2P-Networks. *Telematics and Informatics* 22 (1–2): 41–55.
Barlow, J.P. 1994. The Economy of Ideas [online]. *Wired.* Available from https://www.wired.com/1994/03/economy-ideas/. Accessed 31 May 2017.
Barlow, J.P. 1996. A Declaration of the Independence of Cyberspace [online]. *Electronic Frontier Foundation.* Available from https://projects.eff.org/~barlow/Declaration-Final.html. Accessed 19 Sept 2015.
Barr, K. 2013. Theorizing Music Streaming: Preliminary Investigations. *Scottish Music Review* 3 (2). Available from http://www.scottishmusicreview.org/index.php/SMR/article/view/40
Benkler, Y. 2006. *The Wealth of Networks: How Social Production Transforms Markets and Freedom*. New Haven, CT: Yale University Press.
Burkart, P., and T. McCourt. 2006. *Digital Music Wars: Ownership and Control of the Celestial Jukebox*. Lanham, MD: Rowman & Littlefield.
Carter, D., and I. Rogers. 2014. Fifteen Years of 'Utopia': Napster and Pitchfork as Technologies of Democratization. *First Monday* 19 (10). http://firstmonday.org/ojs/index.php/fm/article/view/5543/4122 or http://dx.doi.org/10.5210/fm.v19i10.5543.
Christman, E. 2013. Fourth Quarter Market Share Report: Indies & Market Share [online]. *Billboard.* Available from http://www.billboard.com/biz/articles/news/5763065/fourth-quarter-market-share-report-indies-market-share. Accessed 28 Nov 2013.
CREATe. 2017. CREATe Copyright and Innovation Network Launch Workshop. London, May 26.
Cummings, A.S. 2010. From Monopoly to Intellectual Property: Music Piracy and the Remaking of American Copyright, 1909–1971. *The Journal of American History* 97 (3): 659–681.
Fleck, J. 1988. *Innofusion or Diffusation? The Nature of Technological Development in Robotics*. Edinburgh: Research Centre for Social Sciences, University of Edinburgh.
Galuszka, P. 2012. Netlabels and Democratization of the Recording Industry. *First Monday* 17 (7). Available from https://journals.uic.edu/ojs/index.php/fm/article/view/3770/3278 or https://doi.org/10.5210/fm.v17i7.3770.
Gayer, A., and O. Shy. 2006. Publishers, Artists, and Copyright Enforcement. *Information Economics and Policy* 18 (4): 374–384.

Geels, F.W. 2002. Technological Transitions as Evolutionary Reconfiguration Processes: A Multi-level Perspective and a Case-Study. *Research Policy* 31: 1257–1274.

Graham, I., G. Spinardi, and R. Williams. 1996. Diversity in the Emergence of Electronic Commerce. *Journal of Information Technology* 11 (2): 161.

Halmenschlager, C., and P. Waelbroeck. 2014. Fighting Free with Free: Freemium vs. Piracy. Available from SSRN https://ssrn.com/abstract=2475641or http://dx.doi.org/10.2139/ssrn.2475641.

Hesmondhalgh, D. 2006. Digitalisation, Copyright and the Music Industries. In *Unpacking Digital Dynamics: Participation, Control and Exclusion*, ed. P. Golding and G. Murdock. New York: Hampton Press.

Hyysalo, S. 2010. *Health Technology Development and Use from Practice-Bound Imagination to Evolving Impacts*. New York, NY: Routledge.

IFPI. 2017. IFPI Global Music Report 2017: Annual State of the Industry. Available from http://www.ifpi.org/news/IFPI-GLOBAL-MUSIC-REPORT-2017.

Jerräng, M. 2009. Documents Reveal Major Labels Own Part of Spotify [online]. *Computer Sweden*. Available from http://computersweden.idg.se/2.2683/1.240046/documents-reveal-major-labels-own-part-of-spotify. Accessed 28 Feb 2016.

Kelly, K. 1998. *New Rules for the New Economy: 10 Ways the Network Economy Is Changing Everything*. London: Fourth Estate.

Kemp, R. 1994. Technology and the Transition to Environmental Sustainability: The Problem of Technological Regime Shifts. *Futures* 26 (10): 1023–1046.

Kemp, R., J. Schot, and R. Hoogma. 1998. Regime Shifts to Sustainability Through Processes of Niche Formation: The Approach of Strategic Niche Management. *Technology Analysis & Strategic Management* 10 (2): 175–198.

Knopper, S. 2009. *Appetite for Self-Destruction: The Spectacular Crash of the Record Industry in the Digital Age*. New York: Free Press.

Ku, R.S.R. 2002. The Creative Destruction of Copyright: Napster and the New Economics of Digital Technology. *The University of Chicago Law Review* 69 (1): 263–324.

Leyshon, A. 2001. Time-Space (and Digital) Compression: Software Formats, Musical Networks, and the Reorganisation of the Music Industry. *Environment & Planning A* 33 (1): 49.

Lie, M., and K.H. Sørensen. 1996. *Making Technology Our Own?: Domesticating Technology into Everyday Life*. Oslo: Scandinavian University Press.

Lynskey, D. 2013. Is Daniel Ek, Spotify Founder, Going to Save the Music Industry … or Destroy It? [online]. *The Observer*. Available from http://www.theguardian.com/technology/2013/nov/10/daniel-ek-spotify-streaming-music. Accessed 27 Jan 2016.

Mikhalkina, T., and L. Cabantous. 2015. Business Model Innovation: How Iconic Business Model Emerges. *Academy of Management Proceedings* 1: 12761.

Mulligan, M. 2014a. Tyranny of Choice. *Music Industry Blog*.

Negroponte, N. 1996. *Being Digital*. New York: Vintage Books.

Nicoll, D.W. 2000. Users as Currency: Technology and Marketing Trials as Naturalistic Environments. *The Information Society* 16 (4): 303–310.

Oberholzer-Gee, F., and K. Strumpf. 2007. The Effect of File Sharing on Record Sales: An Empirical Analysis. *Journal of Political Economy* 115 (1): 1–42.

Page, W., and E. Gradland. 2009. *The Long Tail of P2P*, no. 14. PRS for Music.

Peoples, G. 2015. 'Playola' Infiltrates Streaming Services: Pay for Play 'Definitely Happening' [online]. *Billboard*. Available from http://www.billboard.com/articles/business/6670475/playola-promotion-streaming-services. Accessed 28 Jan 2016.

Pollock, N. 2009. *Software and Organisations: The Biography of the Enterprise-Wide System or How SAP Conquered the World*. London: Routledge.

Reia, J. 2014. Napster and Beyond: How Online Music Can Transform the Dynamics of Musical Production and Consumption in DIY Subcultures. *First Monday* 19 (10). http://firstmonday.org/ojs/index.php/fm/article/view/5552/4131 or http://dx.doi.org/10.5210/fm.v19i10.5552. Accessed 6 Oct 2014.

RIAA. 2007. Who Music Theft Hurts [online]. http://www.riaa.com. Available from http://www.riaa.com//physicalpiracy.php?content_selector=piracy_details_online. Accessed 22 Oct 2015.

Rogers, J. 2013. *The Death and Life of the Music Industry in the Digital Age*. London: Bloomsbury.

Russell, S. 1986. The Social Construction of Artefacts: A Response to Pinch and Bijker. *Social Studies of Science* 16 (2): 331–346.

Shirky, C. 2001. Where Napster Is Taking the Publishing World. *Harvard Business Review* 79 (2): 143–148.

Silverstone, R., and E. Hirsch. 1992. *Consuming Technologies: Media and Information in Domestic Spaces*. London: Routledge.

Simon, H.A. 1971. Designing Organizations for an Information-Rich World. *Computers, Communications, and the Public Interest*, 37–72.

Sørensen, K.H. 1996. *Learning Technology, Constructing Culture: Socio-Technical Change as Social Learning*. Trondheim: University of Trondheim, Centre for Technology and Society, No. 18/96.

Sørensen, K.H., and N. Levold. 1992. Tacit Networks, Heterogeneous Engineers, and Embodied Technology. *Science, Technology & Human Values* 17 (1): 13–35.

Spitz, D., and S. Hunter. 2005. Contested Codes: The Social Construction of Napster. *Information Society* 21 (3): 169–180.

Sun, H. Forthcoming. *Creative Industries Journal (Under Review)*. Resurgence of Market Control.

Teague, E.J. 2012. Saving the Spotify Revolution: Recalibrating the Power Imbalance in Digital Copyright. *Case Western Reserve Journal of Law Technology & Internet* 4: 207.

Théberge, P. 2001. 'Plugged in': Technology and Popular Music. In *The Cambridge Companion to Pop and Rock*, ed. S. Frith, W. Straw, and J. Street, 1–25. Cambridge: Cambridge University Press.

Williams, R. 2000. Public Choices and Social Learning: The New Multimedia Technologies in Europe. *The Information Society* 16 (4): 251–262.

Williams, R., and D. Edge. 1996. The Social Shaping of Technology. *Research Policy* 25 (6): 865.

Williams, R., and N. Pollock. 2012. Research Commentary—Moving Beyond the Single Site Implementation Study: How (and Why) We Should Study the Biography of Packaged Enterprise Solutions. *Information Systems Research* 23 (1): 1–22.

Williams, R., J. Stewart, and R. Slack. 2005. *Social Learning in Technological Innovation: Experimenting with Information and Communication Technologies*. Cheltenham: Edward Elgar.

Zentner, A. 2006. Measuring the Effect of File Sharing on Music Purchases. *The Journal of Law & Economics* 49 (1): 63–90.

Zott, C., and R. Amit. 2010. Business Model Design: An Activity System Perspective. *Long Range Planning* 43 (2): 216–226.

Afterword

This book showed why the promises of revolutionary transformation have not materialised in the digital recording industry. Instead of the anticipated deep structural change, a number of incremental adjustments took place as a result of the intricate interplay between innovation actors and their interactions in the economic, cultural, legal and institutional context. This evolutionary change is manifested with the development of streaming services. The service now seems to have become established as the de facto main means of digital music consumption (Nielson 2016). Streaming services arose as a response to a set of problems posed by digital technology: how to valorise music in the digital environment. The success of this new service and business model provided an effective solution to this dilemma by converting 100 million digital music users to paid music consumers (IFPI 2017). However, this development, though catalysed by technology-focused actors outside the music sector, did not involve the wholesale displacement of existing players. In particular, it allowed the major record labels to retain their power. The major labels have successfully repositioned themselves in the digital sphere by mobilising their massive resources—from financial and social capital to legal and lobbying power. The existing power structure, rather than being overthrown as predicted, has

H. Sun, *Digital Revolution Tamed*, https://doi.org/10.1007/978-3-319-93022-0

survived the so-called digital crisis. The major recording companies invested in new streaming platforms and built partnerships with independent digital music distributors. By establishing indirect vertical integration, they retained much of their market power.

Today, when the costs/barriers of music recording are falling, we find ourselves in an attention economy (Simon 1971). The majority of music listeners tend to listen to popular music and return to the industry's old practice of market manipulation. As a result, the contemporary digital recording industry shows a strong strand of continuity. However, the recording industry is not able to impose solutions unilaterally—the outcome that emerged was also a response to the digital music users' demands and new technological opportunities. The shifting terrain in this arena is therefore producing new dynamics. On the one hand, artists are experiencing unparalleled opportunities and options, and digital music users are enjoying ready access at modest cost to potentially much more diverse music wherever they go on any device. On the other hand, the gatekeepers' roles are becoming increasingly significant and their control over market is resurfacing.

Central to the shifting landscape of contemporary digital recording industry is a rethinking of the future of the music business. Despite the growing optimism primarily induced by increasing digital music revenue, many of the problems are associated with the unresolved issues from the fundamental transformations digital technology has presented. The statement that the digital revolution in the recording industry has been tamed should not be conceived as a judgmental conclusion. Rather, my intention is to trigger broader questions such as what we want from the music industry, what is the current picture, where is the music industry heading and what needs to be done to enable a better future that the diverse range of stakeholders could agree upon. It is my hope that this book has served to raise some of these questions.

Today's streaming services are surely not the end of the process. At the initial stage of the restructuring of the industry, a plethora of new players continue to enter the marketplace and to compete with new distinctive features. Over time, the industry will enter into a stable stage in which a few big players will merge with small and medium players and dominate the market. This is likely to result in a lock-in to one of the technologies. Fundamental problems, if remain unresolved, can lead to a turbulent course in its development. The music industry as the "canary down the mine" has always been at the forefront of facing the challenges and opportunities that disruptive technologies bring and the broader cultural industries learn from the lessons gleaned from their successes and mistakes. A critical reflection on fundamental questions, as well as a further investigation on the new convergence in the music industry, could illuminate insights in understanding other sectors of the digital cultural industries.

Bibliography

Adorno, T.W. 1976. *Introduction to the Sociology of Music*. New York: Seabury Press.

Aguiar, L. 2017. Let the Music Play? Free Streaming and Its Effects on Digital Music Consumption. *Information Economics and Policy* 41: 1–14.

Aguiar, L., and J. Waldfogel. 2015. Streaming Reaches Flood Stage: Does Spotify Stimulate or Depress Music Sales? Working Paper No. 21653, National Bureau of Economic Research.

Akester, P. 2005. Copyright and the P2P Challenge. *European Intellectual Property Review* 27 (3): 106.

Alderman, J. 2002. *Sonic Boom: Napster, MP3, and the New Pioneers of Music*. London: Four Estate.

Allen-Robertson, J. 2013. *Digital Culture Industry a History of Digital Distribution*. Basingstoke: Palgrave Macmillan.

Anderson, C. 2006. *The Long Tail: Why the Future of Business Is Selling Less of More*. New York: Hyperion.

Anderson, C. 2009. *Free: The Future of a Radical Price*. New York: Hyperion.

Apple Press. 2007. Apple Unveils Higher Quality DRM-Free Music on the iTunes Store [online]. *Apple Press*. Available from https://www.apple.com/uk/pr/library/2007/04/02Apple-Unveils-Higher-Quality-DRM-Free-Music-on-the-iTunes-Store.html. Accessed 2 Aug 2014.

H. Sun, *Digital Revolution Tamed*, https://doi.org/10.1007/978-3-319-93022-0

Apple Press. 2009. Changes Coming to the iTunes Store [online]. *Apple Press Info*. Available from https://www.apple.com/uk/pr/library/2009/01/06Changes-Coming-to-the-iTunes-Store.html. Accessed 2 Aug 2014.

Arditi, D. 2014. iTunes: Breaking Barriers and Building Walls. *Popular Music and Society* 37 (4): 408–424.

Arrow, K.J. 1962. The Economic Implications of Learning by Doing. *The Review of Economic Studies* 29 (3): 155–173.

Arthur, W.B. 2009. *The Nature of Technology: What It Is and How It Evolves*. London and New York: Allen Lane.

Attali, J. 1985. *Noise: The Political Economy of Music*. Manchester: Manchester University Press.

Baden-Fuller, C., and M.S. Morgan. 2010. Business Models as Models. *Long Range Planning* 43 (2–3): 156–171.

Baden-Fuller, C., and S. Haefliger. 2013. Business Models and Technological Innovation. *Long Range Planning* 46 (6): 419–426.

Bajarin, T. 2015. How Taylor Swift Saved Apple Music. *Time*.

Bakker, G. 2012. Adopting the Rights-Based Model: Music Multinationals and Local Music Industries Since 1945. *Popular Music History* 6 (3): 307–343.

Bakker, P. 2005. File-Sharing—Fight, Ignore or Compete: Paid Download Services vs. P2P-Networks. *Telematics and Informatics* 22 (1–2): 41–55.

Barlow, J.P. 1994. The Economy of Ideas [online]. *Wired*. Available from https://www.wired.com/1994/03/economy-ideas/. Accessed 31 May 2017.

Barlow, J.P. 1996. A Declaration of the Independence of Cyberspace [online]. *Electronic Frontier Foundation*. Available from https://projects.eff.org/~barlow/Declaration-Final.html. Accessed 19 Sept 2015.

Barna, E. 2017. The Perfect Guide in a Crowded Musical Landscape: Online Music Platforms and Curatorship. *First Monday* 22 (4). Available from https://doi.org/10.5210/fm.v22i4.6914.

Barr, K. 2013. Theorizing Music Streaming: Preliminary Investigations. *Scottish Music Review* 3 (2). Available from http://www.scottishmusicreview.org/index.php/SMR/article/view/40.

Bates, S. 2010. Beatles for Sale: EMI Puts Abbey Road Studios on the Market [online]. *The Guardian*. Available from http://www.theguardian.com/business/2010/feb/16/abbey-road-studios-sale-emi. Accessed 16 Nov 2013.

Bazalgette, P. 2017. *Independent Review of the Creative Industries*. GOV.UK.

BBC News. 2003. Website Offers New View of Music. *BBC*, March 27.

BBC News. 2009. Last.fm to Charge for Streaming. *BBC*, March 25.

Beer, D. 2008. Making Friends with Jarvis Cocker: Music Culture in the Context of Web 2.0. *Cultural Sociology* 2 (2): 222–241.

Bendz, S. 2008. Collaborative Playlists [online]. *Spotify News*. Available from https://news.spotify.com/uk/2008/01/30/collaborative-playlists/. Accessed 27 Feb 2016.

Benkler, Y. 2006. *The Wealth of Networks: How Social Production Transforms Markets and Freedom*. New Haven, CT: Yale University Press.

Bently, L. 1994. Copyright and the Death of the Author in Literature and Law. *The Modern Law Review* 57 (6): 973–986.

Bently, L. 2008. *Intellectual Property Law*, 3rd ed. Oxford: Oxford University Press.

Bergh, A., and T. DeNora. 2009. From Wind-Up to iPod: Techno-Cultures of Listening. In *The Cambridge Companion to Recorded Music*, ed. N. Cook, E. Clarke, D. Leech-Wilkinson, and J. Rink, 102–115. Cambridge: Cambridge University Press.

Bettig, R.V. 1996. *Copyrighting Culture: The Political Economy of Intellectual Property*. Boulder, CO: Westview Press.

Biddle, P., P. England, M. Peinado, and B. Willman. 2002. The Darknet and the Future of Content Distribution. *ACM Workshop on Digital Rights Management*.

Blackburn, D. 2004. Does File Sharing Affect Record Sales. PhD Dissertation at Harvard University.

Blaikie, N.W.H. 2009. *Designing Social Research: The Logic of Anticipation*, 2nd ed. Cambridge, UK and Malden, MA: Polity.

Blankenhorn, D. 2006. Dana Blankenhorn: How Much Further Can Apple Go? [online]. Available from http://www.danablankenhorn.com/2006/12/how_much_furthe.html. Accessed 7 Aug 2014.

Boldrin, M., and D. Levine. 2002. The Case Against Intellectual Property. *American Economic Review* 92 (2): 209–212.

Boytha, G. 1993. The Intellectual Property Status of Sound Recordings. *Iic-International Review of Industrial Property and Copyright Law* 24 (3): 295–306.

BPI. 2018. Rising UK Music Consumption Enjoys Fastest Growth This Millennium [online]. *BPI*. Available from https://www.bpi.co.uk/news-analysis/rising-uk-music-consumption-enjoys-fastest-growth-this-millennium/. Accessed 29 Jan 2018.

Bradshaw, T., A. Edgecliffe-Johnson, and Tim Mitchell. 2009. Spotify Wins High-Profile Backing to Expand iTunes Challenge in US. *Financial Times*, August 4.

Breen, J.C. 2007. YouTube or YouLose: Can YouTube Survive a Copyright Infringement Lawsuit? *Texas Intellectual Property Law Journal* 16 (1): 151–182.

Bridy, A. 2009. Why Pirates (Still) Won't Behave: Regulating P2P in the Decade After Napster. *Rutgers Law Journal* 40 (3): 565–611.

Brown, S.C. 2016. Where Do Beliefs About Music Piracy Come from and How Are They Shared? *International Journal of Cyber Criminology* 10 (1): 21–39.

Burgess, J. 2009. *YouTube: Online Video and Participatory Culture*. Cambridge: Polity.

Burkart, P. 2010. *Music and Cyberliberties*. Middletown, CT: Wesleyan University Press.

Burkart, P., and T. McCourt. 2006. *Digital Music Wars: Ownership and Control of the Celestial Jukebox*. Lanham, MD: Rowman & Littlefield.

Burke, A.E. 2011. Music Business. In *A Handbook of Cultural Economics*, 2nd ed, ed. R. Towse. Cheltenham: Edward Elgar.

Burkitt, D. 2001. Copyrighting Culture-The History and Cultural Specificity of the Western Model of Copyright. *Intellectual Property Quarterly* 2: 146–186.

Burnett, R. 1993. The Popular Music Industry in Transition. *Popular Music and Society* 17 (1): 87–114.

Burnett, R. 1996. *The Global Jukebox: The International Music Industry*. London: Routledge.

Buskirk, E.V. 2008. Free Music Boosts Last.fm's Traffic 58 Percent [online]. *Wired*. Available from http://www.wired.com/2008/02/free-music-boos/. Accessed 10 Feb 2016.

Buskirk, E.V. 2013. What Is It About Sweden and Digital Music? We Ask Some Swedes. *Evolver.fm*.

Byrne, D. 2012. *How Music Works*. San Francisco, CA: McSweeneys.

Byrne, D. 2013. The Internet Will Suck All Creative Content Out of the World [online]. *The Guardian*. Available from https://www.theguardian.com/music/2013/oct/11/david-byrne-internet-content-world. Accessed 31 May 2017.

Byrne, D., and T. Yorke. 2007. David Byrne and Thom Yorke on the Real Value of Music [online]. *Wired*. Available from https://www.wired.com/2007/12/ff-yorke/?currentPage=all. Accessed 10 July 2017.

Cammaerts, B. 2011. The Hegemonic Copyright Regime vs the Sharing Copyright Users of Music? *Media Culture & Society* 33 (3): 491–502.

Cammerts, B., R. Mansell, and B. Meng. 2013. *Copyright & Creation: A Case for Promoting Inclusive Online Sharing*. The London School of Economics and Political Science, Department of Media and Communications. Media Policy Brief 9.

Carter, D., and I. Rogers. 2014. Fifteen Years of 'Utopia': Napster and Pitchfork as Technologies of Democratization. *First Monday* 19 (10). http://firstmonday.org/ojs/index.php/fm/article/view/5543/4122 or http://dx.doi.org/10.5210/fm.v19i10.5543.

Caves, R.E. 2002. *Creative Industries: Contracts Between Art and Commerce.* Cambridge, MA: Harvard University Press.

Christman, E. 2012a. Warner Music's Digital Distribution Going to Sony DADC: Sources [online]. *Billboard.* Available from https://www.billboard.com/biz/articles/news/1098895/warner-musics-digital-distribution-going-to-sony-dadc-sources. Accessed 31 Jan 2018.

Christman, E. 2012b. INgrooves to Purchase Fontana. *Billboard*, March 2.

Christman, E. 2013. Fourth Quarter Market Share Report: Indies & Market Share [online]. *Billboard.* Available from http://www.billboard.com/biz/articles/news/5763065/fourth-quarter-market-share-report-indies-market-share. Accessed 28 Nov 2013.

Christman, E. 2014. IMPALA Files Complaint Against YouTube with European Commission [online]. *Billboard.* Available from http://www.billboard.com/biz/articles/news/global/6141020/impala-files-complaint-against-youtube-with-european-commission. Accessed 25 July 2014.

Christman, E. 2017. Sony Merges RED Into The Orchard: What the Music Giant's Latest Consolidation Means for Indie Labels [online]. *Billboard.* Available from https://www.billboard.com/articles/business/7817640/sony-music-orchard-red-indie-distributors-merged. Accessed 27 Feb 2018.

Clair, W.S. 2004. *The Reading Nation in the Romantic Period.* Cambridge: Cambridge University Press.

Clark, D. 2013. Amanda Palmer: Proof That Social Media Is the Future of Business. *Forbes.*

CNW. 2010. Cinram Signs New Agreements with Warner Music Group [online]. Available from http://www.prnewswire.com/news-releases/cinram-signs-new-agreements-with-warner-music-group-108702959.html. Accessed 24 Feb 2016.

Coleman, E.G., and A. Golub. 2008. Hacker Practice: Moral Genres and the Cultural Articulation of Liberalism. *Anthropological Theory* 8 (3): 255–277.

Coleman, M. 2004. *Playback: From the Victrola to MP3, 100 Years of Music, Machines, and Money.* New York: Da Capo Press.

Constine, J. 2014. Inside the Spotify—Echo Nest Skunkworks. *TechCrunch.*

Craft, K.L. 2001. The Webcasting Music Revolution Is Ready to Begin, as Soon as We Figure Out the Copyright Law: The Story of the Music Industry at War with Itself. *Hastings Communications and Entertainment Law Journal* 24: 1.

CREATe. 2017. CREATe Copyright and Innovation Network Launch Workshop. London, May 26.

Crisell, A. 2002. Radio: Public Service, Commercialism and the Paradox of Choice. In *The Media. An Introduction*, ed. A. Briggs and P. Cobley. Harlow: Longman.

Cummings, A.S. 2010. From Monopoly to Intellectual Property: Music Piracy and the Remaking of American Copyright, 1909–1971. *The Journal of American History* 97 (3): 659–681.

Cunningham, M. 1998. *Good Vibrations: A History of Record Production*. London, UK: Sanctuary Publishing.

Dale, P. 2008. It Was Easy, It Was Cheap, so What?: Reconsidering the DIY Principle of Punk and Indie Music. *Popular Music History* 3 (2): 171–193.

Danaher, B., and M.D. Smith. 2014. Gone in 60 Seconds: The Impact of the Megaupload Shutdown on Movie Sales. *International Journal of Industrial Organization* 33: 1–8.

Danielsen, Anne D., and Yngvar K. Kjus. 2017. The Mediated Festival: Live Music as Trigger of Music Streaming and Social Media Engagement. *Convergence: The International Journal of Research into New Media Technologies*. Online First, 1–21.

Davies, G. 1979. The Rome Convention 1961: A Brief Summary of Its Development and Prospect. *European Intellectual Property Review* 2: 154.

Deazley, R. 2003. The Myth of Copyright at Common Law. *The Cambridge Law Journal* 62 (1): 106–133.

Deazley, R. 2004. *On the Origin of the Right to Copy: Charting the Movement of Copyright Law in Eighteenth-Century Britain (1695–1775)*. Oxford: Hart.

Deazley, R. 2010. What's New About the Statute of Anne? In *Global Copyright: Three Hundred Years Since the Statute of Anne, from 1709 to Cyberspace*. Cheltenham: Edward Elgar.

Delaney, K.J., and E. Smith. 2006. YouTube Model Is Compromise Over Copyrights. *Wall Street Journal*, September 19.

Delchin, R.J. 2004. Musical Copyright Law: Past, Present and Future of Online Music Distribution. *Cardozo Arts & Entertainment Law Journal* 22: 343.

DeNora, T. 2000. *Music in Everyday Life*. Cambridge, UK: Cambridge University Press.

DeVoss, D.N., and J.E. Porter. 2006. Why Napster Matters to Writing: Filesharing as a New Ethic of Digital Delivery. *Computers and Composition: An International Journal for Teachers of Writing* 23 (2): 178–210.

Dickey, J. 2014. Taylor Swift Talks Business. *Time*.

DiMaggio, P. 1977. Market Structure, the Creative Process, and Popular Culture: Toward an Organizational Reinterpretation of Mass-Culture Theory. *The Journal of Popular Culture* 11 (2): 436–452.

Dosi, G. 1982. Technological Paradigms and Technological Trajectories: A Suggested Interpretation of the Determinants and Directions of Technical Change. *Research Policy* 11 (3): 147–162.

Dosi, G. 1988. The Nature of the Innovative Process. In *Technical Change and Economic Theory*, ed. G. Dosi, C. Freeman, N. Richard, S. Gerald, and S. Luc. London: Pinter Publishers.

Dosi, G., and L. Orsenigo. 1988. Coordination and Transformation: An Overview of Structures, Behaviours and Change in Evolutionary Environments. In *Technical Change and Economic Theory*, ed. G. Dosi, C. Freeman, N. Richard, S. Gerald, and S. Luc. London: Pinter Publishers.

Drahos, P. 2002. *Information Feudalism: Who Owns the Knowledge Economy?*. London: Earthscan.

Dredge, S. 2012. Spotify's Daniel Ek: 'We Want Artists to Be Able to Afford to Create the Music They Want to Create'. *The Guardian*, December 6.

Dredge, S. 2013a. Spotify Launches Artist Spotlight Feature with Haim and Lorde [online]. *Musically*. Available from http://musically.com/2013/10/01/spotify-launches-artist-spotlight-feature-with-haim-and-lorde/. Accessed 18 Feb 2016.

Dredge, S. 2013b. Thom Yorke Calls Spotify 'the Last Desperate Fart of a Dying Corpse'. *The Guardian*, October 7.

Dredge, S. 2013c. Billy Bragg: Labels Not Spotify Deserve Streaming Music Payouts Scrutiny. *The Guardian*, November 7.

Dredge, S. 2014. Musician Zoe Keating Reveals iTunes, Spotify and YouTube Payouts for 2013. *The Guardian*, February 24.

Drumm, H.M. 2003. Life After Napster: Will Its Successors Share Its Fate? *Texas Review of Entertainment & Sports Law* 5: 157.

ECSA. 2015. ECSA Position Paper—What Music Creators Want—ECSA-Composer Alliance [online]. *European Composer & Songwriter Alliance*. Available from http://composeralliance.org/ecsa-position-paper-what-music-creators-want/. Accessed 25 Aug 2015.

Edge, D. 1974. Technological Metaphor and Social Control. *New Literary History* 6 (1): 135–147.

Edwards, L. 2011. *Role and Responsibility of the Internet Intermediaries in the Field of Copyright and Related Rights*. Geneva: WIPO. Available from http://www.wipo.int/meetings/en/doc_details.jsp?doc_id=170839.

Ehrlich, C. 1985. *The Music Profession in Britain Since the Eighteenth Century: A Social History*. Oxford: Clarendon Press.

Eijk, van, J.P. Poort, and P. Rutten. 2010. Legal, Economic and Cultural Aspects of File Sharing. *Communications & Strategies* 77 (1): 35–54.

Ek, D. 2011. Say Hello to Spotify Apps. *Spotify News*.

Erickson, K. 2015. Five Things to Understand About That Spotify Contract Leak [online]. *Future of Music Coalition*. Available from http://www.future-ofmusic.org/blog/2015/05/27/five-things-understand-about-spotify-contract-leak. Accessed 25 Aug 2015.

Feather, J. 2006. *A History of British Publishing*. London and New York : Routledge.

Feather, J. 2007. Copyright and the Creation of Literary Property. In *A Companion to the History of the Book*, ed. S. Eliot and J. Rose. Malden, MA: Blackwell.

First Kiss. 2014. Available at https://www.youtube.com/watch?v=IpbDHxCV29A.

Fitzpatrick, A. 2016. Streaming Showdown: Amazon Music Unlimited vs. Spotify [online]. *Time*. Available from http://time.com/4533923/amazon-music-unlimited-spotify/. Accessed 5 Feb 2018.

Flanagan, A. 2014. YouTube Re-negotiating with Indies Following Outcry [online]. *Billboard*. Available from http://www.billboard.com/biz/articles/news/digital-and-mobile/6150292/youtube-re-negotiating-with-indies-following-outcry. Accessed 12 July 2014.

Fleck, J. 1988. *Innofusion or Diffusation? The Nature of Technological Development in Robotics*. Edinburgh: Research Centre for Social Sciences, University of Edinburgh.

Fred von Lohmann 'Copyright and Innovation Policy'. 2012. Available at https://www.youtube.com/watch?v=kd4BprytFFk.

Freeman, C., and C. Perez. 1988. Structural Crises of Adjustment: Busines Cycles and Investment Behaviour. In *Technical Change and Economic Theory*, ed. G. Dosi, C. Freeman, R. Nelson, G. Silverberg, and L. Soete. London: Pinter Publishers.

Freeman, C., 1992. *The Economics of Hope : Essays on Technical Change, Economic Growth and the Environment*. London: Pinter.

Frith, S. 1978. *The Sociology of Rock*. London: Constable.

Frith, S. 1981. *Sound Effects: Youth, Leisure, and the Politics of Rock'n'roll*. New York: Pantheon Books.

Frith, S. 1986. Art Versus Technology: The Strange Case of Popular Music. *Media, Culture & Society* 8 (3): 263–279.

Frith, S. 1987. The Industrialization of Popular Music. In *Popular Music and Communication*, ed. J. Lull. Newbury Park, Calif: Sage Publications, 53–77.

Frith, S. 1988. Copyright and the Music Business. *Popular Music* 7 (1): 57–75.

Frith, S. 1990. Picking up the Pieces. In *Facing the Music: Essays on Pop, Rock and Culture*, ed. S. Frith. London: Mandarin.

Frith, S. 2002. Music and Everyday Life. *Critical Quarterly* 44 (1): 35–48.

Frith, S. 2007. Live Music Matters. *Scottish Music Review* 1 (1): 1–17.

Galuszka, P. 2012. Netlabels and Democratization of the Recording Industry. *First Monday* 17 (7). Available from https://journals.uic.edu/ojs/index.php/fm/article/view/3770/3278 or https://doi.org/10.5210/fm.v17i7.3770.

Galuszka, P. 2015. New Economy of Fandom. *Popular Music & Society* 38 (1): 25–43.

Galuszka, P., and B. Brzozowska. 2017. Crowdfunding: Towards a Redefinition of the Artist's Role—The Case of MegaTotal. *International Journal of Cultural Studies* 20 (1): 83–99.

Gardner, E. 2014a. Viacom, Google Settle Long-Running YouTube Copyright Lawsuit [online]. *The Hollywood Reporter*. Available from http://www.hollywoodreporter.com/thr-esq/viacom-google-settle-long-running-689291. Accessed 7 Aug 2014.

Gardner, E. 2014b. What Viacom Has to Show for Seven Years of Pursuing YouTube [online]. *Billboard*. Available from http://www.billboard.com/biz/articles/news/legal-and-management/5937673/what-viacom-has-to-show-for-seven-years-of-pursuing. Accessed 16 July 2014.

Garofalo, R. 1999. From Music Publishing to MP3: Music and Industry in the Twentieth Century. *American Music: A Quarterly Journal Devoted to All Aspects of American Music and Music in America* 17 (3): 318–353.

Gayer, A., and O. Shy. 2006. Publishers, Artists, and Copyright Enforcement. *Information Economics and Policy* 18 (4): 374–384.

Geels, F.W. 2002. Technological Transitions as Evolutionary Reconfiguration Processes: A Multi-level Perspective and a Case-Study. *Research Policy* 31: 1257–1274.

Gensler, A. 2017. Lyor Cohen on the Streaming Business, Combining YouTube Red and Google Play, and SoundCloud's 'Sad Experience' [online]. *Billboard*. Available from http://www.billboard.com/articles/business/7881753/lyor-cohen-streaming-business-youtube-red-google-play-soundcloud. Accessed 31 Oct 2017.

Ghafele, R. 2014. Europe's Lost Royalty Opportunity: A Comparison of Potential and Existing Digital Music Royalty Markets in Ten Different

EU Member States. *Review of Economic Research on Copyright Issues* 11 (2): 60–91.
Giblin, R. 2011. *Code Wars 10 Years of P2P Software Litigation*. Cheltenham: Edward Elgar.
Gilfillan, S.C. 1970. *The Sociology of Invention: An Essay in the Social Causes, Ways and Effects of Technic Invention, Especially as Demonstrated Historicly in the Author's 'Inventing the Ship'*. Cambridge, MA: MIT Press.
Ginsburg, J.C. 2001. Copyright and Control Over New Technologies of Dissemination. *Columbia Law Review* 101 (7): 1613–1647.
Goldsmith, J.L., and T. Wu. 2006. *Who Controls the Internet?: Illusions of a Borderless World*. Oxford: Oxford University Press.
Goldstein, P. 1994. *Copyright's Highway: From Gutenberg to the Celestial Jukebox*. Stanford, CA: Stanford University Press.
Goodell, J. 2003. Steve Jobs: Rolling Stone's 2003 Interview [online]. *Rolling Stone*. Available from http://www.rollingstone.com/music/news/steve-jobs-rolling-stones-2003-interview-20111006. Accessed 31 July 2014.
Google. 2006. Google to Acquire YouTube for $1.65 Billion in Stock [online]. *Google News*. Available from http://googlepress.blogspot.co.uk/2006/10/google-to-acquire-youtube-for-165_09.html. Accessed 10 Feb 2016.
Graham, I., G. Spinardi, and R. Williams. 1996. Diversity in the Emergence of Electronic Commerce. *Journal of Information Technology* 11 (2): 161.
Green, C. 2008. Radiohead Sales Show Fans' Loyalty to Illegal Sites. *The Independent*, August 4.
Greenburg, Z.O. 2012. INgrooves: Proof You Can Make Money on Music, Even If You're Not Apple. *Forbes*.
Greenfeld, K.T. 2000. Meet the Napster. *Time*.
Gronow, P. 1983. The Record Industry: The Growth of a Mass Medium. *Popular Music* 3: 53–75.
Grossman, L. 2006. You—Yes, You—Are TIME's Person of the Year. *Time*.
Halmenschlager, C., and P. Waelbroeck. 2014. Fighting Free with Free: Freemium vs. Piracy. Available from SSRN https://ssrn.com/abstract=2475641or http://dx.doi.org/10.2139/ssrn.2475641.
Handke, C. 2010. The Creative Destruction of Copyright—Innovation in the Record Industry and Digital Copying. SSRN Working Paper Series.
Hardin, G.J. 1968. The Tragedy of the Commons. *Science* 162: 1243–1248.
Helft, M., and G. Fabrikant. 2007. WhoseTube? Viacom Sues Google Over Video Clips. *The New York Times*, March 14.

Hennion, A. 1989. An Intermediary Between Production and Consumption: The Producer of Popular Music. *Science, Technology, & Human Values* 14 (4): 400–424.

Hennion, A. 2001. Music Lovers: Taste as Performance. *Theory, Culture & Society* 18 (5): 1–22.

Hern, A. 2016. Amazon Launches Spotify and Apple Music Competitor [online]. *The Guardian*. Available from http://www.theguardian.com/technology/2016/oct/12/amazon-music-unlimited-launch-spotify-apple-streaming-competitor-echo. Accessed 5 Feb 2018.

Hesmondhalgh, D. 1997. Post-Punk's Attempt to Democratise the Music Industry: The Success and Failure of Rough Trade. *Popular Music* 16 (3): 255–274.

Hesmondhalgh, D. 2006. Digitalisation, Copyright and the Music Industries. In *Unpacking Digital Dynamics: Participation, Control and Exclusion*, ed. P. Golding and G. Murdock. New York: Hampton Press.

Hesmondhalgh, D. 2009. The Digitalisation of Music. In *Creativity, Innovation and the Cultural Economy*, ed. A.C. Pratt and P. Jeffcutt. Hoboken: Taylor and Francis.

Hiatt, B. 2002. Which Online Music Service Is Worth Paying for? [online]. *Entertainment Weekly*. Available from http://ew.com/article/2002/08/28/which-online-music-service-worth-paying/. Accessed 16 Apr 2018.

Hill, B. 2018. The Digital Songstream: Mastering the World of Digital Music (Paperback)—Routledge [online]. *Routledge.com*. Available from https://www.routledge.com/The-Digital-Songstream-Mastering-the-World-of-Digital-Music/Hill/p/book/9780415942034. Accessed 17 Apr 2018.

Himanen, P. 2001. *The Hacker Ethic: And the Spirit of the Information Age*. London: Secker & Warburg.

Hippel, E.V. 2005. *Democratizing Innovation*. Cambridge, MA: MIT Press.

Hirsch, P. 1969. *The Structure of the Popular Music Industry: An Examination of the Filtering Process by Which Records are Preselected for Public Consumption*. Ann Arbor, Mich.: Institute for Social Research, The University of Michigan.

Hirsch, P.M. 1972. Processing Fads and Fashions: An Organization-Set Analysis of Cultural Industry Systems. *American Journal of Sociology* 77 (4): 639–659.

Hirsch, P.M. 2000. Cultural Industries Revisited. *Organization Science* 11 (3): 356–361.

Hirschhorn, J. 2015. Less Money, Mo' Music & Lots of Problems: A Look at the Music Biz [online]. Available from https://www.linkedin.com/pulse/

less-money-mo-music-lots-problems-look-biz-jason-hirschhorn. Accessed 22 Jun 2017.

Holt, F. 2010. The Economy of Live Music in the Digital Age. *European Journal of Cultural Studies* 13 (2): 243–261.

Holton, K. 2007. Warner Music Announces Last.fm Content Deal [online]. *Reuters*. Available from http://uk.reuters.com/article/industry-warner-last-fm-dc-idUKL0662451720070207. Accessed 10 Feb 2016.

Hopkins, J. 2006. Surprise! There's a Third YouTube Co-founder [online]. *USA Today*. Available from http://usatoday30.usatoday.com/tech/news/2006-10-11-youtube-karim_x.htm?csp=34. Accessed 28 Feb 2016.

Hormann, K.C. 2009. The Death of the DMCA? How Viacom v. Youtube May Define the Future of Digital Content. *Houston Law Review* 46 (4): 1345–1377.

Hughes, T.P. 1986. The Seamless Web: Technology, Science, Etcetera, Etcetera. *Social Studies of Science* 16 (2): 281–292.

Hull, G.P. 2004. *The Recording Industry*. New York, NY: Routledge.

Hunter, D. 1986. Music Copyright in Britain to 1800. *Music & Letters* 67 (3): 269–282.

Huygens, M., C. Baden-Fuller, F.A.J. Van Den Bosch, and H.W. Volberda. 2001. Co-evolution of Firm Capabilities and Industry Competition: Investigating the Music Industry, 1877–1997. *Organization Studies (Walter de Gruyter GmbH & Co. KG.)* 22 (6): 971.

Hyysalo, S. 2010. *Health Technology Development and Use from Practice-Bound Imagination to Evolving Impacts*. New York, NY: Routledge.

IFPI. 2000. IFPI Music Piracy Report 2000. Available from http://www.ifpi.org/content/library/Piracy2000.pdf.

IFPI. 2009. Digital Music Report 2009: New Business Models for a Changing Environment. Available from http://www.ifpi.org/content/library/DMR2009.pdf.

IFPI. 2010. Digital Music Report 2010: Music How, When, and Where You Want It. Available from http://www.ifpi.org/content/library/DMR2010.pdf.

IFPI. 2013. Digital Music Report 2013: Engine of a Digital World. Available from http://www.ifpi.org/downloads/dmr2013-full-report_english.pdf.

IFPI. 2015. Digital Music Report 2015: Charting the Path to Sustainable Growth. Available from http://www.ifpi.org/downloads/Digital-Music-Report-2015.pdf.

IFPI. 2017. IFPI Global Music Report 2017: Annual State of the Industry. Available from http://www.ifpi.org/news/IFPI-GLOBAL-MUSIC-REPORT-2017.

IFPI. 2018. Global Music Report 2015: Annual State of the Industry. Available from http://www.ifpi.org/downloads/GMR2018.pdf.

IMPALA. 2001. Independent Record Labels Strike Historical Deal with Napster [online]. *IMPALA*. Available from http://www.impalamusic.org/docum/04-press/press_0106_1.html. Accessed 21 Jan 2015.

Ingham, T. 2014. Living on the Pledge. *Music Week*.

International Intellectual Property Alliance. 2006. *International Intellectual Property Alliance 2006 Special 301 Special Mention Sweden*. International Intellectual Property Alliance.

Jarrett, K. 2008. Beyond Broadcast Yourself™: The Future of Youtube. *Media International Australia* 126 (1): 132–144.

Jenkins, H. 2006. *Convergence Culture: Where Old and New Media Collide*. New York: New York University Press.

Jeremy Fry—Celtics Fan Dancing to Bon Jovi Living on a Prayer at a Celtics Game. 2009. Available from https://www.youtube.com/watch?v=mOHkRk00iI8.

Jerräng, M. 2009. Documents Reveal Major Labels Own Part of Spotify [online]. *Computer Sweden*. Available from http://computersweden.idg.se/2.2683/1.240046/documents-reveal-major-labels-own-part-of-spotify. Accessed 28 Feb 2016.

JK Wedding Entrance Dance. 2009. Available from https://www.youtube.com/watch?v=4-94JhLEiN0.

Jobs, S. 2007. Apple—Thoughts on Music [online]. Available from http://web.archive.org/web/20080517114107/http://www.apple.com/hotnews/thoughtsonmusic. Accessed 31 July 2014.

Jones, S. 1992. *Rock Formation: Music, Technology, and Mass Communication*. Newbury Park, CA: Sage.

Jozuka, E. 2014. Last Fugitive Pirate Bay Member Arrested [online]. *Wired UK*. Available from http://www.wired.co.uk/news/archive/2014-11/04/last-fugitive-member-of-pirate-bay-arrested. Accessed 14 Nov 2014.

Kaplan, B. 1966. *An Unhurried View of Copyright*. New York: Columbia University Press.

Kassabian, A. 2001. *Hearing Film: Tracking Identifications in Contemporary Hollywood Film Music*. New York: Routledge.

Kassabian, A. 2013. *Ubiquitous Listening: Affect, Attention, and Distributed Subjectivity*. Berkeley: University of California Press.

Katz, C. 2013. Music for Everyone. Now Free on Your Mobile. *Spotify Blog*. December 11.

Katz, R.A., and R. Hepworth-Sawyer. 2009. *From Demo to Delivery: The Process of Production*. Boston: Elsevier/Focal Press.

Kelly, K. 1998. *New Rules for the New Economy: 10 Ways the Network Economy Is Changing Everything*. London: Fourth Estate.
Kelly, K. 2008. The Technium: Better Than Free [online]. *The Technium*. Available from http://kk.org/thetechnium/better-than-fre/. Accessed 28 Feb 2016.
Kemp, R. 1994. Technology and the Transition to Environmental Sustainability: The Problem of Technological Regime Shifts. *Futures* 26 (10): 1023–1046.
Kemp, R., J. Schot, and R. Hoogma. 1998. Regime Shifts to Sustainability Through Processes of Niche Formation: The Approach of Strategic Niche Management. *Technology Analysis & Strategic Management* 10 (2): 175–198.
Kernfeld, B. 2011. *Pop Song Piracy: Disobedient Music Distribution Since 1929*. Chicago: University of Chicago Press.
King, J. 2007. *Steal This Film*. Artefact Films.
Kiss, J. 2007. Last.fm Fetches $280m. *The Guardian*, May, 30.
Kjus, Y. and A. Danielsen. 2014. Live Island in the Seas of Recordings: The Music Experience of Visitors at the Oya Festival. *Popular Music and Society* 37 (5): 660–679.
Knopper, S. 2009. *Appetite for Self-Destruction: The Spectacular Crash of the Record Industry in the Digital Age*. New York: Free Press.
Koh, B., B.P.S. Murthi, and S. Raghunathan. 2014. Shifting Demand: Online Music Piracy, Physical Music Sales, and Digital Music Sales. *Journal of Organizational Computing and Electronic Commerce* 24 (4): 366–387.
Kreitz, G., and F. Niemela. 2010. Spotify–Large Scale, Low Latency, P2P Music-on-Demand Streaming. 2010 IEEE Tenth International Conference on Peer-to-Peer Computing (P2P), 1–10.
Kretschmer, M. 2000. Intellectual Property in Music: A Historical Analysis of Rhetoric and Institutional Practices. *Studies in Cultures, Organizations & Societies* 6 (2): 197–223.
Kretschmer, M., G.M. Klimis, and R. Wallis. 1999. The Changing Location of Intellectual Property Rights in Music: A Study of Music Publishers, Collecting Societies and Media Conglomerates. *Prometheus* 17 (2): 163.
Kretschmer, M., G.M. Klimis, and R. Wallis. 2001. Music in Electronic Markets—An Empirical Study. *New Media & Society* 3 (4): 417–441.
Krueger, A.B. 2005. The Economics of Real Superstars: The Market for Rock Concerts in the Material World. *Journal of Labor Economics* 23 (1): 1–30.
Ku, R.S.R. 2002. The Creative Destruction of Copyright: Napster and the New Economics of Digital Technology. *The University of Chicago Law Review* 69 (1): 263–324.

Kuhn, T.S. 1970. *The Structure of Scientific Revolutions*, 2nd ed. Chicago: University of Chicago Press.

Kusek, D., G. Leonhard, and S.G. Lindsay. 2005. *The Future of Music: Manifesto for the Digital Music Revolution*. Boston: Berklee Press.

Laing, D. 2004. Copyright, Politics and the International Music Industry. In *Music and Copyright*, ed. S. Frith and L. Marshall. Edinburgh: Edinburgh University Press.

Laing, D. 2013. The Recording Industry in the Twentieth Century. In *The International Recording Industries*, ed. L. Marshall. Milton Park: Routledge.

Lalonde, P.-E. 2014. Study Concerning Fair Compensation for Music Creators in the Digital Age [online]. *CIAM*. Available from http://www.songwriters.ca/studyconcerningfaircompensation2014.aspx. Accessed 2 Aug 2015.

Lampel, J., A. Bhalla, and P. Jha. 2006. Back to the Digital Future: The Role of Copyrights in Sustaining Creativity and Diversity in the Music Industry. Project Report. Cass Business School.

Landes, W.M., and R.A. Posner. 1989. An Economic Analysis of Copyright Law. *Journal of Legal Studies (0047–2530)* 18 (2): 325.

Lane, D. 2014. The Top 10 Most Streamed Songs and Artists of All Time Revealed! [online]. Available from http://www.officialcharts.com/chart-news/the-top-10-most-streamed-songs-and-artists-of-all-time-revealed-3107/. Accessed 24 July 2014.

Lane, M.A. 2011. 'Interactive Services' and the Future of Internet Radio Broadcasts. *Alabama Law Review* 62: 459.

Larkin, J. 2006. Live Boom Raises Data Question. *Music Week* 10: 10–11.

Larsson, S. 2011. The Path Dependence of European Copyright. *SCRIPT-ed* 8 (1): 8–31.

Last.fm Blog. 2008. Free the Music [online]. *Last.fm Blog*. Available from http://blog.last.fm/2008/01/23/free-the-music. Accessed 10 Feb 2016.

Last.fm Blog. 2009. Last.fm Radio Announcement [online]. Available from http://blog.last.fm/2009/03/24/lastfm-radio-announcement. Accessed 11 Feb 2016.

Last.fm Blog. 2010. April 12 Site Update—Track Page Beta, Streaming Changes—Feedback and Ideas [online]. *Last.fm*. Available from http://www.last.fm/forum/21717/_/617074. Accessed 11 Feb 2016.

Lathrop, T. 2007. *This Business of Global Music Marketing*. New York: Billboard Books.

Lauinger, T., M. Szydlowski, K. Onarlioglu, G. Wondracek, E. Kirda, and C. Kruegel. 2013. Clickonomics: Determining the Effect of Anti-piracy Measures for One-Click Hosting. NDSS Symposium.

Lee, S. 1995. Re-examining the Concept of the 'Independent' Record Company: The Case of Wax Trax! Records. *Popular Music* 14 (1): 13–31.

Leeds, J. 2006. Warner Music Makes Licensing Deal with YouTube [online]. *New York Times*. Available from http://www.nytimes.com/2006/09/19/business/media/19tube.html. Accessed 28 Feb 2016.

Lemley, M.A., and R.A. Reese. 2004. Reducing Digital Copyright Infringement Without Restricting Innovation. *Stanford Law Review* 56 (6): 1345–1434.

Lessig, L. 2001. *The Future of Ideas: The Fate of the Commons in a Connected World*. New York: Random House.

Lessig, L. 2004. *Free Culture: How Big Media Uses Technology and the Law to Lock Down Culture and Control Creativity*. New York: Penguin Press.

Lessig, L. 2008. *Remix*. New York: Penguin Press.

Lewen, Ulric M. 2008. Internet File-sharing: Swedish Pirates Challenge the U.S. *Cardozo Journal of International & Comparative Law* 16 (1): 173–206.

Levy, N.N. 2000. Method to Their Madness: The Secure Digital Music Initiative, a Law and Economics Perspective. *Virginia Journal of Law and Technology* 5: 1.

Levy, S. 2001. *Hackers: Heroes of the Computer Revolution*. New York: Penguin Press.

Levy, S. 2006. *The Perfect Thing: How the iPod Shuffles Commerce, Culture, and Coolness*. New York: Simon and Schuster.

Leyshon, A. 2001. Time-Space (and Digital) Compression: Software Formats, Musical Networks, and the Reorganisation of the Music Industry. *Environment & Planning A* 33 (1): 49.

Lie, M., and K.H. Sørensen. 1996. *Making Technology Our Own?: Domesticating Technology into Everyday Life*. Oslo: Scandinavian University Press.

Liebowitz, S.J. 2006. File Sharing: Creative Destruction or Just Plain Destruction? *Journal of Law and Economics* 49 (1): 1–28.

Lindvall, H. 2010. Behind the Music: An Interview with Pitchfork Founder Ryan Schreiber. *The Guardian*, October 21.

Litman, J. 2001. *Digital Copyright: Protecting Intellectual Property on the Internet*. Amherst, NY: Prometheus Books.

von Lohmann, F. 2006. Thoughts on Google, YouTube [online]. *Electronic Frontier Foundation*. Available from https://www.eff.org/deeplinks/2006/10/thoughts-google-youtube. Accessed 10 Feb 2016.

Lowndes, S. 2016. *The DIY Movement in Art, Music and Publishing: Subjugated Knowledges*. New York: Routledge.

Lynskey, D. 2013. Is Daniel Ek, Spotify Founder, Going to Save the Music Industry … or Destroy It? [online]. *The Observer*. Available from http://www.theguardian.com/technology/2013/nov/10/daniel-ek-spotify-streaming-music. Accessed 27 Jan 2016.

Maasø, A. 2016. Music Streaming, Festivals, and the Eventization of Music. *Popular Music and Society*, 1–23. https://doi.org/10.1080/03007766.2016.1231001.

MacKenzie, D.A., and J. Wajcman. 1985. *The Social Shaping of Technology: How the Refrigerator Got Its Hum*. Milton Keynes: Open University Press.

Mann, C.C. 2000. The Heavenly Jukebox. *The Atlantic*.

Mäntymäki, M., and A.K.M.N. Islam. 2015. Gratifications from Using Freemium Music Streaming Services: Differences Between Basic and Premium Users. In *ICIS 2015 Proceedings*.

Marshall, L. 2004. Infringers. In *Music and Copyright*, ed. S. Frith and L. Marshall. Edinburgh: Edinburgh University Press.

Marshall, L. 2005. *Bootlegging: Romanticism and Copyright in the Music Industry*. London: Sage.

Marshall, L. 2013. The 360 Deal and the 'New' Music Industry. *European Journal of Cultural Studies* 16 (1): 77–99.

Marshall, L. 2015. 'Let's Keep Music Special. F—Spotify': On-Demand Streaming and the Controversy Over Artist Royalties. *Creative Industries Journal* 8 (2): 177–189.

Marshall, L., J. Williamson, and M. Cloonan (eds.). 2013. Contextualising the Contemporary Recording Industry. In *The International Recording Industries*. Milton Park: Routledge.

McCarthy, C. 2006. Paris Hilton Showcases YouTube's New ad Concepts [online]. *CNET*. Available from http://www.cnet.com/uk/news/paris-hilton-showcases-youtubes-new-ad-concepts/. Accessed 29 Feb 2016.

McCarthy, C. 2007. What Does CBS Want with Last.fm? [online]. *CNET*. Available from http://www.cnet.com/news/what-does-cbs-want-with-last-fm/. Accessed 25 Feb 2016.

McIntyre, H. 2015. Apple Music Has Lost 40% of Users After Its Free Trial—Forbes [online]. *Forbes*. Available from http://www.forbes.com/sites/hughmcintyre/2015/10/20/apple-music-has-lost-40-of-users-after-its-free-trial/#7e4e6d041c1c. Accessed 9 Feb 2016.

McKay, G. (ed.). 2015. *The Pop Festival: History, Music, Media, Culture*. New York: Bloomsbury.

McLeod, K. 2005. MP3s Are Killing Home Taping: The Rise of Internet Distribution and Its Challenge to the Major Label Music Monopoly. *Popular Music and Society* 28 (4): 521–531.

McNulty, B. 2017. Has the UK's Festival Scene Reached Saturation Point? [online]. *Financial Times*. Available from https://www.ft.com/content/622d56e2-157f-11e7-b0c1-37e417ee6c76. Accessed 27 Feb 2018.

Medford, C. 2008. Report: Apple Killed Music Industry. *Red Herring*, 2–2.

Mikhalkina, T., and L. Cabantous. 2015. Business Model Innovation: How Iconic Business Model Emerges. *Academy of Management Proceedings* 1: 12761.

Miles, M.B., and A.M. Huberman. 1984. *Qualitative Data Analysis: A Sourcebook of New Methods*. Beverly Hills: Sage.

Miller, L.S. 2017. Paradigm Shift: Why Radio Must Adapt to the Rise of Digital. *Entertainment and Sports Lawyer* 28 (16).

Minsker, E. 2014. Indie Labels Unite to Launch 'Fair Digital Deals Declaration' Initiative [online]. *Pitchfork*. Available from http://pitchfork.com/news/55909-indie-labels-unite-to-launch-fair-digital-deals-declaration-initiative/. Accessed 25 July 2014.

Mitroff, S. 2015. Apple Music vs Spotify: What's the Difference? [online]. *CNET*. Available from http://www.cnet.com/uk/news/apple-music-vs-spotify-whats-the-difference/. Accessed 9 Feb 2016.

Mortimer, J.H., C. Nosko, and A. Sorensen. 2012. Supply Responses to Digital Distribution: Recorded Music and Live Performances. *Information Economics and Policy* 24 (1): 3–14.

Moses, A. 2007. Nails Frontman Urges Fans to Steal Music—Web—Technology—smh.com.au. *The Sydney Morning Herald*, September 18.

Mulligan, M. 2014a. Tyranny of Choice. *Music Industry Blog*.

Mulligan, M. 2014b. Why the Music Aficionado Was to Blame for Declining Music Sales. *Music Industry Blog*.

Mulligan, M. 2015. Why the Music Aficionado Was to Blame for Declining Music Sales in 2014. *Music Industry Blog*.

Mulligan, M. 2016. Cross Border Listening: Borderless Hits and Curated Playlists. *MIDiA Research*.

Mulligan, M. 2017a. Announcing MIDiA's Streaming Services Market Shares Report. *Music Industry Blog*.

Mulligan, M. 2017b. Amazon Is Now the 3rd Biggest Music Subscription Service. *Music Industry Blog*.

Music Managers Forum. 2016. *Dissecting The Digital Dollar*. CMU Insights.

Napier-Bell, S. 2014. *Ta-ra-ra-boom-de-ay: The Business of Popular Music*. London: Unbound.

Nash, E. 2011. How Steve Jobs Saved the Music Industry. *Wall Street Journal*, October 21.

Nasir, C. 2005. Taming the Beast of File-Sharing—Legal and Technological Solutions to the Problem of Copyright Infringement Over the Internet. *Entertainment Law Review* 16 (4): 82–88.

Nathan, J. 1999. *Sony: The Private Life*. London: HarperCollins.

Negroponte, N. 1996. *Being Digital*. New York: Vintage Books.

Negus, K. 1992. *Producing Pop: Culture and Conflict in the Popular Music Industry*. London: Edward Arnold.

Nelson, R.R., and S.G. Winter. 1977. In Search of Useful Theory of Innovation. *Research Policy* 6 (1): 36–76.

Nelson, R.R., and S.G. Winter. 1982. *An Evolutionary Theory of Economic Change*. Cambridge, MA: Belknap Press.

Nicolaou, A. 2017. Taylor Swift Changes Her Tune and Returns to Spotify. *Financial Times*, June 9.

Nicoll, D.W. 2000. Users as Currency: Technology and Marketing Trials as Naturalistic Environments. *The Information Society* 16 (4): 303–310.

Nielsen Music. 2017. Nielsen Music 360 Report 2017. Nielsen.

O'Brien, D.S., and B.F. Fitzgerald. 2006. Mashups, Remixes and Copyright Law. *Internet Law Bulletin* 9 (2): 17–19.

Oberholzer-Gee, F., and K. Strumpf. 2007. The Effect of File Sharing on Record Sales: An Empirical Analysis. *Journal of Political Economy* 115 (1): 1–42.

Oram, A. (ed.). 2001. *Peer-to-Peer: Harnessing the Power of Disruptive Technologies*. Beijing and Sebastopol, CA: O'Reilly Media.

Osborne, R. 2016. *Vinyl: A History of the Analogue Record*. London: Routledge.

Owsinkski, B. 2011. *Music 3.0: A Survival Guide for Making Music in the Internet Age*. 2nd ed. Milwaukee, WI: Hal Leonard Books.

Page, W. 2013. Adventures in the Netherlands: New Spotify Study Sees Encouraging Downwards Trend in Music Piracy in the Netherlands. *Spotify Press*.

Page, W., and E. Gradland. 2009. *The long tail of p2p*. PRS for Music, No. Issue 14.

Page, W., and K. Ning. 2014. Anatomy of a Hit: How Meghan Trainor Made the UK Chart Without Selling Downloads. *Spotify Insights*.

Palmås, K., J. Andersson Schwarz, and S. Larsson. 2014. The Liability of Politicalness: Legitimacy and Legality in Piracy-Proximate Entrepreneurship. *International Journal of Entrepreneurship and Small Business* 22 (4): 408–425.

Pareles, J. 2002. David Bowie, 21st-Century Entrepreneur. *The New York Times*, June 9.

Parker, N. 2004. *Music Business: Infrastructure, Practice and Law*. London: Sweet & Maxwell.

Pasquale III, F.A., K.G. Weatherall, and M.B. Fagin. 2002. Beyond Napster: Using Antitrust Law to Advance and Enhance Online Music Distribution. *Boston University Journal of Science & Technology Law* 8 (2): 451–573.

Passman, D.S. 2011. *All You Need to Know About the Music Business*. London: Penguin.

Patterson, L.R. 1968. *Copyright in Historical Perspective*. Nashville: Vanderbilt University Press.

Peacock, A.T., and R.B. Weir. 1975. *The Composer in the Market Place*. London: Faber Music.

Pelly, L. 2017. The Secret Lives of Playlists [online]. *WATT*. Available from https://watt.cashmusic.org/writing/thesecretlivesofplaylists. Accessed 24 Aug 2017.

Peoples, G. 2013. Spotify Throws Its Weight Behind Artist Marketing [online]. *Billboard*. Available from http://www.billboard.com/biz/articles/news/digital-and-mobile/5740703/spotify-throws-its-weight-behind-artist-marketing. Accessed 18 Feb 2016.

Peoples, G. 2015. 'Playola' Infiltrates Streaming Services: Pay for Play 'Definitely Happening' [online]. *Billboard*. Available from http://www.billboard.com/articles/business/6670475/playola-promotion-streaming-services. Accessed 28 Jan 2016.

Peterson, R.A. 1990. Why 1955? Explaining the Advent of Rock Music. *Popular Music* 9 (1): 97–116.

Peterson, R.A., and D.G. Berger. 1975. Cycles in Symbol Production: The Case of Popular Music. *American Sociological Review* 40 (2): 158–173.

Peterson, R.A., and R.M. Kern. 1996. Changing Highbrow Taste: From Snob to Omnivore. *American Sociological Review* 61 (5): 900–907.

Pham, A. 2013a. The Evolution of iTunes: The Birth of a Colossus: The Creation of the World's Biggest Music Retailer Seemed to Happen Almost in spite of the Record Labels, but They Knew a Good Thing When Steve Jobs Showed It to Them. *Billboard* 125 (17): 24.

Pham, A. 2013b. Vevo Pumps Up the Volume with More Than 1 Billion Monthly Views on Mulitple Platforms, Vevo Has Become Crucial. *Billboard* 125 (45): 36.

Pham, A. 2013c. Questions Answered: Robb McDaniels, Founder/CEO of INgrooves/Isolation Network [online]. *Billboard*. Available from http://www.billboard.com/biz/articles/news/1560617/questions-answered-robb-mcdaniels-founderceo-of-ingroovesisolation-network. Accessed 9 Oct 2014.

Plumb, J.H. 1973. *The Commercialisation of Leisure in Eighteenth-Century England*. Reading: University of Reading.

Pollack, N. 2009. *Software and Organisations: The Biography of the Enterprise-Wide System or How SAP Conquered the World*. London: Routledge.

Pollack, N. 2010. Spotify Is the Coolest Music Service You Can't Use. *Wired*.

Pollack, N., 2011. Spotify's Celestial Jukebox [online]. *Wired UK*. Available from http://www.wired.co.uk/magazine/archive/2011/02/start/spotify-celestial-jukebox. Accessed 28 Feb 2016.

Pollack, W.M. 1999. Tuning In: The Future of Copyright Protection for Online Music in the Digital Millennium. *Fordham Law Review* 68: 2445.

Poort, J., J. Leenheer, J. van der Ham, and C. Dumitru. 2014. Baywatch: Two Approaches to Measure the Effects of Blocking Access to The Pirate Bay. *Telecommunications Policy* 38 (4): 383–392.

Porter, M.E. 1980. *Competitive Strategy: Techniques for Analyzing Industries and Competitors*. New York: Free Press.

Posner, R.A. 1998. *Economic Analysis of Law*, 5th ed. New York: Aspen Law & Business.

Preston, P., and J. Rogers. 2011. Social Networks, Legal Innovations and the 'New' Music Industry. *Info* 13 (6): 8–19.

Price, J. 2012. How Technology Destroyed The Traditional Music Industry. *Hypebot*.

Prior, N. 2010. The Rise of the New Amateurs: Popular Music, Digital Technology and the Fate of Cultural Production. In *Handbook of Cultural Sociology*, ed. J.R. Hall, L. Grindstaff and M. Lo, 398–407. Routledge.

Quan, M. 1999. SDMI Releases Portable-Player Spec [online]. *EETimes*. Available from http://www.eetimes.com/document.asp?doc_id=1139861. Accessed 28 Feb 2016.

Rapaport, D.S. 2003. *A Music Business Primer*. Upper Saddle River, NJ: Prentice Hall.

Raven, J. 2007. *The Business of Books: Booksellers and the English Book Trade, 1450–1850*. New Haven: Yale University Press.

Reed, M. 2006. Publishers vs. YouTube: Does Either Side Win? [online]. *USC Annenberg Online Journalism Review*. Available from http://www.ojr.org/?s=Publishers+vs.+YouTube%3A+Does+Either+Side+Win. Accessed 22 Feb 2016.

Reia, J. 2014. Napster and Beyond: How Online Music Can Transform the Dynamics of Musical Production and Consumption in DIY Subcultures. *First Monday* 19 (10). http://firstmonday.org/ojs/index.php/fm/article/view/5552/4131 or http://dx.doi.org/10.5210/fm.v19i10.5552. Accessed 6 Oct 2014.

Rethink Music. 2015. Fair Music: Transparency and Payment Flows in the Music Industry [online]. *Rethink Music*. Available from http://www.rethink-music.com/research/fair-music-transparency-and-payment-flows-in-the-music-industry. Accessed 15 Aug 2015.

Reuters. 2006. YouTube Serves Up 100 Million Videos a Day Online [online]. *USA Today*. Available from http://usatoday30.usatoday.com/tech/news/2006-07-16-youtube-views_x.htm. Accessed 7 Aug 2014.

Reuters. 2007. French Pact Aims to Fight Unauthorized Downloading. *The New York Times*, November 24.

Reynolds, S. 2006. *Rip It Up and Start Again: Postpunk 1978–1984*. New York: Penguin Books.

Reynolds, S. 2011. *Retromania: Pop Culture's Addiction to Its Own Past*. London: Faber and Faber.

RIAA. 2007. Who Music Theft Hurts [online]. http://www.riaa.com. Available from http://www.riaa.com//physicalpiracy.php?content_selector=piracy_details_online. Accessed 22 Oct 2015.

Ricketson, S. 2006. *International Copyright and Neighbouring Rights: The Berne Convention and Beyond*, 2nd ed. Oxford: Oxford University Press.

Rip, A., and R. Kemp. 1998. Technological Change. In *Human Choice and Climate Change*, ed. S. Rayner and E.L. Malone. Columbus, OH: Battelle Press.

Rip, A., T.J. Misa, and J. Schot. 1995. *Managing Technology in Society: The Approach of Constructive Technology Assessment*. London: Pinter.

Roberts, R. 2011. Critic's Notebook: With Spotify, the Future of Music Is Here. *LA Times Blogs—Pop & Hiss*.

Robinson, R. 2016. *Music Festivals and the Politics of Participation*. London: Routledge.

Rogers, J. 2013. *The Death and Life of the Music Industry in the Digital Age*. London: Bloomsbury.

Rogers, J. 2014. Canary Down the Mine: Music and Copyright at the Digital Coalface. *Socialism and Democracy* 28 (1): 34–50.

Rogers, J., and P. Preston. 2016. Crisis and Creative Destruction: New Modes of Appropriation in the Twenty-First Century Music Industry. In *Business Innovation and Disruption in the Music Industry*, ed. P. Wikström and R. DeFillippi, 53–72. Cheltenham, UK: Edward Elgar.

Rose, F. 2007. Secret Websites, Coded Messages: The New World of Immersive Games. *Wired Magazine* 20: 16–01.

Rose, M. 1993. *Authors and Owners: The Invention of Copyright*. Cambridge, MA: Harvard University Press.

Rosen, R.S. 2008. *Music and Copyright*. New York and Oxford: Oxford University Press.

Rosenberg, N. 1982. *Inside the Black Box: Technology and Economics*. Cambridge: Cambridge University Press.

Rossow, C., D. Andriesse, T. Werner, B. Stone-Gross, D. Plohmann, C.J. Dietrich, and H. Bos. 2013. SoK: P2PWNED—Modeling and Evaluating the Resilience of Peer-to-Peer Botnets. In *2013 IEEE Symposium on Security and Privacy*. Presented at the 2013 IEEE Symposium on Security and Privacy, 97–111.

Rozat, P. 2011. Deezer: Profitability Down the Line? [online]. *InaGlobal*. Available from http://www.inaglobal.fr/en/music/article/deezer-profitability-down-line. Accessed 1 Feb 2018.

Russell, S. 1986. The Social Construction of Artefacts: A Response to Pinch and Bijker. *Social Studies of Science* 16 (2): 331–346.

Russell, S., and R. Willams. 2002. Social Shaping of Technology: Frameworks, Findings and Implications for Policy with Glossary of Social Shaping Concepts. In *Shaping Technology, Guiding Policy: Concepts, Spaces, and Tools*, ed. K.H. Sørensen and R. Williams. Cheltenham: Edward Elgar.

Rutter, P. 2011. *The Music Industry Handbook*. London: Routledge.

Samuel, M.C. 2014. Winds of Change. Journey of UK Music from the Old World to the New World. *Review of Economic Research on Copyright Issues* 11 (2): 27.

Sandoval, G. 2008. Source: Universal Music Group Plans 'Hulu-Like' Site [online]. *CNET*. Available from http://www.cnet.com/uk/news/source-universal-music-group-plans-hulu-like-site/. Accessed 24 July 2014.

Sassard, S. 2017. The French Music Streaming Service Taking on Spotify, Apple and Amazon [online]. *The Independent*. Available from http://www.independent.co.uk/news/business/analysis-and-features/deezer-music-streaming-spotify-amazon-apple-subscritpiton-hans-holger-albrecht-len-blavatnik-a7940896.html. Accessed 1 Feb 2018.

Scheirer, E. 1999. The End of SDMI [online]. *MP3.com Technology*. Available from http://web.archive.org/web/20000229055832/www.mp3.com/news/394.html. Accessed 10 Feb 2016.

Scherer, F.M. 2004. *Quarter Notes and Bank Notes: The Economics of Music Composition in the Eighteenth and Nineteenth Centuries*. Princeton: Princeton University Press.

Schreiber, D. 2016. The Influence of Disruptive Technologies on Radio Promotion Strategies in the Music Industry: A Case Study of One Micro-Firm's Decision-Making Practice. In *Business Innovation and Disruption in the Music Industry*, ed. P. Wikström and R. DeFillippi, 13–32. Cheltenham, UK: Edward Elgar.

Schumpeter, J.A. 1950. *Capitalism, Socialism and Democracy*. London: G. Allen & Unwin.

Schwarz, J.A. 2014. *Online File Sharing Innovations in Media Consumption*. New York: Routledge.

Scott, S. 2014. The Moral Economy of Crowdfunding and the Transformative Capacity of Fan-ancing. *New Media & Society*. https://doi.org/10.1177/1461444814558908.

Severin, K. 2014. Music Consumer Segmentation: From Lagging Indicators to Leading Indicators. *MIDiA Research*.

Sharpe, N.F., and O.B. Arewa. 2006. Is Apple Playing Fair—Navigating the iPod FairPlay DRM Controversy. *Northwestern Journal of Technology and Intellectual Property* 5: 332.

Sheffner, B. 2011. The Antitrust Case Against Major Record Labels, in Perspective [online]. *Billboard*. Available from http://www.billboard.com/biz/articles/news/1179723/the-antitrust-case-against-major-record-labels-in-perspective. Accessed 5 Aug 2014.

Shirky, C. 2001. Where Napster Is Taking the Publishing World. *Harvard Business Review* 79 (2): 143–148.

Silverstone, R., and E. Hirsch. 1992. *Consuming Technologies: Media and Information in Domestic Spaces*. London: Routledge.

Simon, H.A. 1971. Designing Organizations for an Information-Rich World. *Computers, Communications, and the Public Interest*, 37–72.

Sisario, B. 2012. TuneCore Chief Shakes Up Music with His Own Words. *The New York Times*, May 6.

Sisario, B. 2014. Beats Music Enters Online Streaming Market—The New York Times [online]. Available from http://www.nytimes.com/2014/01/12/arts/music/beats-music-enters-online-streaming-market.html. Accessed 28 Feb 2016.

Siwek, S.E. 2007. *The True Cost of Sound Recording Piracy to the U.S. Economy*. Policy Report, Institute for Policy Innovation.

Smith, C. 2014. How Spotify, Netflix and Amazon Control Your Online Habits [online]. *TechRadar*. Available from http://www.techradar.com/us/news/internet/how-spotify-netflix-and-amazon-s-powerful-discovery-tools-control-our-habits-1216211. Accessed 18 Feb 2016.

Solon, O. 2013. Pirate Bay Interview: You Can't Beat Politics with Technology Says Peter Sunde [online]. *Wired UK*. Available from http://www.wired.co.uk/news/archive/2013-11/18/peter-sunde-hemlis-political-apathy. Accessed 7 Feb 2016.

Sørensen, K.H. 1994. Adieu Adorno: The Moral Emancipation of Consumers. In *Domestic Technology and Everyday Life—Mutual Shaping Processes: Proceedings from COST A4 Workshop in Trondheim, Norway, October 28–30, 1993*, ed. A.-J. Berg and M. Aune. Brussels: Europese Commissie, Directorate General Science, Research and Development.

Sørensen, K.H. 1996. *Learning Technology, Constructing Culture: Socio-Technical Change as Social Learning*. Trondheim: University of Trondheim, Centre for Technology and Society, No. 18/96.

Sørensen, K.H., and N. Levold. 1992. Tacit Networks, Heterogeneous Engineers, and Embodied Technology. *Science, Technology & Human Values* 17 (1): 13–35.

Sparks, D. 2017. Apple Music Subscribers Hit 30 Million, but It's not as Impressive as It Sounds [online]. *Business Insider*. Available from http://www.businessinsider.com/apple-music-subscribers-30-million-2017-9. Accessed 15 Dec 2017.

Spellman, P. 1996. Creative Marketing: Making Media Waves: Creating a Scheduled Publicity Plan Music Business Insights [online]. Available from http://www.mbsolutions.com/biz/Info3.html#creative_marketing. Accessed 28 Feb 2016.

Spencer, A. 2005. *DIY: The Rise of Lo-fi Culture*. London: Marion Boyars.

Spilker, H.S. 2012. The Network Studio Revisited: Becoming an Artist in the Age of 'Piracy Cultures'. *International Journal of Communication* 6: 773–794.

Spitz, D., and S. Hunter. 2005. Contested Codes: The Social Construction of Napster. *Information Society* 21 (3): 169–180.

Spotify. 2013. Spotify Explained [online]. *Spotify for Artists*. Available from http://www.spotifyartists.com/spotify-explained/. Accessed 28 Feb 2016.

Spotify. 2014. Spotify Acquires the Echo Nest. *Spotify Press*.

Spotify. 2017. Fast Facts—Spotify. *Spotify Press*.

Stabell, C.B., and Ø.D. Fjeldstad. 1998. Configuring Value for Competitive Advantage: On Chains, Shops, and Networks. *Strategic Management Journal* 19 (5): 413.

Stanford's Entrepreneurship Corner. 2014. *Stanford's Entrepreneurship Corner: Daniel Ek, Spotify*. Available from http://ecorner.stanford.edu/authorMaterialInfo.html?mid=2964. Accessed 28 June 2018.

Strahilevitz, L.J. 2003. Charismatic Code, Social Norms, and the Emergence of Cooperation on the File-Swapping Networks. *Virginia Law Review* 89 (3): 505–595.

Sun, H. 2018. The Times They Are a-Changin': Digital Music Value in Transition from Piracy to Streaming. In *Digital Piracy: A Global, Multidisciplinary Account*, ed. S.C. Brown and T.J. Holt. Arbington, Oxon and New York.

Sun, H. Forthcoming. *Creative Industries Journal (Under Review)*. Resurgence of Market Control.

Sunde, P. 2015. The 'Pirate Movement' Is Dead. *TorrentFreak*.

Swash, R. 2009. Lily Allen: Social Networker of the Decade. *The Guardian*, November 29.

Taylor, J., A. Bennett, and I. Woodward (eds.). 2016. *The Festivalization of Culture*. London: Routledge.

Taylor, T.D., M. Katz, and T. Grajeda. 2012. *Music, Sound, and Technology in America: A Documentary History of Early Phonograph, Cinema, and Radio*. Durham, NC: Duke University Press.

Teague, E.J. 2012. Saving the Spotify Revolution: Recalibrating the Power Imbalance in Digital Copyright. *Case Western Reserve Journal of Law Technology & Internet* 4: 207.

TechRadar. 2006. Digital Music Award Winners Announced [online]. *TechRadar*. Available from http://www.techradar.com/news/portable-devices/other-devices/phone-and-communications/mobile-phones/internet/web/audio/portable-audio/digital-music-award-winners-announced-159274. Accessed 23 Feb 2016.

Teller, B. 1990. Toward Better Protection of Performers in the United States: A Comparative Look at Performers' Rights in the United States, Under the Rome Convention and in France. *Columbia Journal of Transnational Law* 28 (2): 775.

Tepper, S.J., and E. Hargittai. 2009. Pathways to Music Exploration in a Digital Age. *Poetics* 37 (3): 227–249.

The New York Times. 2007. CBS Buys Last.FM, an Online Radio Site. *The New York Times*, May 31.

Théberge, P. 1997. *Any Sound You Can Imagine: Making Music/Consuming Technology*. Hanover, NH: Wesleyan University Press.

Théberge, P. 2001. 'Plugged in': Technology and Popular Music. In *The Cambridge Companion to Pop and Rock*, ed. S. Frith, W. Straw, and J. Street, 1–25. Cambridge: Cambridge University Press.

Théberge, P. 2006. Everyday Fandom: Fan Clubs, Blogging, and the Quotidian Rhythms of the Internet. *Canadian Journal of Communication* 30 (4): 485–502.

This Week in Music—Interview with Robb McDaniels. 2012. Interview. Music Biz 2012.

Thompson, D. 2014. The Shazam Effect. *The Atlantic*.

Thompson, E. 1986. Performers and Technological Change 25 Years After the Rome Convention. *International Labour Review* 125 (5): 575.

Thorpe, V. 2015. Zane Lowe to leave BBC Radio 1 for Apple. *The Guardian*, February 15.

Towse, R. 1999. Copyright and Economic Incentives: An Application to Performers' Rights in the Music Industry. *Kyklos* 52 (3): 369–390.

Towse, R. 2001. *Creativity, Incentive, and Reward: An Economic Analysis of Copyright and Culture in the Information Age*. Cheltenham, UK: Edward Elgar.

Towse, R. 2004. Copyright and Economics. In *Music and Copyright*, ed. S. Frith and L. Marshall. New York: Routledge.

Towse, R. 2014. *Advanced Introduction to Cultural Economics*. Cheltenham, UK: Edward Elgar.

Toynbee, J. 2004. Musicians. In *Music and Copyright*, ed. S. Frith and L. Marshall. Edinburgh: Edinburgh University Press.

Trent Reznor—Steal This Music. 2007. Available from https://www.youtube.com/watch?v=IFXivarypE4.

Tschmuck, P. 2012a. *Creativity and Innovation in the Music Industry*, 2nd ed. Berlin: Springer.

Tschmuck, P. 2012b. The Emergence of the Phonographic Industry Within the Music Industry. In *Creativity and Innovation in the Music Industry*, 225–251. Berlin: Springer.

Tschmuck, P. 2015. Music Streaming Revisited—The Problem of Income Distribution [online]. *Music Business Research*. Available from https://musicbusinessresearch.wordpress.com/2015/07/18/music-streaming-revisited-the-problem-of-income-distribution/. Accessed 21 Jun 2017.

Tschmuck, P. 2016. From Record Selling to Cultural Entrepreneruship: The Music Economy in the Digital Paradigm Shift. In *Business Innovation and Disruption in the Music Industry*, ed. P. Wikström and R. DeFillippi, 13–32. Cheltenham, UK: Edward Elgar.

Turner, F. 2006. *From Counterculture to Cyberculture: Stewart Brand, the Whole Earth Network, and the Rise of Digital Utopianism*. Chicago: University of Chicago Press.

Turow, J. 1997. The Organizational Underpinnings of Contemporary Media Conglomerates. In *The Political Economy of the Media. Volume 1*, ed. P. Golding and G. Murdock, 351–373. Elgar Reference Collection. International Library of Studies in Media and Culture, vol. 2.

Twohey, M. 2000. Land of the Free and MP3. *National Journal* 32 (3): 182–183.

Tynan, D. 2006. The 25 Worst Tech Products of All Time [online]. *PCWorld*. Available from http://www.pcworld.com/article/125772/worst_products_ever.html. Accessed 10 Feb 2016.

UK Intellectual Property Office. 2017. Online Copyright Infringement Tracker Survey (7th Wave)—GOV.UK [online]. Available from https://www.gov.uk/government/publications/online-copyright-infringement-tracker-survey-7th-wave. Accessed 12 Dec 2017.

UK Music. 2016. *Measuring Music 2016*. London: UK Music. Available from https://www.ukmusic.org/assets/general/measuring-music-2016.pdf.

UK Music. 2017. *Music Tourism: Wish You Were Here—The Contribution of Live Music to the UK Economy*. London: UK Music. Available from https://www.ukmusic.org/assets/general/Report_WYWH_17.pdf.

Universal Music Group. 2008. Universa l Music Group Distribution (UMGD) Expands Digital Services with INgrooves Strategic Alliance [online]. Available from http://www.universalmusic.com/corporate/detail/544. Accessed 8 Oct 2014.

Vaidhyanathan, S. 2001. *Copyrights and Copywrongs: The Rise of Intellectual Property and How It Threatens Creativity*. New York: New York University Press.

Viacom Newsroom. 2014. Viacom and Google Resolve Copyright Lawsuit [online]. Available from http://news.viacom.com/press-release/legal/viacom-and-google-resolve-copyright-lawsuit. Accessed 8 Aug 2014.

Wallis, R. 2006. The Changing Structure of the Music Industry: Threats to and Opportunities for Creativity. In *Music and Manipulation: On the Social Uses and Social Control of Music*, ed. S. Brown and U. Volgsten. New York: Berghahn.

Watson, S., D. Zizzo, and P. Fleming. 2014. Determinants and Welfare Implications of Unlawful File Sharing: A Scoping Review. *CREATe*.

Waugh, M. 2015. 'Music That Actually Matters'? Post-Internet Musicians, Retromania and Authenticity in Online Popular Musical Milieux. Ph.D. Dissertation, Anglia Ruskin University.

Webb, S.W. 2000. RIAA v Diamond Multimedia Systems: The Recording Industry Attempts to Slow the MP3 Revolution-Taking Aim at the Jogger Friendly Diamond Rio. *Richmond Journal of Law & Technology* 7: 5–34.

Weinman, J.J. 2011. How Jobs Rescued Old Media: Music Was Free Online, Until He Showed That People Still Wanted to Pay. *Maclean's* 124 (41): 48.

Weissman, D. 2010. *Understanding the Music Business*. Upper Saddle River, NJ: Prentice Hall.

Wikström, P. 2013. *The Music Industry: Music in the Cloud*, 2nd ed. Cambridge, England: Polity.

Williams, R. 1997. The Social Shaping of Information and Communications Technologies. In *The social shaping of information superhighways : European and American roads to the information society*, ed. H. Kubicek, W.H. Dutton, and R. Williams. Frankfurt: New York: Campus Verlag St. Martin's Press.

Williams, R. 2000. Public Choices and Social Learning: The New Multimedia Technologies in Europe. *The Information Society* 16 (4): 251–262.

Williams, R., and D. Edge. 1996. The Social Shaping of Technology. *Research Policy* 25 (6): 865.

Williams, R., and N. Pollock. 2012. Research Commentary—Moving Beyond the Single Site Implementation Study: How (and Why) We Should Study the Biography of Packaged Enterprise Solutions. *Information Systems Research* 23 (1): 1–22.

Williams, R., J. Stewart, and R. Slack. 2005. *Social Learning in Technological Innovation: Experimenting with Information and Communication Technologies*. Cheltenham: Edward Elgar.

Williamson, O.E. 1975. *Markets and Hierarchies: Analysis and Antitrust Implications; A Study in the Economics of Internal Organization*. New York: Free Press.

Williamson, J., and M. Cloonan. 2007. Rethinking the Music Industry. *Popular Music* 26 (2): 305–322.

WIN. 2017. WINTEL 2017—Worldwide Independent Market Report.

Wingfield, N., and E. Smith. 2007. Music's New Gatekeeper. *Wall Street Journal*, March 9.

Wlömert, N., and D. Papies. 2016. On-Demand Streaming Services and Music Industry Revenues—Insights from Spotify's Market Entry. *International Journal of Research in Marketing* 33 (2): 314–327.

World Intellectual Property Organization. 1981. *Guide to the Rome Convention and to the Phonograms Convention*. Geneva: World Intellectual Property Organization.

Wu, T. 2003. When Code Isn't Law. *Virginia Law Review* 89 (4): 679–751.

Yin, R.K. 2009. *Case Study Research: Design and Methods*, 4th ed. Thousand Oaks, CA: Sage.

Young, S., and S. Collins. 2010. A View from the Trenches of Music 2.0. *Popular Music & Society* 33 (3): 339–355.

YouTube. 2006. YouTube Unveils New Advertising Concepts [online]. *YouTube News Room*. Available from http://www.marketwired.com/press-release/youtube-unveils-new-advertising-concepts-697771.htm. Accessed 29 Feb 2016.

Zentner, A. 2005. File Sharing and International Sales of Copyrighted Music: An Empirical Analysis with a Panel of Countries. *The BE Journal of Economic Analysis & Policy* 5 (1): 1–17.

Zentner, A. 2006. Measuring the Effect of File Sharing on Music Purchases. *The Journal of Law & Economics* 49 (1): 63–90.

Zhu, K., and B. Macquarrie. 2003. The Economics of Digital Bundling: The Impact of Digitization and Bundling on the Music Industry. *Communications of the ACM* 46 (9): 264–270.

Zittrain, J. 2007. *The Future of the Internet: And How to Stop it*. New Haven: Yale University Press.

Zott, C., and R. Amit. 2010. Business Model Design: An Activity System Perspective. *Long Range Planning* 43 (2): 216–226.

Index

H. Sun, *Digital Revolution Tamed*, https://doi.org/10.1007/978-3-319-93022-0

The manufacturer's authorised representative in the EU is Springer Nature Customer Service Centre GmbH, Europaplatz 3, 69115 Heidelberg, Germany. If you have any concerns regarding our products, please contact ProductSafety@springernature.com

Printed and bound by CPI Group (UK) Ltd, Croydon, CR0 4YY
25/09/2026
02222849-0010